14-120-1200

THE PUBLIC JUNIOR
COLLEGE

Officers of the Society
1955–1956

THE PUBLIC JUNIOR COLLEGE

The Fifty-fifth Yearbook of the
National Society for the Study of Education

PART I

Prepared by the Yearbook Committee: B. LAMAR JOHNSON (*Chairman*),
LAWRENCE L. BETHEL, W. A. BROWNELL, NORMAN BURNS,
and JAMES W. REYNOLDS

Edited by

NELSON B. HENRY

1 9 NSSE 5 6

Distributed by THE UNIVERSITY OF CHICAGO PRESS · CHICAGO, ILLINOIS

The responsibilities of the Board of Directors of the National Society for the Study of Education in the case of Yearbooks prepared by the Society's committees are (1) to select the subjects to be investigated, (2) to appoint committees calculated in their personnel to insure consideration of all significant points of view, (3) to provide appropriate subsidies for necessary expenses, (4) to publish and distribute the committees' reports, and (5) to arrange for their discussion at the annual meetings.

The responsibility of the Yearbook Editor is to prepare the submitted manuscripts for publication in accordance with the principles and regulations approved by the Board of Directors.

Neither the Board of Directors, nor the Yearbook Editor, nor the Society is responsible for the conclusions reached or the opinions expressed by the Society's yearbook committees.

Published 1956 by

THE NATIONAL SOCIETY FOR THE STUDY OF EDUCATION

5835 Kimbark Avenue, Chicago 37, Illinois

The Society's Committee on the Public Junior College

LAWRENCE L. BETHEL
President, Fashion Institute of Technology, State University of New York
New York, New York

WILLIAM A. BROWNELL
Dean, School of Education, University of California
Berkeley, California

NORMAN BURNS
Professor of Education, University of Chicago
Chicago, Illinois

B. LAMAR JOHNSON
(Chairman)
Professor of Higher Education, University of California
Los Angeles, California

JAMES W. REYNOLDS
Professor of Junior College Education, University of Texas
Austin, Texas

Associated Contributors

GRACE V. BIRD
Associate Director, Relations with Schools, University of California
Berkeley, California

JESSE P. BOGUE
Executive Secretary, American Association of Junior Colleges
Washington, D.C.

DAN W. DODSON
Professor of Education, New York University
New York, New York

PAUL L. DRESSEL
Professor and Head, Board of Examiners, The Basic College
Michigan State University of Agriculture and Applied Science
East Lansing, Michigan

RALPH R. FIELDS
Director, Division of Instruction, Teachers College, Columbia University
New York, New York

ELBERT K. FRETWELL, JR.
Assistant Professor of Education, Teachers College, Columbia University
New York, New York

ROBERT J. HANNELLY
Dean, Phoenix College
Phoenix, Arizona

L. L. JARVIE
Executive Dean for Institutes and Community Colleges
State University of New York
Albany, New York

MALCOLM S. MAC LEAN
Professor of Higher Education, University of California
Los Angeles, California

S. V. MARTORANA
Specialist for Community and Junior Colleges, Division of Higher Education
Office of Education, Department of Health, Education, and Welfare
Washington, D.C.

LELAND L. MEDSKER
Director, East Contra Costa Junior College
Concord, California

A. M. MEYER
President, Amarillo College
Amarillo, Texas

JAMES W. THORNTON, JR.
Vice-President, Orange Coast College
Costa Mesa, California

Editor's Preface

At the conclusion of his comprehensive inquiry into the work and the worth of the junior colleges as they were developing in the early 1920's, Koos listed approximately a score of the seemingly legitimate claims for the junior-college program and its place in the American system of education. Among these claims, none received greater emphasis in the evaluation of this new unit of school organization than those reflecting an appreciable popularizing of the first two years of higher education. In detail, these popularizing influences included: establishing post-high-school classes close to the homes of greater numbers of high-school graduates; giving more attention to the individual needs and interests of students; providing more opportunities for training for social leadership; and improving instruction over that available in the lower divisions of the four-year colleges and the universities. Perhaps it is not without significance that Koos refers to the numerous claims then being made for the junior college as "the aspirations entertained for this new unit [of our system of education] by its friends." He reported, however, that the findings of his extensive investigation included factual support for each of the several claims mentioned here.

The suggestion that the National Society provide for a yearbook on the junior college was first considered by the Board of Directors at its regular meeting in October, 1953. A tentative outline of a yearbook on this subject had been prepared by Professor B. Lamar Johnson at the request of the Board in advance of that meeting. Mr. Johnson was then requested to review that outline in conference with several other persons identified with the junior college and then to make arrangements for a meeting of the yearbook committee at an early date.

The volume which has been prepared as a result of these preliminary activities is presented as a cordial tribute to the "aspirations" of earlier friends of the junior-college movement. In addition to its liberal confirmation of former appraisals of the effectiveness of the junior-college program in the improvement of the kinds of educational advantages available to the youth of America, the yearbook provides guidance for future planning in the interest of making these advantages available to the young people of every community. It is a timely publication in view of the predictions regarding the population of college age in the near future. It contributes also to the further stimulation of interest in adult-education programs and furnishes inspiration for the intelligent citizenry already engaged in promoting measures directed toward the effective integration of collegiate education and community life.

NELSON B. HENRY

Table of Contents

SECTION II

Accomplishing the Purposes of the Institution

CHAPTER I

Purpose and Plan of the Yearbook

B. LAMAR JOHNSON

Seven hundred and eight students, aged from sixteen to sixty, attend state-supported Mayville College in a village of eighteen hundred in an agricultural region of Midwest State. Half of the students live in dormitories where lodging and meals are provided at cost (thirty-eight dollars a month for board and room); one-third drive to the college each day from farms and villages within commuting distance; and the remainder, adults, come to the campus for evening classes one or two evenings a week. With a curriculum planned on the basis of regional surveys, and developed with the help of lay-advisory boards, the college features two-year programs in agriculture, homemaking, secretarial-training, and preparation for transfer to State University or to State Agricultural College.

Serving as a regional educational center, the college annually attracts to its campus more than twenty-five thousand who participate in and attend a wide variety of educational, cultural, social, and athletic events—including stock-judging contests and demonstrations, regularly scheduled radio broadcasts by children from fifteen public schools in the region, educational conferences, livestock sales, music festivals, rodeos, Future Farmers of America conferences and contests, speech and business meets, and meetings of such organizations as the Boy Scouts Area Council, Regional Bankers Association, garden clubs, and county agents conferences.

———

Metropolis, one of the largest cities in the United States, has two publicly controlled city colleges planned to prepare students for employment following the completion of a two-year curriculum of studies. Since the colleges recognize the importance of general education, both in preparation for earning a livelihood and for day-by-

I

day living, approximately 40 per cent of the curriculum of all students is devoted to general education.

One of the colleges, Tech Institute, has an enrolment of twenty-five hundred full-time and thirty-eight hundred part-time students. Located in the heart of the city's industrial area, Tech is housed in two large buildings, one originally a high school, the other a former manufacturing plant. Courses at the college relate primarily to the technologies in which skilled workers are needed in Metropolis, including electronics, building construction, petroleum, and food administration. One-third of Tech's support comes from the state, one-third from the city, and one-third from tuition charges.

The second college, Textile Institute, prepares its sixteen hundred students (four hundred full-time and twelve hundred part-time) for work in textile design, apparel design, and management positions in the textile and clothing industry. The college secures its financial support from the city, from the state, from fees charged part-time students, and from Industrial Foundation, which was established specifically to contribute to the costs of operating Textile Institute. Scholarships which pay total tuition charges are awarded to all students admitted to full-time work.

———

Situated in a midwestern city of twenty thousand, Moulton College offers courses in English, science, social studies, and foreign languages planned to parallel Freshman-Sophomore requirements at State University. Limited offerings in secretarial training are also provided. Classes are taught by instructors who also teach in the senior high school which is located in the same building. The college, which is governed by the Moulton Board of Education is jointly supported by local taxation and by an annual tuition charge of one hundred dollars.

The 192 students at Moulton College have all graduated from high school within the past four years, and most of them plan to continue their education at a senior college or university. Only occasionally (as, for example, the housewife planning a trip to Europe who took a course in French) does an adult enrol in a class at the college.

Suburban Junior College is a part of the public school system of an upper-middle-class suburban community. Except for modest fees for the adult program, the college is supported entirely by tax funds. Seventy per cent of the regular students transfer to senior colleges, for the most part to State University. Major emphasis in the curriculum is on general education, designed both for those who will complete their formal education at Suburban and for those who will continue their schooling after graduation from the Junior College. Vocational courses are offered only in business and secretarial studies.

Citizens of the community in sizable numbers enrol in adult evening classes and forums. Lecture series and discussion groups enjoy great popularity in such fields as current social and economic development, modern literature, American foreign policy, child care, home construction and maintenance, interior decoration, and photography.

In Seaside, a West Coast city, one out of every five citizens eighteen years of age or over enrols each year at tuition-free Seaside City College. Seven thousand attend college full-time, some preparing for advanced study at a senior college or university, but most preparing for immediate employment in such fields as aircraft construction, building trades, merchandising, secretarial work, petroleum technology, welding, and real estate.

More than thirty-eight thousand adults take part-time work at one of the more than forty college centers located throughout the city. Featured in the adult program are vocational education, citizenship training, public affairs forums, geriatics workshops, and family-life education—including courses in marriage and the family, mental hygiene of the family, family finances and management, home planning and furnishing, nutrition, and clothing.

Here are six greatly different colleges. Though located in six very different communities, they nevertheless have at least three characteristics in common: each is an institution of post-high-school education; each limits its offerings to programs of less than four (ordinarily two) years; and each is publicly supported and controlled. These distinguishing features identify all as public junior colleges. It is with these institutions, and others more or less like them, that we are concerned in the present yearbook.

As the foregoing illustrations have demonstrated, public junior colleges vary greatly and in many ways. Some are large, others small. Some are rural, others urban or suburban. Some are locally controlled, others state controlled. Some are entirely supported by tax funds and are, therefore, tuition-free; others receive major support from tuition and fees. Some emphasize preparation for advanced study, others emphasize preparation for earning an immediate livelihood. Some enrol a predominantly adult and part-time student body, others enrol full-time students only. Some have programs which emerge from the characteristics and needs of their particular communities. These differences are characteristic of the public junior college as it is developing in widely distributed communities of our nation.

Purposes of the Yearbook Committee

We have noted the general field of this volume. Our purposes are:

1. To report the sociological, technological, and psychological factors giving rise to the demand for more education beyond high school on the part of vastly increasing numbers of youth and adults.
2. To define the role of the public junior college in helping to satisfy this demand.
3. To identify and report selected practices by means of which the public junior college can better fulfil its functions and accomplish its purposes.

The public junior college has emerged from a historical background to which the private junior college has made major contributions. The great majority of early junior colleges were privately supported and controlled. In 1915, for example, 75 per cent of the enrolment in junior colleges was in private institutions. Even today, 45 per cent of the junior colleges are private. Many independent junior colleges, both in the past and at present, have furnished outstanding leadership in research, in program development, and in achieving national recognition for the junior college.

The private and the public junior colleges have a number of features in common, including a similarity in the length of their programs. For these reasons it would seem that in this volume we might have dealt as completely with private as with public institutions.

On the other hand, these two types of college are markedly dissimilar not only in source of support and agency of control but also typically in clientele, purposes, and curriculums. Writing about both types of junior college would demand two quite different treatments. To deal with both adequately would clearly be impossible within the confines of a single yearbook.

Accordingly, we have been faced with the choice of selecting *either* the public *or* the private junior college as the subject of this volume. We have elected to concentrate on the public institution, not primarily because of its accelerated growth or even because of its dominance in enrolment, but particularly because educators, students of public affairs, legislators, citizens, and taxpayers in general are actively and increasingly studying the public junior college and its place in American education.

But the independent junior college is not wholly neglected. Developments in private institutions will occasionally be described. Moreover, readers who are acquainted with the history of the junior college will also observe that we repeatedly report practices in public junior colleges which historically have been initiated by independent institutions.

The Junior College Today

The junior college represents more than a promise for the future. It is a vital present-day reality, a vigorous institution. The first public junior college which is still in existence was founded at Joliet, Illinois, in 1902. Since that date, this new educational agency has multiplied and spread until it currently numbers 598, of which 338 are public institutions and 260 are private. At the close of its first half-century, the number of junior colleges is 40 per cent of the number of four-year colleges and universities in America, institutions which have a history of more than three hundred years.

The junior college is presently in a period of especially rapid growth and expansion. From the last prewar year, 1940–41, to 1953–54, junior-college enrolment has more than doubled, the increase being from 267,406 to 622,864.[1] This expansion is particularly notable because it occurred at a time when three major conditions militated against the growth of the public junior college:

1. Enrolment data used here are based upon the publications of the American Association of Junior Colleges, including the *Junior College Directory* published annually by the Association.

1. World War II took large numbers of actual and prospective college students out of education, reducing junior-college enrolments conspicuously.
2. The more recent Korean conflict and the "cold war" have necessitated the continued drafting of manpower for our armed forces. In particular, this need has drawn off youth of junior-college age who might otherwise have continued their education.
3. Unprecedented levels of production and prosperity during much of the past decade have created a demand even for untrained workers at high wage-scales. Accordingly, high-school graduates in large numbers have entered employment instead of continuing their schooling.

In addition to its rate of growth, at least two other notable observations should be made about the junior college:

1. A constantly increasing percentage of students is attending public junior colleges. In 1915, only 25 per cent of the junior-college enrolment was in public institutions. In the intervening years this percentage has consistently increased to its present 88 per cent. Between 1940–41 and 1953–54 public junior-college enrolment expanded more than 170 per cent (from 197,375 to 553,008) while that of independent institutions decreased slightly (from 70,003 to 69,856).
2. More than half (59 per cent in 1953–54) of the junior-college enrolment consists of adult and special students. This high percentage undoubtedly reflects something of the extent to which the junior college is meeting the needs of the people of its particular locale.

Plan of the Yearbook

In this chapter we have identified the public junior college as the subject of this yearbook. We have noted, too, something of its status and have explained our purposes in preparing the present volume.

The plan of the yearbook emerges from its purposes. In Section I, consideration is given first to those characteristics of society (chap. ii) and those needs and purposes of individuals (chap. iii) which make post-high-school education necessary for growing numbers of youth and adults. Secondly, the role of the junior college is defined (chap. iv) in terms of its unique contributions to the community's efforts to meet the demands for more education.

In the four chapters of Section II emphasis is placed on the part the junior college can play in providing more education beyond the high school: preparation for advanced study (chap. v), preparation for vocation (chap. vi), general education (chap. vii), and community service (chap. viii). In each of these chapters the value and importance of the objective under consideration and the practices which junior colleges follow to achieve this purpose are noted, problems and obstacles are identified, and plans for future development are suggested.

The five chapters of Section III are devoted to plans and programs for institutional improvement: program planning and development (chap. ix), student personnel services (chap. x), the improvement of instruction (chap. xi), legislation and accrediting (chap. xii), and finance (chap. xiii).

In the two chapters of Section IV, preliminary plans for and problems related to the establishment of new junior colleges are considered. In chapter xiv procedures for identifying a need for a new junior college are indicated; principles and practices to aid in planning and setting up the new institution are explained. In chapter xv recommended directions for the future are outlined and some anticipated developments are noted.

Following Section IV is an annotated list of selected readings on the junior college.

SECTION I

THE EMERGING INSTITUTION

CHAPTER II

Educational Needs Emerging from the Changing Demands of Society

MALCOLM S. MACLEAN

AND

DAN W. DODSON

It is the function of this chapter to deal briefly with some of the powerful social, political, economic, scientific, and technological forces that move in and through American society, and to suggest something of their impact upon post-high-school education. Clearly, the planning of the future roles of the multiform institutions devoting themselves to the education of our youth and adults, the identification of their unfolding purposes, and the effective management and development of their operations, all depend in large measure upon sharpening our perceptions of dynamic societal changes and their implications for education.

In this chapter, then, we take a look, first, at the changing community. We use the concept of "community" in its current meaning which attaches to the word such modifiers as local, state, regional, national, and world. We assume that, in these meanings, every institution of higher education, from the most local junior college to the universities of world repute, is in a very real sense a community institution. As such, the forces that cause communities, large or small, to grow and flourish or to decline and die must perforce carry their colleges with them whichever trend prevails. Second, we consider population trends: the increasing birth rate and the declining death rate which have produced a shifting of the proportions in numbers of the different age groups; immigration; and the feverish mobility and migration of people within our borders which may give clues as to where students at these upper levels are now, and where they may be in the future. Third, we attempt to sketch a few of the extraor-

dinary forces unleashed by science and technology: the development
of new forms of energy; trends toward mechanization, automation,
and gigantism; the growth of mass media of communication; and the
technologies of war. Fourth, and finally, we try to picture a few of
the most significant changes in our American mores, attitudes, and
customs resulting in large part from the developments previously
described: the shifting status of women at work, at home, and in
public affairs; the impact of many forces upon the family and upon
the individual; emerging attitudes toward work and play, toward
culture and recreation. All of these will be reviewed in light of their
implications for post-high-school education.

The Changing Community

If we take the concept of "community" to mean basically a gathering and grouping of people with common purposes, interests, and
concerns, it may refer to a tiny village, a town, a suburb, a city, a
region, a nation, or a community of nations. Whatever the size and
location of the communities with which we may be dealing, we have
clear examples of colleges and universities which are serving the interests and needs of those communities. Thus, we may have a junior
college with an enrolment of 200, of which 195 students live within
a radius of ten miles. We may have a state college that serves few
from outside the borders of the state. We may have a national university like that of Ankara, Turkey, or a national normal college like
that of the Philippines; and, at the extreme, there are the great universities which, for many years, have drawn students from all parts
of the world, for example, Oxford, Cambridge, Paris, Harvard,
Michigan, to name but a few.

Each institution undergoes change as the character of its community changes. It grows, expands, and flourishes, or it declines and dies
with its community. To illustrate: While the authors know of no
full-fledged historical study of the interaction between a college and
its community, we have found in the catalogues, and some other
sources, striking pictures of the changes wrought in Princeton[1] and
in the University of Michigan[2] in approximately one hundred years.

1. Catalogues of the College of New Jersey, 1851–52, and of Princeton University, 1951–52.
2. Catalogues of the University of Michigan 1859–60 and 1952–53.

In 1851–52, Princeton was The College of New Jeresy, located in a small village. It drew its students, 255 undergraduate and one graduate, chiefly from New York and New Jersey, with a sprinkling from near-by states. Its total teaching staff, including the president, consisted of thirteen men, who taught a total of 41 courses in a single four-year curriculum. By 1951–52, there were 421 teachers of all ranks from instructor to professor offering instruction to 3,148 undergraduates from many parts of the world in 517 courses, given in two colleges by 29 departments.

The University of Michigan offers an even more startling portrait of growth and change in service to the world community. In 1859, our first sample year, Ann Arbor was, like Princeton, just a tiny village. By 1953 it was a city of 50,000 and, in effect, a suburb of Detroit, which has a population of nearly 2,000,000. In this time the College of Science, Literature, and Arts had grown from an enrolment of 254 undergraduate and 31 graduate students, drawn from points only so far away as New England, to more than 11,000 students who came from every corner of the United States and from 72 foreign areas. The foreign students totaled more than the entire enrolment of the earlier year. In this college alone, to serve these large numbers and to meet the educational demands of this vast community, the teaching staff had increased from 17 to 570, and the number of courses offered, from 48 to 1,116. In addition, the one college had proliferated to fifteen colleges, and these served a total of some 32,000 students.

Obviously, for anything like a full understanding of the forces in local and world society that bring about the extraordinary changes suggested by these illustrations, we need many longitudinal case studies of post-high-school institutions and their communities, large and small. Awaiting such studies, we can do no more here than to ask the reader to recall the communities he has known since childhood and to assess in his memory and his present knowledge the changes wrought in them by migration of peoples, by births and deaths, by the building of highways and the vast increase in automobiles, by the great networks of communication—telephone, radio, television, movies, the press—by the discovery of oil or uranium, by the ebb and flow of employment, by the changing role of women, by the development of business and industry, and by the establishment of plants for the generation of power and of bases for national defense. Leaving it to the imagination of the reader to create his own feeling of difference and change in community and of the consequences in terms of educational demand, organization, and process, we turn to examine some of the major forces at work, bringing changes in their wake, and some of the problems these changes breed for post-high-school education.

Population Changes

A major force in society is that of population change. Human fertility, birth rates, deaths; immigration; ethnic and religious composition; the ratios of the young to the old; the restless movement of peoples seeking work, health, a better climate, or greater security— all of these in any one year or decade will determine where youth and their elders will be, the communities they will inhabit, and their availability as students in junior colleges and the higher institutions. To gather the data on these many factors, to analyze and intercorrelate them, and to derive from the total process predictions of some accuracy requires the teamwork of many high-order specialists, the most advanced techniques in statistics, and more than a touch of the wisdom of Solomon in interpretation. They demand organizations and money.[3] Even with these resources, gross errors occur in prediction.

For example, in 1925, Dr. Raymond Pearl, the acknowledged leader in the field, projected the growth of our population to a final leveling-off figure of 197 million in the year 2100. He was accurate within tolerable limits in 1930 and again in 1940. But by 1950 he was three million low, and his forecast of 159 million by 1960 had already been exceeded by two millions in 1954. Neither he nor his associate specialists foresaw either the phenomenal rise in our birth

3. Some of the leading organizations for population study are the Scripps Foundation for Research in Population Problems; the Milbank Memorial Fund, Division of Research; the Population Reference Bureau, Washington, D.C., whose eight annual bulletins are an invaluable source; the Office of Population Research, Princeton University with its quarterly bibliography, the "Population Index." The ten-year official United States Census reports, the bulletins of the Bureau of Vital Statistics in the United States Public Health Service, and the annual "Statistical Abstracts" of the United States Department of Commerce are basic sources. The United Nations maintains a Population Commission and provides for a population division in the Secretariat to furnish technical aid. Materials for this section have been drawn from these sources.

rate or the parallel decline in death rate that has occurred in the past thirteen years. Taking these new trends into account, the experts still disagree to some extent, but the general consensus is that we will reach 190 millions by 1975 and at least 200 millions by the year 2000.

BIRTH RATE

The magnitude of the educational problem is, in part, a result of the astonishing rise in the birth rate. An all-time low was reached in the years of the great depression when, in 1935, the rate was only 16.9 per 1,000 inhabitants. It changed little until 1942, when it jumped to 20.8 per 1,000. In 1947 it reached an all-time high of 25.8 per 1,000 and, with minor fluctuations, has stayed right around the 25 per 1,000 mark. This rate was greater than that of India, for example, for the years 1952, 1953, and 1954. Moreover, it should be remembered that this increase is happening at a time when parents in the age-span of fertility are low in number and in proportion to those of earlier or later periods, for these parents were born in the depression years when the rate was around 17 per 1,000. To cite a single example, in 1935 there was a total of only 2,155,105 births, but in 1952 there were 3,824,000. What, then, will be the number when the majority of those born in 1952 become parents?

As we are all uncomfortably aware, the swelling flood of American children has been increasingly overcrowding the elementary schools for some time, is now pressing on into the high schools, and will soon be knocking on the doors of higher institutions. If we consider youth of 18 to 21 years of age as being the major core of initial enrolments in the colleges, we find that we had close to 8 million potential enrolees in this country in 1954, and that we will probably have 9.25 million by 1960, and more than 13.5 million by 1970.

Even so, it might not be too difficult for educators to plan to take care of the new increments in school population if the enrolments in school and college kept an even pace, step by step, with the number of children born and growing up. But this does not happen. Enrolments in educational institutions have, in our past history, run far ahead of population growth. In 70 years, while the number of people more than tripled, school attendance doubled each decade. College attendance increased from a fraction of 1 per cent of the youth of college age to more than 15 per cent in the same period of time. We do not yet know how far such factors as compulsory attendance, parental and student ambition, established habits of schooling, or society's demands for people trained in technical skills and general education will increase the proportion of youth who will include advanced training in their life plans. There is a limit somewhere, but we may not see it for many years. Continuance of these trends will likely make the 1947 prediction of the President's Commission on Higher Education of 4,600,000 students in attendance in college in another ten to twenty years seem conservative indeed.

DEATH RATE AND LIFE EXPECTANCY

Dramatic as is the rise in the birth rate and bewildering as are the emerging problems of post-high-school education, these are no more dramatic and bewildering than the contemporary decline in death rate and the increase in life expectancy. Since adults are becoming more and more the beneficiaries of the community services of our educational institutions, it is mandatory that we modify our accent on youth and give more attention to what is happening to the older segments of the population. They are increasingly seeking instruction in recreational skills, hobbies, and handicrafts; in social, political, and economic trends; in guidance in what to read, what to see, what to do to make themselves useful and happy. A number of junior and metropolitan colleges have many adults enrolled as regular students, and, in general, the enrolment of part-time adults in public junior colleges is greater than that of full-time young people. What then is happening to the death rate and life expectancy in the United States?

The number of persons over 65 in our population has quadrupled since 1900 and has increased by 50 per cent since 1940. The census of 1950 showed 12,269,547 of them in a total of just under 151 million. This group showed increases of 33 per cent between the census enumeration of 1920 and 1930; 33.7 per cent between 1930 and 1940; and 36 per cent between 1940 and 1950. Population specialists estimate that by 1980 there will be between 20 and 24 million people over 65 years of age, making up 11 to 15 per cent of the total population of the nation.

As already suggested, older people are becoming increasingly the users of college-community services and are likely, therefore, to become important factors in future changes in educational organization, in development of curriculums, and in requirements for the kinds of teachers to be employed since adult students may not, probably will not, be satisfied with all aspects of the materials and methods used for the instruction of youth. But beyond these considerations, local, state, and national political power and influence will increasingly rest in the hands of adults. College youth cannot vote at present until age twenty-one, but our society has not yet reached the point where it will take away the franchise from old people for reasons of reactionary attitudes or failing judgment.

In any case, it is probable that elderly persons will increasingly influence the policies and operations of post-high-school education. They will sit on boards of trustees, regents, and school districts, will vote on bond issues and tax rates, and may help revise legislation affecting the public colleges in the states. As legislators, lobbyists, or members of pressure groups, they will influence Congress in its attitudes and actions toward the Department of Health, Education, and Welfare and toward the activities of the United States Office of Education. They may help determine the amounts and kinds of federal appropriations for higher education. They will influence federal, state, and local civil-service policies affecting the employment of junior-college and college graduates; they may help set the policies of the selective service and the national manpower commissions. In sum, the old-age group appears to be in the way of becoming one of the most powerful political, social, and economic blocs this country has yet seen.

It is likely that the attitudes, policies, and actions of this bloc will be more or less strongly colored by conservatism and desire for security. It seems unlikely that, without great wisdom and foresight, our society can avoid the development of competition between the older and the younger citizens for a share of tax dollars. For example, the Commission on Financing Higher Education reports[4] that, in 1915, education received 12.6 per cent of the expenditures of state governments for operation and capital outlay. In 1949 this

4. H. K. Allen, in collaboration with Richard G. Axt, *State Public Finance and State Institutions of Higher Education in the United States*, p. 56. Published for the Commission on Financing Higher Education. New York: Columbia University Press, 1952.

proportion had dropped to 9.4 per cent. In the same period "welfare" expenditures rose from 7.2 to 12.7 per cent of the cost of state governments. While few will question the wisdom of society's making every possible provision for the comfort, usefulness, and happiness of the aged, most will agree that it must not do so at the expense of educational opportunities for children and youth. It would seem that post-high-school institutions can play a major role in protecting young people by rendering the greatest possible services to the old.

IMMIGRATION

Midcentury and future policies and practices concerning immigration to the United States will certainly affect the majority of higher institutions to an extent deserving at least brief consideration. Visas and permits for teacher and student exchange with other countries, the stimulation or restriction of foreign scholarships and fellowships, and the freedom of travel to international meetings are part of the picture. But of as great significance is the indrift of foreigners who become United States citizens. Serving their needs is not only a question of developing courses in "English for Foreigners" or of collaborating with International Institutes and similar agencies to offer special night courses in American history and the Constitution for those who are applying for citizenship but it also involves the broader and deeper task of helping them understand American customs, learn to meet American standards in the mastery of tools and techniques, and acquire the knowledges and skills that will prepare them for employment.

In past years, the population pattern of the United States has been deeply affected by immigration. There was the grim side of the importation of Negro slaves to support the economy of the South, and the later drafting of great numbers of cheap, unskilled laborers from Europe and the Orient to build our vast agricultural, industrial, and transportation systems. From 1820 through 1952 nearly 40 million persons migrated to us. During World War II the number dropped to the lowest figure since 1820, that for 1943 being only 23,725. However, since 1950 close to a quarter of a million have been admitted each year, and, in addition, in 1953 the Congress passed a special act allowing approval of 214,000 visas for refugee aliens above regular quotas.

The effects of these immigrations are sharply felt in the colleges of certain areas. Unique is the New York city region with from 350,000 to a half-million Spanish-speaking persons from Puerto Rico. New York and the eastern seaboard draw concentrations of other immigrants as well, although it is the general policy of agencies which take care of these people to distribute them as widely over the country as possible. On the West Coast is felt the flow from the Orient and the Pacific Islands. Also, along with the southwestern states, the West Coast has the continuous quota immigration of natives of Mexico, Central America, and South America and the knotty problem of the "wetback." A further source of legitimate incomers—which is likely to continue so long as we keep armed divisions and military and naval bases abroad while continuing to expand our diplomatic and business and cultural services in many parts of the world—is the marriage of American men and women to foreign mates. As a result of this factor after World War II, this country received 114,691 war brides, 333 war husbands, and their 4,669 "alien" children by 1950, and many of these parents got a part of their induction into American life through higher institutions.

In the near future, development of our policies in southeastern Asia may deeply affect our post-high-school education. If, along the lines of the Marshall and Truman plans for Europe and the Point-Four Program for undeveloped territories, the United States works to improve agriculture, industry, health, and education in southeastern Asia, it is more than probable that we shall have an increasing flow of college and postgraduate students from that area and shall, in turn, be sending perhaps thousands of specialists of many kinds, professionals, and technicians to Asian countries. The evolving patterns of these overseas ventures have educational implications.

INTERNAL MIGRATION AND SHIFTING POPULATION

Of far greater moment than immigration to all higher education is the internal migration of United States citizens. Americans have always moved about restlessly as a people. But with the development of the automobile and other forms of transportation, and under the impact of other social and economic forces, this movement has steadily accelerated. The figures are startling.

We have already mentioned the 350,000 to a half-million Puerto

Ricans coming from the island to the continent. Within the borders of our continent, and within the sample year of April, 1951, to April, 1952, a total of 29,840,000 persons moved their homes. While many of these moves were local, from home to home within a city, 4,854,-000 moved from one county to another, and 5,112,000 moved from one state to another.[5] This sample is quite typical of migration year after year.

What problems do these migrations raise for higher education? First, there is the flow from rural to urban places. In 1820, 72 per cent of our entire labor force worked and lived on farms; in 1950 only 12 per cent were so situated. The 1950 census showed also that 168 metropolitan areas contained 83,930,000 people, or 55.7 per cent

TABLE 1

POPULATION CHANGE BY REGIONS

Region	1940	1950
Northeast.........	35,976,275	39,477,986
North Central......	40,143,332	44,460,762
South............	41,665,901	47,197,088
West.............	13,883,265	19,551,525

of the entire population.[6] Some of these cities have had phenomenal growth, particularly those in the west and southwest. As examples, the net gain in the decade 1940–50 was 10 per cent for New York City; 13.5 per cent for Chicago; 14.9 per cent for Scranton; 43.9 per cent for Seattle; 48.8 per cent for Los Angeles; 51.6 per cent for Houston; and 82.5 per cent for Miami. By regions, in this same decade, we find the pictures as shown in Table 1.

An analysis by states shows that Arkansas, Mississippi, North Dakota, and Oklahoma lost small percentages of population in this period, whereas seven western states gained 28 to 53 per cent and Florida gained 46.1 per cent. Maryland and Virginia increased heavily with the concentration of governmental activities, and a few

5. Joseph Monserrat, "Industry and Community—A Profitable Partnership," *Journal of Educational Sociology*, XXVII (December, 1953), 180. See, also, the *Statistical Abstracts of the United States Department of Commerce*, referred to earlier, for year-by-year summaries of these migrations.

6. Walter G. Bowerman, "Metropolitan Areas of the United States," *Journal of Educational Sociology*, XXV (May, 1952), 526.

southern states were climbing in population with the shift of industry to those areas. Meanwhile, in the same decade the farm population dwindled another 6.6 per cent—while nonfarm employment rose 63 per cent. These trends indicate the dwindling and possible abandonment of some higher institutions in the drained areas and the establishment of many new ones in the areas that are mushrooming.

Other aspects of the population shift are significant in planning the future of post-high-school education in the United States. The drift of people is *away from the interior to the periphery* of the nation with inevitably consequent changes in the balance of political and economic power and social influence. This trend may be slowed in time or reversed, either by the decentralization of defense production or by the development of atomic energy. For example, in September, 1954, near Pittsburgh, in an area marked as economically "sick" because of changes in social and economic life, ground was broken for the first private atomic energy plant in the United States. The resuscitating effect of this new power source remains to be seen, especially since, with the great increase in population in the West and South, there is a corresponding development of power sources there.

Another characteristic of population migration is that it is *selective.* For more than three decades there has been a strong and steady movement of Negro Americans from the South to other parts of the country, and chiefly to metropolitan districts. In the wake of this migration have come several developments of significance to communities and their colleges, particularly in the light of the 1954 decision of the United States Supreme Court barring segregation in all public schools and colleges. Some of these developments are: (*a*) greater political and social concern about civil rights, not only for Negroes but also for other minorities; (*b*) increased planning and effort on the part of the colleges, other educational agencies, and welfare institutions to accelerate the tempo of adjustment of people from a farm and folkway cultural background to urban and sophisticated ways of life; (*c*) a heightening of the expectations of Negroes and other minorities as to what democratic, public education can do for them in enhancing their acceptance by the majority, in preparing them for jobs that they can get and hold, and in improving their social, economic, and political status; and (*d*) a growing identification of labor unions with the cause of minority rights and an increasing integration of minorities into the unions. These trends are of special importance to the junior colleges and technical institutes because of the closeness with which they must work with unions in the development of their vocational and technical, work-study and apprentice programs.

Another phase of this pattern of internal migration is what might be called "mobile drift." In part, it represents the movement of the flotsam and jetsam of indigency, the Jodes of *The Grapes of Wrath*, the "Okies" trekking from the Dust Bowl to Arizona, New Mexico, and California. In part, it is the movement of migrant labor—"wetbacks" and others who follow the harvest whether it be dates, nuts, lima beans, citrus fruits, wheat, corn, or any other of the seasonal crops. Basically, it is the flow of skilled, semiprofessional, professional, and managerial labor to defense plants, to power and energy developments, to oil, or to iron and uranium fields. These movements bring demands at the technical and professional levels of teaching, medicine, nursing, engineering, and law, for migrations of thousands to whatever new concentrations of population need their services.

Mobility also includes that part of the population which moves, lives, and has its being in the ubiquitous American trailer. In 1953 there were 330,000 families living full time in these mechanized and mobile homes which ranged from little two-wheeled, tight and tidy carriers of food and shelter for two to land yachts that sleep and feed and transport a family of eight. Singly, in groups of two or three, or in droves of hundreds, these mobile homes may move twenty or 2,000 miles. Some stop only for a few days, many settle down at a work-site for one or several years, thus making a community of their own or attaching themselves by light, sewer, telephone, and by fraternization to the already established community. What has this to do with post-high-school education? Much indeed, for not only do these trailer nomads change communities which the colleges serve but it is becoming increasingly common practice for college students and their families to park their homes beside the college grounds. So long as our population remains so fluid and so mobile, so long as there continues to be in many communities a housing shortage, those who are responsible for college development may expect and must provide for these itinerant students.

Technological Changes

If the population changes summarized in the preceding pages present broad demographic background as a guide for the development of post-high-school education, the technological changes stemming from the continuing scientific and industrial revolution bring into sharpened focus some of the specific problems of education at this level. These technological developments revolve around and interact with both social and economic factors. We may deal briefly with them under four headings.

SOURCES OF POWER

The shift from man and animal muscle-power to steam, oil, electricity, and atomic power has taken place in little more than two generations.

To illustrate this shift, the number of horses and mules in the United States had decreased from 26.7 million in 1918 to 7.5 million by 1950. The number of tractors increased from 1.5 million in 1939 to 4 million by 1952. Stated in another way, the increase in the use of power per employed worker has been at the average rate of 3 per cent per year over the past twenty years so that now the average American worker on the job commands the equivalent of 250 human slaves. Nor is the end in sight. Atomic power is now only in the first experimental stages of public and private development and use. Some glimpse of the future may be had in the startling announcement of the chairman of the Atomic Energy Commission on September 16, 1954, when he predicted, "Our children will enjoy in their homes electrical energy too cheap to meter." This he thought would happen in only five to fifteen years, depending on the vigor of inventive and experimental effort.[7]

These developments in sources and abundance of power suggest several problems of great importance to higher education. The first is that they are bound to bring in their wake the elimination of many jobs for which these institutions now train so that the obsolescence of current vocational and technical courses is likely to speed up and may leave any new educational program out of date in a matter of months. It is not to be forgotten, for example, that many colleges

7. *New York Times*, September 17, 1954.

accepted with delight World War II surplus airplane engines and other aviation equipment, established courses for training students in design, repair, and operation, only to have jets and turbojets outmode them. The second problem is that new jobs will be born by the hundreds, each one, or each allied group, requiring new housing, new equipment, new instructors, texts, methods, and processes. Implications of these changes for college administration, staff, course programs, and financing are far-reaching.

Accompanying the kaleidoscopic shifts in technical and vocational programming will come a number of impelling needs. Guidance and counseling services will have to be improved to help students adapt their interests, ambitions, knowledges, and skills to these rapid changes in the selection of their courses of study, plan their careers, adjust to training programs, and achieve understanding of the broader aspects of technological change. Research on an extended scale will be required to refine present diagnostic tests and develop new ones. The colleges will need to put pressure on the psychologists and test-makers of the universities to carry on research and to develop training programs for counselors able to keep pace with these swift and sometimes drastic changes.

Another need of the colleges will be to struggle even more valiantly than they have in the past to bring their cultural, liberal, and general-education offerings into balance with those in the professional, technical, vocational, and commercial fields. The youth of tomorrow will have to learn to handle these new sources of power in technical skills. They will also be confronted with developments flowing out of new power sources which change the requirements of many other jobs and will profoundly affect the workers' hours of leisure and most of the pattern of American living. There are meanings with which we have not yet come to grips in the colleges in the current and growing "do-it-yourself" movement, a sort of revival of man's earlier desire to create through handicrafts but which now calls for the use of power tools, new chemicals, and novel techniques. How important these considerations may become is seen in the present beginnings of talk of the four-day, thirty-four-hour week.[8] The increasing opportunity for leisure under the impact of

8. Daniel Seligman, "The Four-Day Week: How Soon?" *Fortune*, XLIX (January, 1954), 81.

the development of new sources of power would seem to place at a high premium college programs for self-improvement on the part of the students.

MECHANIZATION AND AUTOMATION

The trend toward mechanization and automation of production and distribution is, perhaps, the most discussed of pending changes in American life. Put simply, it means that science and technology are making more and more processes partially or fully automatic with a hazard of reducing millions of workers to becoming little more than nursemaids to machines. The increasing tempo of the competitive processes has bred the invention and use of electronic and other automatic devices on a massive scale. For example, although net employment in the telephone industry has remained relatively steady, roughly 50,000 operators have been displaced by local dial conversion which is now nearly nation-wide. Moreover, with thousands of other telephone employees presently installing, repairing, and maintaining hundreds of thousands of miles of lines and millions of poles, there is imminent the replacement of all of these processes by microwave transmission.[9] In an article on "Push Button Labor" in *Fortune*, August, 1954, there are striking illustrations of the progress of automation in the United States. In the field of petro-chemicals, many plants were then on the verge of complete automation. The Ford plant in Cleveland now processes an engine block in 14.6 minutes, an operation which takes nine hours at the "old-fashioned" River Rouge plant. In the packing industry, hide-pulling machines and other devices have boosted production 20 per cent per man hour. Nor is automation confined to skilled technical work alone; it is moving swiftly into white-collar processes[10] with the introduction of the "Univac" and other electronic "memory" machines. The Metropolitan Life Insurance Company, for example,

9. Robert L. Conley, "New Miracles of the Telephone Age," *National Geographic*, CVI (July, 1954), 87–120. For further important analyses and predictions of effects of automation on society and education, see the pamphlet by Peter F. Drucker, *America's Next Twenty Years* (published in 1955 by Harper's Magazine), and "The Age of the Thinking Robot and What It Will Mean to Us" by Robert Bendiner in *The Reporter*, April 7, 1955, pp. 12–18.

10. For extended treatment of this problem and its implications, see C. Wright Mills, *White Collar: The American Middle Classes*. New York: Oxford University Press, 1951.

has replaced with a single univac computator 100 punch-card machines and 135 punch-card operators. To train college youth to live and work in a new world of automation and to help adults understand the meaning and significance of automation would seem to be a paramount task for post-high-school education.

COMMUNICATION THROUGH MASS MEDIA

The pressure that is exerted by the mass media of communication upon youth of college age and upon older students has grown greater with the years and is changing its patterns. There is increasing need for critical training in the analysis of these media and the significance of their impact upon the minds, emotions, attitudes, and value systems of all of us lest we become a nation of stereotypes and intellectual automatons. Advertising hucksters refine their techniques for turning us into ravenous and unthinking consumers, making use of all media—press, movies, radio, and television. The press itself is undergoing change with a slow choking-out of small and independent newspapers and the alliance of those of mass circulation, chain ownership, and policy control with the dominant networks of radio and television. As a result, for the most part, our students from Maine to California and Duluth to Miami read the same by-line writers, hear the same commentators, view the same TV programs, and are dinned at by the same commercials. In the magazine field, except for the special-interest journals serving small publics, circulations are in the millions, and the trend toward standardization and stereotyping is obvious. The result of these trends is a powerful pull toward uniformity in thinking, feeling, and action in our society and a consequent loss of freedom. They present increasing difficulty for the colleges and other educational institutions to develop critical and imaginative thinking, creative abilities, and the varied and unique talents which are the main strength of democracy.

Corollary to these main currents are others of specific concern to education. Whereas, for centuries, our main source of instruction was *reading*, it has now become essential that we learn how to teach by means of *listening* and *viewing*, in both of which our ignorance is abysmal, although research is under way in both fields in a few universities and colleges. While the colleges are making increasing use of slides, film strips, movies, radio, and some television, they are doing so with as yet inadequate knowledge of the new methods and techniques, with but indefinite impressions regarding the effects of these instruments on learning and retention, and with still less comprehension of the influence of such procedures on student emotions, attitudes, and values.

YOUTH, DEFENSE, AND THE NEW TECHNOLOGY OF WAR

The threat of global war, the seemingly endless persistence of "cold" war, our national policies of defense by "massive retaliation" or peaceful "coexistence," the organization and programs of selective service, of veterans affairs, of manpower commissions, of civil defense, all are of deep and continuing concern to the colleges of the nation. Upon these policies depend questions of enrolment, since the majority of young men, and perhaps many women, may be drafted in universal military training in the armed services. If so, they may perhaps return to advanced schooling at a later time with greater maturity and higher motivation. There depend, too, questions of finance through subsidy not only of veteran students but also of much expanded student reserve corps on the campuses with their essential staffs and technical equipment. On the technological side, defense or war and the development of the weapons, machines, and electronic devices to support them commit our military strength to extremely destructive, extremely mobile, and extremely complicated machines and techniques. Guided missiles, jet propulsion, atomic-powered submarines, 25-mile cameras, and 1,000-mile television sets in 700-mile-an-hour planes are not toys for amateurs. The whole pattern of future war and the use and co-ordination of these instruments demand technical skills, emotional stability, and a psychological maturity such as American youth have never known. To prepare them to handle these extremely complex and interrelated problems is one of the most pressing needs of our time, and the colleges must be one of the basic agencies for this preparation.

Occupational Changes

As has been suggested, the population shifts and the technological changes outlined in the preceding pages will produce a new array of jobs and job change. Patently the American notion of upward occupational mobility is part of the dream of most American families. In recent years there has been a marked change in thinking and feeling about this upward mobility. Formerly most youth desired to move "up" from skilled labor and its wages to "white collar" jobs and salaries. Now, however, this view is being reconsidered because the advance of technology and automation has put such premium upon advanced professional and technical knowledges and skills that people who do not wear the white collar in many instances make more money than those who do. The weekly average wage of the technical earner is already several dollars above that of the bank clerk. This democratization of job status has already brought some troublesome results, such as a tremendous shortage of secretarial help which is by no means, at least as yet, balanced by the automation of office processes. There is some evidence, too, that the shortage of teachers, especially in the scientific and mechanical fields, is in part due to this shift toward higher earnings for technicians and professionals in these fields. Further developments in electronics, plastics, chemicals, metals, and atomic energy will doubtless change the whole pattern of our occupational life.

To illustrate, the Bureau of Labor Statistics shows wage increases between 1939 and 1953 as follows: building construction, 202 per cent; coal mining, 258 per cent; paper production, 207 per cent; textiles, 217 per cent. In contrast, it reports wage increases in retail trades during the same period of only 137 per cent and in telephone of 102 per cent.

In the article on automation in *Fortune* (January, 1954), the writers point to some striking changes occurring in the status of labor within the labor force itself. With the rapidly rising prestige and wages for the skilled and highly skilled, and with automation under way, there is less and less need for unskilled laborers of dull mind, however powerful in muscle they may be. How such marginal men and women may be employed, and for what, is becoming a major problem. Further striking changes in wage payments are coming, for, with automation, the worker can neither speed up nor slow down the output of his machine. Therefore, piecework or by-the-hour payment is diminishing and being replaced by weekly or monthly salaries, and the unions are putting on pressure for a guaranteed annual wage.

While the foregoing is important background, of specific and major importance for colleges are the trends in preprofessional training and in employment in clerical, sales, and distributive occupations and in the semiprofessions. In the two decades between 1920 and 1940 the biggest growth in the labor force was in clerical and sales personnel. Since 1940 the curves of both have been flattening out slowly, but for many years to come it is probable that the economy can absorb all that the post-high-school institutions can train. At present the curves are rocketing upward for the semiprofessional workers such as junior engineers; technicians in electronics, plastics, chemicals, and oil; "vocational" or "practical" nurses; dietitians; medical and dental technologists, and the like, all of whom must have considerable training beyond high school. Most insistent of all is the country's requirement for professionals in engineering, teaching, medicine, social and welfare work, which demand Master's or Doctor's degrees. Governmental civil service—local, state, and federal—requires a high-school certificate for minimal jobs and college degrees for all others. With the United States struggling to learn its role as a leading world power, with the previously described complexity of social forces and their consequences in terms of change, this country will need to identify and develop to its highest capacity every sort of talent and at all levels (see chap. iii). These trends clearly demand of the colleges a strengthening and refinement of their counseling and teaching processes to identify, persuade, and prepare students of many kinds of intelligence and ability for advanced work in the junior colleges, colleges, and universities.

As we look at this picture of occupational change, plus the high mobility of a large proportion of our national labor force, certain demands upon higher education become clear. It is not alone in job training that education at these levels is urgently needed but just as importantly in the development of social intelligence through general education and through expanded activities programs. Upon these may hang the fate of our democracy. The central problem of our time is how to control gigantism, to profit by its benefits, and to retain individual freedom and initiative.[11] It is apparently impossible to have large-scale mass production and not to have gigantic industry. Titans such as Ford and General Motors have, throughout their

11. See David Riesman, *Individualism Reconsidered*. Glencoe, Illinois: Free Press, 1954.

history, absorbed one after another of the smaller companies and, by competition, have forced huge, second-line companies to merge. In like manner, governmental services have expanded to the point where they employ more people than the whole of agriculture in America. The armed forces direct the occupational lives of two or three million of us a year. And the labor unions are now Gargantuan enterprises, with the smaller units continually affiliating with the larger and the C.I.O. merging with the A.F. of L.

With just these few illustrations we can see that one of the foremost problems of the colleges for years to come is how to prepare youth to handle themselves in their relationships with these giants of organization, to work for and with them, to draw wages and salaries from them, but to maintain their independence, their dignity, their personal integrity, their delight in the exercise of political power, and their satisfaction in home and family life and in recreation in leisure hours. This clearly indicates an impelling need for the education of youth and adults in both the liberal and the cultural heritage of the past and, through general education, in how to come to grips with current and future problems.

Another factor in occupational change that will be of continuing importance to post-high-school institutions is that of the migration of industry. Sometimes this occurs because an area is becoming over-industrialized; sometimes because of heavy taxation as compared with little or none; sometimes because of the availability of land, labor supply, or cheap power; sometimes because of the discovery of new natural resources in oil, coal, and other materials; sometimes because of revised policies of national defense. Whatever the causes, industry is on the move, carrying with it hundreds of thousands of mobile workers and precipitating community changes, such as demands for the training of youth in desired skills and techniques and demands for such services as colleges can render in behalf of youth and of those adults whose interests and abilities can be served, whether or not they are gainfully employed.

In Yonkers, New York, for example, the Alexander Smith Carpet Mills closed down their vast plants and moved to South Carolina. At Norwalk, Connecticut, the A.F. of L. Hatters Union carried on a strike of many months against the Hat Corporation of America in an attempt to limit the company's right to transfer its operations to the

South. Twenty years ago, over one-third of the hosiery knitting machines of the country were located in Philadelphia as compared with
7 per cent for the entire South. By 1952 the South had acquired 47
per cent, and Philadelphia had less than 4 per cent. What this industrial migration does in terms of draining people away from some
communities, swelling others, or creating new ones is suggested by
the figures on increase of nonfarm employment. A survey[12] indicates an over-all national increase of 63 per cent; but by regions,
New England gained only 37.4 per cent; Middle Atlantic states, 44
per cent; and the Pacific Coast, 104.6 per cent; with the South rapidly rising into the higher brackets.

Changing Social Mores, Attitudes, and Customs

Stemming more or less directly from the ponderous and powerful
flow of the forces already sketched—population changes, cold war
and defense psychology, occupational shift, automation, and gigantism—come profound changes in the thinking, feeling, attitudes, and
behavior of our people. Each of these has meaning for the future of
our colleges. A few of the most significant of these changes are here
noted.

THE "SICK" COMMUNITY

In the opinion of many sociologists and anthropologists, American
community life in general is sick. In their view, there are few places
where people have put down roots, where they have a feeling of
having achieved a progressively wholesome community life. Neighbors scarcely know one another, nor do they have much, if any,
feeling of interdependence and mutual need. As distance increases,
the feeling of belongingness, of concern, and of desire to co-operate
in the performance of the duties of citizenship diminishes. Control of
community affairs is frequently left to little-known or unknown politicians and, when things go wrong, the only cure seems to be to
"throw the rascals out." Of great moment in these times is the fact
that this destruction of the sense of local community is paralleled by
lack of understanding, sympathy, and out-reaching to the larger
communities of state, nation, and world upon which rest the lives,
the growth, and the happiness of all of us. The sense of "drifting"

12. *Fortune*, L (July, 1954), 35.

and of helplessness is increasingly characteristic of the psychology of our people.[13]

Baker Brownell goes so far as to charge that higher education has been a major culprit in this destruction of community life by "siphoning off" students from active citizenship in their own home town and thus leaving the community devoid of its potential leadership.[14] The implications of all this for the public junior college are of the utmost significance. It is basically a local institution. Well wrought, it can extend its powers and services to counteract a community's sense of drift and helplessness. It can operate as a major centralizing agency to bring neighbors together on many fronts—cultural, recreational, occupational, civic, and political. It can train directly for citizenship in both its course work and its activities and can help to extend the sense of belonging beyond the borders of the town or district to the larger world. And it can avoid or postpone for at least a year or more the "siphoning off" Brownell describes and give youth that much more chance to get their roots down into the nourishing soil of the community.

MARRIAGE, HOME, FAMILY, AND THE "PLACE" OF WOMEN

The deep-rooted tradition in most cultures is that the family is the core of all civilized living, is the basic unit of society. Changes in any of the established characteristics of family life affect not only individuals and communities but also the structure, organization, and health of society itself. Some of the changes in American attitudes and customs in this area are of great and growing significance for post-high-school education. The majority of youthful students are in the throes of preparing to mate; many of them are living at home and struggling to attain adult independence from it. Some are newly married and absorbed in the problems of marital adjustment, child-bearing, and child-rearing. In meeting their need of general education for knowledge and insight into these relationships, the college has a most important role. Moreover, the college has much to do to help adults in the community understand both the marriage and fam-

13. See David Riesman, *Individualism Reconsidered, op. cit.,* and his earlier work, *The Lonely Crowd.* New Haven, Connecticut: Yale University Press, 1950.

14. Baker Brownell, *The Community and the College.* New York: Harper & Bros., 1952.

ily problems of youth and the effects of their own parts in compli-
cating these problems or in helping the young people work out their
solution. We leave it to authors of later chapters to draw the full
implications and here sketch only some of the changes evident in our
society.

Youth Are Marrying Younger. In the half-century from 1890 to
1940 there was a persistent decline in the median age of first marriage. During the following decade, 1940–50, the decline was as great
as during the previous 50 years. There was also a continuing narrow-
ing of the age difference of the two sexes at marriage. In 1890, the
median age of first marriage was 26.1 for men and 22 for women. By

TABLE 2

Marital Status of American Youth

Age	1940			1952		
	Married	Widowed	Divorced	Married	Widowed	Divorced
Male:						
14–19....	106,000	1,000	1,000	206,000	6,000	4,000
20–24....	1,557,000	8,000	18,000	2,168,000	2,000	20,000
Female:						
14–19....	717,000	7,000	9,000	872,000	6,000	24,000
20–24....	3,026,000	33,000	56,000	3,888,000	10,000	84,000

1951, it was 22.6 for men and 20.4 for women. More startling are the
changes revealed in the table of marriage and divorces among those
whom most adults used to consider far too young and immature to
marry (Table 2).

These figures speak, perhaps grimly, for themselves and for their
implications for the colleges since these people were of high-school
and college age. We can think of nothing that more clearly points
up the need for general education in marriage, home, and family life
and for intensified guidance and counseling.

More Women Are Working. Not long ago our mores declared
that "woman's place is in the home" and that "a young man should
not think of marriage until he is able to support a wife in the manner
to which she is accustomed." With the "emancipation" of women,
with the growing demand for her entering the national labor force,
and with the powerful lure of having two monthly checks to raise

the family income to new and satisfying heights, women have increasingly trained themselves in school and college and have gone to work. Between 1870 and 1950, the number of men in the labor force of this country increased four times, but the number of women increased nine times; and there is every indication that this trend will continue. By 1954, according to the Labor Department, there were 19,500,000 women at work, and their median age was 38 years, one-third of them between 45 and 64. Implications for the colleges are clear, in terms of vocational counseling and the development of further training in occupational refresher courses as well as of the extension of general education to prepare for personal and family adjustments.

Learning What To Do with Leisure. One of the great, unsolved problems of both youth and adults is how to occupy fruitfully and with personal, familial, and community satisfaction the growing hours, days, and weeks of freedom from the compulsions of work. These increases in leisure time have, in the past, been forced upon us before we were ready for them, and we have, as a people, by no means caught up with the lag. The probability of a thirty-hour, four-day week is already a subject of discussion. Technological unemployment seems to be a continuing aspect of such an economy as ours. The necessity for finding ways to keep the aged and retired not only alive but lively has been indicated. We have not treated the all-too-familiar picture of the grim business of juvenile delinquency and youthful crime. But obvious enough is the fact that the leisure activities in the average community are far short of adequately involving individuals in community services. Obvious, too, is the fact that most of us spend far too much of our leisure in a fruitless spectator role, whether it be watching television for endless hours or attending competitive sports, concerts, and movies.

If colleges are to help reverse this unsatisfactory trend, there will be a need for a swift change in attitude. Under the influence of our tradition of puritanism and pioneering, we still have stern residuals of attitude and feeling against idleness, play, or recreation. In education we tend to look upon standard academic courses and intellectual activities as the solid substance of our work and upon leisure-time activities as fads, froth, and frills. The values of a course in fly- or bait-casting is considered far below one in mathematics, whereas in terms of human happiness and mental health it may be far above. We can see, outside the college walls, strong trends toward essential change in these attitudes in the "do-it-yourself" movement, in the sales of fishing and hunting licenses, in the purchase of recordings and muscial instruments for amateur delight. But we know of no college which has given adequate attention to the development of programs for all the many kinds of leisure-time activities needed by the community which it serves.

Educational Implications of Social Change

The powerful forces that move in and through human society, only a few of which have been sketched in the preceding pages, have many important implications for the future development of post-high-school education in the United States. The complexity of these forces, their vast energy, and the swift and kaleidoscopic changes they generate demand constant watchfulness and intense study on the part of all who are responsible for higher schooling. Without rapidly increasing knowledge of the nature of the forces and of their impact upon our people and our institutions, we can do no more than thrash and flounder in blind opportunism with a certainty of enormous wastage of human talents and energies and a threatening shadow of disaster. On the other hand, with knowledge and insight into scientific, technological, political, economic, social, and humanistic trends, we may be able to use these very forces to give higher education new blood, bone, and sinew, and to chart the direction and speed of its development in an expanding universe of junior colleges, colleges, and universities.

COMMUNITY AND PUBLIC EDUCATION

The implication here is that each institution needs to define its community in order to study it, to be alert to changes wrought in it by social forces, and to serve it. This principle applies whether the institution be a public junior college, a municipal college, a regional college, a state college, or a state university. From grass roots to global scope, the community and its relationships with public education require constant vigilance, for upon the service rendered by the college to the community will depend in large measure the health and growth of both.

POPULATION TRENDS AND HIGHER EDUCATION

Birth Rate. Barring atomic and hydrogen war and other unforeseeable disasters, the present and apparently continuing high birth rate will give post-high-school education a tremendous and increasing potential enrolment for all levels and all kinds of institutions. The birth rate alone guarantees this flood of many sorts of young people needing and demanding schooling at the upper levels.

Life Expectancy. The rapidly declining death rate with its resultant huge increase in number and proportion of older people in our population has further implications. (*a*) The adult-education processes of all higher institutions must be organized to meet the demands for college training of those who have missed it and for occupational refresher courses to keep adults abreast of developments in the techniques and processes of their current employment; to train for transfer to new jobs when necessary; to help adults keep aware of progress in those fields that affect them and interest them most; to offer escape from the humdrum routine of daily tasks into the "realms of gold" of music, poetry, drama, and art; and to enhance their interests, know-how, and skills in all the arts of leisure-time activities. (*b*) All educators must be alerted to the facts of the enormously increasing power and influence of older people, in the policy-making of our society.

It seems inevitable that adults from forty-five years of age and up will more and more control most of the planning and operation of higher institutions. Tendencies toward conservatism and reaction or the desire for placid security and safety rather than adventure and progress must be watched for. Especially in the economic and political field there appears to be a hazard that this domination by the aged may lead to proposals and actions for curtailing the education of children and young people in order to make the aged comfortable with pensions, insurance, and social security. It is essential, in our view, that educators see clearly the implications of this evolving conflict of youth and age and put forth every effort to see to it that both are served.

Immigration. National policies and practices in immigration have profound meanings for the future of higher education. It is clear that we are likely to have increasing demands put upon our educational system to welcome and educate thousands of people from many parts of the world; to train our own students to familiarize themselves with hitherto strange or unknown areas, peoples, and languages, and to prepare many of them to teach and train faraway natives in their own home grounds.

Mobility. Internal migration of our peoples is significant for the future of post-high-school education. What this mobility means in terms of rich and varied educational and other experiences, on the one hand, or in terms of rootlessness, instability, and drifting, on the other, we by no means clearly know. However, several aspects of the migratory problem bear strongly on higher education: (*a*) The shifting of families from East to West, North to South, farm to city, interior to periphery, drains old communities and establishes or expands new ones. A college in a sick and dying community must expand its area of service or itself collapse. In those of the West and South, particularly Florida, where a "four corners" may become a city in a decade, the demand for post-high-school education requires from one to a dozen brand-new institutions. (*b*) Students of varied backgrounds, schooling, interests, abilities, customs, and language patterns will increasingly make up the enrolments of our colleges. Despite every effort to achieve homogeneity, to set simple and clear standards of admission and performance, heterogeneity and variability are inevitable. (*c*) Of special significance is the swelling hegira of Negroes and, to some extent, other minority groups to regions where post-high-school education and ensuing higher-level employment is open to them and where, at intermediate levels, the labor unions are supporting the drive of these groups for junior-college vocational and technical training. Similar trends may be found increasingly among the offspring of migrant workers who follow seasonal employment.

TECHNOLOGICAL CHANGES

Science and technology, invention and production, are shifting the life patterns of Americans at a breathless pace. The need for gross human and animal muscle power dwindles almost to the vanishing point. This trend implies much of profound significance for higher education. Not only is it essential that enormous numbers of our youth and adults be trained to master the operation of the machines and processes of this new, startling technological world, but they must somehow be taught through liberal and through general education the personal and social meanings of them. The following trends are of the deepest import:

The trend toward mechanization and automation of production and distribution is fast making old routines of teaching and learning at the higher levels as obsolete as the fish-grabbing and horse-socking of *The Saber-Tooth Curriculum*. What automation will come to mean can be only dimly foreseen. Whatever its meanings may be, it is certain that post-high-school students will have to be taught to understand them and to adjust to the changes brought about.

Current trends in communication through mass media threaten to pour us all into standard molds of thought, feeling, and action and to curtail the very freedoms of the mind, of radical thought, and of inquiry which are the life blood of higher education. On the brighter side it seems probable that the new instruments of high-fidelity recording, of television, and of electromicroscopy will swiftly open up new worlds of learning, although as yet we know far less about what and how students learn through listening and viewing than we do about reading.

The new technology of defense and war implies much for the colleges of our nation. It requires the preliminary institutional training of a continuous flow of many thousands of high-order technicians and professional junior officers in the reserve corps, for modern complex tools of destruction are not toys for amateurs. Nor are the ordering of combat, the strategy and tactics of atomic warfare problems to be handled by militiamen leaving the plow to pick up a muzzle-loading rifle. The broader concerns of selective service, war manpower, civil defense, and veterans' affairs are matters demanding the fullest co-operative planning by higher institutions and the federal government.

OCCUPATIONAL CHANGES

Population shifts, growing and dying communities, development of new sources of power, scientific and technological advances, all bring in their wake a mighty turbulence in the employment market for men and women. One general result of such changes is the rapid elimination of unskilled jobs, the continuous proliferation and elaboration of processes into semiskilled, skilled, and highly skilled techniques requiring more and more advanced training, and finally into automation and mechanization that wipe out most of the tasks which have been learned. Another general trend of significance is a clearly emerging pattern of supporting the work of each high-level professional—whether he be doctor, engineer, teacher, lawyer, army commander, business executive, or industrial manager—with a large corps of specially trained assistants of several or many kinds: technicians, personnel people, salesmen, and public relations operators. In practically all instances these require training at post-high-school levels for initial employment and, thereafter, both in-service and adult refresher courses. Some important social problems have emerged from these broad trends:

1. The problem of maintaining full employment, especially for youth, if and when peace in the world is established. The United States cannot in any way afford another economic depression such as that of the 1930's when more than four million young people were out of work and out of school, subject to the dry-rot of idleness. In that time, temporary expedients were found in the National Youth Administration and the Civilian Conservation Corps. These, with the onset of World War II, saved the bulk of our youth from deterioration, but the war itself killed and maimed many thousands. At the war's end, the G.I. bills flooded the colleges with veterans, kept them temporarily off the job market. Then the new crop of high-school graduates and college young people were drafted for the Korean war and for national defense. In view of these experiences in our immediate past, what solutions can society find? Is atomic war the solution? Or a vast system of federal, state, and local public works to employ young people until they can be absorbed in the regular labor force? Or continued schooling at post-high-school levels? Or, optimistically, an economy expanding to an annual product of more than 500 billions so that the nation can afford both an expanded higher education and work for all hands?

2. The problem of how to teach our youth to maintain their independence, initiative, and personal freedoms in the face of the trend toward gigantism. Involvement in world affairs, vast and expanding productivity apparently require giant organization in business, industry, government, labor, and in education itself. Employment in any of these massive enterprises tends to induce feelings of isolation,

loneliness, and futility. How to educate youth to resist these pressures, to engage in the pursuit of happiness and the joy of living on the job, with home and family, and in their hours of leisure becomes increasingly a critical question.

3. The enormous increase in the number of women working in the national labor force. It seems clear that an increasingly higher proportion of young women will enter and complete junior-college, college, and university training since (*a*) employers require it; (*b*) employers have liberalized policies on leaves for pregnancy; (*c*) our mores have changed so that young husbands no longer are ashamed to have their wives working, but, instead, both are delighted to have a doubled income; (*d*) women who have received training and practiced a profession for a while and then withdrew to devote themselves to family life, on their return to the job, will need and demand refresher training. Further, if family life is not to be disrupted and destroyed by this process, the colleges must educate both men and women in how to preserve and enhance it under these radically changed conditions. Concentration upon these basic problems of modern women by higher institutions seems mandatory.

Conclusion

The social forces and the changes they produce, treated all too briefly in this chapter, indicate to the authors a clear need in nearly every community in America for post-high-school institutions as a flexible and growing part of community structure. Such institutions, well managed, will serve both youth and age in accord with all healthy local and national and world trends and against those that are evil and destructive. Working through liberal and general education, they will help to preserve the best and soundest of our traditions but will modify them as social change requires. They will be alert to needs for training for jobs, for counseling, for developing citizenship and neighborliness, and for active and fruitful employment of leisure hours. They will be a center and a resource to which our citizens will turn to meet their educational needs whatever they may be. At best they may exercise a compelling, directive force for the preservation of American liberties, lives, and pursuits toward happiness, and an antidote for the confusions and conflicts which are inevitably attendant upon the new world that is being born.

CHAPTER III

Educational Demands Arising from Individual Needs and Purposes

PAUL L. DRESSEL

The Nature of Individual Needs

The individuals who seek or need more education differ widely in ability, in adjustment, in beliefs, and in physical and mental health. While some needs are more potent in determining interest in further education, others are equally potent in determining the kind and amount. Some individuals desire only a few months of training while others aim at the professions. Some have heavy responsibilities and few resources while others are in the most favorable position. Financial need and accessibility are major elements in determining whether individuals can acquire education beyond the high-school level. Equally important is the availability of a wide range of programs adapted to the varying needs, interests, and abilities of the prospective students. Then, too, the programs must be so related to the economy of the community as to give reasonable insurance of placement. The six brief sketches which follow will illustrate the variability and the complexity of the patterns of need which cause individuals to seek more education.

Pete Smith has been clerking in a supermarket for six years since he graduated from high school. His salary, though adequate for himself and his wife, is not large and is not likely to become much larger. Advancement in his work is a possibility, but it is not attractive since Pete finds his job steadily less interesting.

Pete believes that with further instruction he can equip himself for something that will challenge more fully the ability he knows he has and that others assure him he has. At age twenty-eight he is confident that he can still learn. A friend has told him of openings in the personnel offices of a large local industrial plant, and Pete believes that with his combination of intelligence and personal characteristics he can, in time, qualify for the duties and responsibilities of such a position. He has talked about the problem with his wife, and she is ready to co-operate in every way in helping Pete see his plan through to a successful conclusion.

Pete has a legitimate need for more education. Will there be facilities to help him satisfy this need?

———————

Mrs. Ellen Brewster is forty-five years old. The last of her four children, a daughter, has just married and established her own home. Mrs. Brewster's husband died ten years ago but left her in comfortable circumstances so that she was able to see all four children through college. She herself had only three years of high-school education, but she is an intelligent woman and has maintained a vigorous mental outlook, partly because of the stimulation provided by her own children's maturing interests.

While her youngest child was in college, Mrs. Brewster began to take a more active part than formerly in community activities, particularly in those relating to social equality and interracial relations. As she met with like-minded persons and participated in their discussions, she became more uncomfortably aware of her limited knowledge. At first she undertook to enlighten herself by reading books recommended by friends or by the local library. However, she found this none too satisfying—it was easy to neglect the reading she had set herself to do; and even as she did it, she was aware of gaps and disturbing discontinuities in what she was reading.

Mrs. Brewster, like Pete Smith, has a legitimate educational need, no less important by reason of her being in middle life. She is determined to do something about this need. What can she do? Is she correct in her belief that somewhere she should be able to find the kind of instructional service she wants?

———————

Fred Beaver is the only son of a small-town businessman. In high school he made a fair academic record but participated only slightly in the extraclassroom activities. He was not unpopular among his peers, but neither was he popular. Instead of belonging to the drama group or to the basketball squad, he seemed to prefer to spend his time at home. Although not maladjusted, he is clearly not a happy person, and even a casual observer might predict that without attention he will become even less happy. Yet, up to this point, if one may judge from the lack of tangible assistance for Fred, even this casual observer has been lacking.

Fred's parents have noted his increasing dependence upon them and are now worried about it. They are debating the wisdom of putting him "on his own" by sending him away to college.

grocery clerk, has realized the necessity of more education in achieving certain aims and now needs only to be provided the opportunity.

THE PROBLEMS OF YOUTH

College-age youth are on the threshold of a much-desired independence, but their lack of experience in self-direction and in self-discipline results in a mixture of hopes, fears, and doubts, all magnified by a variety of problems which they are just beginning to recognize as their own. These recurring common problems fall into several different categories, and no one individual necessarily faces difficulties in all categories.

Vocational Problems. Despite the vocational guidance provided for high-school students, many have not reached a firm decision by the date of high-school graduation. In a study of junior-college Freshmen, Todd found that only 19 per cent lacked a vocational choice, but 38 per cent of those with a choice would have chosen differently if they could have overcome existing handicaps. Forty per cent of the students with a choice indicated doubt as to their prospects of actually working in their chosen field.[1] The vocational interests and choices of the students reflected their uncertainty and represented much wishful thinking which was subject to change. Five of the six persons mentioned at the beginning of this chapter had clearly identified vocational needs, but their dilemmas show that earning a living is such a pervasive part of life that vocational problems inevitably affect and are affected by all other aspects of a person's experience.

Social and Emotional Problems. In Doane's survey of the needs of 2,069 rural and urban youth, the need for help in development of social abilities ranked next to that pertaining to vocational choice and placement.[2] Acquiring poise, social status as an adult, and greater independence are important phases of this need. So is the cultivation of emotional control and self-assurance to the point where pleasure

1. Lindsey O. Todd, "Meeting the Needs of Junior College Students," p. 156. Unpublished Doctor's dissertation, George Peabody College for Teachers, June, 1943.

2. Donald C. Doane, *The Needs of Youth*, p. 116. New York: Bureau of Publications, Teachers College, Columbia University, 1942.

and satisfaction rather than strain and frustration result from adult behavior and contacts.

The process of acquiring independence as an adult is particularly difficult for the college student who lives at home and lacks the status imparted by a job, for personal and parental views of the amount of independence desirable may be in continual conflict. Such problems as those of Fred Beaver are recurring and often go unrecognized.

Health Problems. Most teen-agers are reasonably healthy, accidents being the principal cause of death at this age.[3] For most youth, life and health are taken for granted, although Lantagne's study of Pasadena City College and Ventura Junior College students reported a high degree of interest in health programs and pointed to a higher degree of interest in health problems on the part of junior-college than of high-school students.[4] Douglas and Rack found that lack of time for sleep was the most frequent health problem of junior-college students.[5] The survey by Diehl and Shepard, now somewhat dated but still one of the most comprehensive reports available, points up the presence of numerous, serious, but not disabling, physical defects.[6] Underweight or overweight, visual defects, dental caries, chronic nasal obstruction, chronic tonsillitis, and spinal curvature were found to be quite prevalent. Such defects lower efficiency and, if untreated, may lead to even more serious difficulties.

It has been estimated that from 10 to 15 per cent of college students have mental-health problems requiring psychiatric attention. Such services are now more readily sought than formerly. Longstaff's[7] comparison of beliefs in 1923 and 1946 indicated that the

3. *Health of Teen-Agers,* pp. 1–4. Metropolitan Life Insurance Company Statistical Bulletin No. 34, August, 1953.

4. Joseph E. Lantagne, "An Analysis of Health Interests of 1,000 Junior-College Students in California," *Junior College Journal,* XXI (April, 1951), 429–33.

5. O. B. Douglas and Lucille Rack, "Problems of Junior-College Students," *Junior College Journal,* XX (March, 1950), 377–89.

6. H. S. Diehl and C. E. Shepard, *The Health of College Students,* p. 46. Washington: American Council on Education, 1939.

7. Howard P. Longstaff, "A Note on Popular Pseudo-Psychological Beliefs in 1923 and in 1946," *Journal of Applied Psychology,* XXXI (February, 1947), 91–93.

percentage of students believing in the value of psychotherapy increased from 45 in 1923 to 89 in 1946.

Religious Problems. Surveys suggest that students consider moral and religious issues of less importance than the other problem areas here listed, although for individuals religious problems may be of paramount importance, especially when differences in the views and affiliations of parents result in conflicting pressures and loyalties. Congdon reported that only 3.25 per cent of college Freshmen checked problems of morals and religion as compared with 9 to 20 per cent who checked other problems.[8] Apparently, for most students, the span of years ahead makes such problems seem less immediate and, therefore, less urgent. Yet, the importance of moral and religious values in giving meaning to life suggests that education cannot be indifferent to needs in this area.

Financial Problems. At least three of our six illustrations of educational needs (pp. 41–44) point to the fact that the expense of college attendance is one of the major hurdles for those seeking post-high-school education. Proximity and tuition rates become important factors in the decision to continue education beyond high school. Even the lessened expense of attendance at a local college does not always eliminate the problem. Wedemeyer reported in 1951 that 75 per cent of the students enrolled at the Racine Extension Center worked outside of school.[9] Approximately 70 per cent of these working students claimed to be responsible for 50 per cent or more of their total living expenses. Moreover, 63 per cent of all students enrolled stated that financial considerations were a major factor in selecting the Extension Center. Surveys in Minnesota, Illinois, and California junior colleges have revealed similar conditions. Orange Coast College found that 63.1 per cent of its students held jobs outside of school, and over half of these supported one or more persons partially or in full.[10]

Esthetic Problems. As Mrs. Brewster (p. 42) exemplifies, knowl-

8. Nora A. Congdon, "The Perplexities of College Freshmen," *Educational and Psychological Measurement*, III (Winter, 1943), 67–75.

9. Charles A. Wedemeyer, "Morale-type Survey on the College Level," *Junior College Journal*, XXI (1951), 434–43.

10. *Educational and Occupational Needs*, p. 86. An appraisal made by the staff of Orange Coast College. Costa Mesa, California: Orange Coast College, 1954 (mimeographed).

edge of art, architecture, music, and literature is a mark of culture and a social advantage to which many persons aspire. However, as new standards are acquired, conflict may be generated by their incompatibility with those implicit in the home. The plight of the student who finds that her home and its furnishings are very different from, if not actually inferior to, those of her friends is understandable, but the dismay of the parents who have sacrificed to send a daughter to college only to find her dissatisfied with their home and their standards is pathetic.

Dating and Marriage Problems. "Adolescents are marrying earlier each decade, and marrying people more nearly their own age. One-third of the girls and 7 per cent of the boys married by age 19. Two-thirds of the girls and over 40 per cent of the boys married by age 25. The younger the marriage, the more likely it was to fail."[11] (See chap. ii.) Following World War II, married G.I.'s brought about acceptance of the marital state as a respectable one for both male and female college students. The realization even developed that marriage removed certain types of behavior from the area of disciplinary action! However, the changed attitude of colleges does not solve the problems of youth, for further education may enforce a delay of marriage with consequent tensions and moral conflicts. Conversely, marriage may enforce discontinuance of education; indeed, a large percentage of drop-outs among women students is attributable to marriage. The problem of Betty Willsen, the young widow (p. 43), points to the desirability of encouraging young women to continue their education until they have acquired the means for self-support. For married couples, one or both of whom are enrolled in college, marital conflicts, children, and finance may give rise to problems which seriously interfere with progress in college work.

Academic Adjustment. Problems of adjustment to their educational programs are typically rated by students as their most common and pressing problems. This finding is perhaps less surprising and rather different in meaning than it at first appears. The uncertainty of being able to meet a new set of experiences satisfactorily creates

11. Midcentury White House Conference on Children and Youth, *Children and Youth at the Midcentury:* A Chart Book. Raleigh, North Carolina: Health Publications Institute, 1951 (unpaged).

the immediate problem of educational adjustment. Thus, for five of the individuals discussed at the beginning of this chapter, it would seem quite likely that some difficulties would be faced in adjusting to the academic routine.

THE PROBLEMS OF ADULTS

Differences between Youth and Adults. Age, the most obvious distinction between youth and adults, has only limited significance for educational purposes. With due allowance for some discontinuity in education, the age range of college youth may be regarded as running from 18–24 for four-year colleges and from 18 to 21 for junior colleges. Since persons in this age group are usually treated as adults, the problem areas of youth are, with only slight reinterpretation, applicable to adults. But adults are distinguishable from youth in regard to their assumption of such responsibilities as the following:

1. Participation in the functions of government through voting and holding offices
2. Maintenance of economic stability for themselves and their families
3. Parenthood, home, and family life
4. Determination of the social, cultural, and spiritual environment for present and future generations

For many young people, college may be regarded complacently as a continuation of schooling with a degree or a terminal certificate as the immediate goal. The adult commonly comes to class with a more specific and immediate need. Since education for the adult is ordinarily a part-time affair and the completion of a degree is often too remote to be satisfying as an objective, education must be related and adjusted to his present responsibilities and associated concerns.

Contrasting Characteristics of Youth and Adults.[12,13] The adults portrayed in our case studies illustrate that adults enrol for further education because they want it. Therefore, they are well motivated and eager to learn. They seem to be more sensitive than youth to

12. *Handbook for Teachers of Adults.* Bulletin of the California State Department of Education (Sacramento, California), XX, No. 4 (1951).

13. Summary prepared by Dr. John B. Schwertman of remarks made by Dr. Raymond Kuhlen, "What Adults Are Like." The summary is available from the Center for the Study of Liberal Education for Adults, 940 East Fifty-eighth Street, Chicago 37, Illinois.

environmental factors such as seating, lighting, and ventilation. They demand and appreciate good instruction. Adults are more fixed in their ways, and their responsibilities make them more realistic and also more hesitant about commitments requiring extra work for long periods. Thus, they like materials in short, complete units which they can relate directly to daily problems. Conflicting pressures, such as problems on the job and sickness at home, make it difficult or impossible to give much attention to educational materials outside of class unless these relate directly to such difficulties. Important as education is to Pete Smith, his responsibilities as a husband and father and the necessity of continuing to perform effectively as a grocery clerk must often result in his giving less time to his educational preparation than he would wish.

Adults view the future as part of the present much more than do youth. The adult often seeks to extend his present-future concept by interest in genealogy, by identification with his children, and by increased concern with immortality. Having attained some measure of security, yet having basic insecurities, adults are apt to be disturbed by change in procedure or policy, or by tests or requirements which threaten to make their deficiencies apparent to themselves or others. Time is tremendously important to adults because of the many roles and responsibilities which they have. The sense of urgency thus created makes adult students appreciative of systematic and business-like handling of classes. Yet, education added onto a full-time job cannot be entirely a formal, serious experience. The adult demands opportunity for participation in class activity; he wants a congenial atmosphere and good fellowship, and he expects to enjoy the class. Denied these satisfactions, he is likely to discontinue.

OTHER FACTORS PREDISPOSING INDIVIDUALS
TO SEEK MORE EDUCATION

Sociological and Technological Change. In the preceding chapter MacLean and Dodson have discussed the impetus given to post-high-school education by sociological and technological change. An increasing number of specialized jobs, the increasing complexity of modern civilization, and the ideals of democracy mold the view that each person should have all the education which he can profitably assimilate.

Education is still the major means of upward social mobility.[14] In fact, the expectation that college-level education will lead into executive and professional occupations commanding a high income is a major difficulty in dealing with individuals for whom desire has outraced ability. Also, as college training and degrees have become requirements for a larger number of occupations, an increasing percentage of youth must face the necessity of college training as a means of maintaining the status already achieved by the family.

Social Background and Motivation. Motivation for more education is molded from the earliest years, and any attempt to encourage more individuals to attend college must begin early. The importance of motivation is exemplified by the estimate that perhaps two-thirds of the youth who do not go to college lack the motivation to do so.[15]

Havighurst and Rodgers argue that motivation is closely related to social status and that the social patterns of the lower class lead these youth to ignore college or consider it as unrelated to their aspirations and beyond their means. Certainly, parental hopes and pressures have a profound effect on youth, and college attendance by close friends is often the incentive for similar planning by both youth and adults. Encouragement, financial aid, and the immediate availability of education can do much to develop motivation. Many adults whose early contacts did not encourage their seeking more education may later need only to have the opportunities made clear to them.

International Tension and General Uncertainty. The uncertainties of the past ten years have made higher education more attractive than it might otherwise have been. To youth, the value of college training has been emphasized by the possibility of deferment of military service and of better assignment once in the service. With the future uncertain, it has seemed to many people, also, that a level of education which would make for flexibility in selection of an occupation offers the best possible assurance of satisfactory employment.

14. Carson McGuire, "Adolescent Society and Social Mobility." Unpublished Doctor's Dissertation, University of Chicago, 1949.

15. Robert J. Havighurst and Robert R. Rodgers, "The Role of Motivation in Attendance at Post-High-School Education Institutions," in Byron S. Hollinshead's *Who Should Go to College*, p. 162. New York: Columbia University Press, 1952.

WHY INDIVIDUALS WANT AND NEED MORE EDUCATION

A broad range of problems and needs of individuals has been briefly presented earlier in this chapter. A number of forces in present-day society which emphasize the value of and need for education have also been noted. Although the reasons why individuals seek more education are to be found in these problems, needs, and forces, this advantage is too vague. The factors are so numerous and affect individuals so differently that the ultimate reasons for seeking further education may not be identical for any two persons. Indeed, few individuals can explain fully their reasons for wanting more education. Furthermore, wants and needs do not always correspond and, in fact, may sometimes be antithetical.

Accepting the entire range of problems and needs and the various social forces as factors which strongly condition the decision of an individual to undertake and to persist in further education, among the more immediate motivations for more education there are three which command attention: vocational preparation and advancement, the acquiring of a general or cultural education, and the development of recreational or practical skills.

Vocational Preparation and Advancement. Both youth and their parents commonly regard education, whether or not it is vocational in nature, as having definite vocational advantages. This attitude is not surprising, for even liberal-arts colleges have often "sold" education by emphasizing the increased earnings of college graduates. Nicholson, surveying 5,211 adults attending evening schools, trade and business schools, and day colleges, found that 73 per cent of the men and 45 per cent of the women gave economic-occupational reasons for attending those classes.[16]

General and Cultural Education. Neither youth nor adults are solely vocationally minded in their search for more education. In many cases where the initial impetus is entirely vocational, interest in cultural values soon develops. Perhaps the real explanation is that the students are much less conscious of a distinction between cultural and useful learning. With appropriate interpretation, those deficient in such skills as writing, speaking, or mathematics want such courses when they see the need for these skills in their work or in

16. David H. Nicholson, "Why Adults Attend School," *Adult Education Bulletin*, VIII (August, 1949), 172–77.

the home, in social relationships, and citizenship activities. Most youth and adults are quite aware that vocational proficiency is not the only factor upon which advancement depends; they are equally aware that their job does not encompass all of life and that an understanding of man's cultural heritage is relevant to the aesthetic, social, emotional, and religious concerns of individuals.

Recreational and Practical Skills. Home-planning and home-maintenance interests have both a practical and an avocational aspect. Some persons are interested in building, remodeling, or redecorating a home. Others, out of a desire for a hobby, want to learn woodworking, upholstering, bridge, jewel polishing, photography, or other recreational or maintenance skills. It is entirely natural that many adults with no experience in such tasks look for evening classes where they can learn how to do some of their own work. For youth there may be somewhat less immediate interest in recreational and practical skills. Yet, for youth as well as for adults, such activity provides some aesthetic satisfaction. Practical, vocational, and cultural values are not entirely separable, and most education experiences contribute in varying degrees to all three.

THE ROLE OF OTHER PROBLEM AREAS AND NEEDS

The three major reasons for seeking further education which have just been discussed do not obviously include the others discussed earlier. Except as emotional problems are intertwined with vocational, aesthetic, or practical interests, few students seek further education for emotional adjustment. With rare exceptions, problems of health, religion, finances, marriage, and academic success are not so much reasons for seeking further education as they are considerations which help him select an institution and an educational program or to continue his studies to the completion of that program. In any case, these characteristics become important in planning the educational experience for such students. Therefore, no college can afford to ignore the diverse problems and needs of its students.

Reasons for Selection of a Particular College. The findings of a survey of students' reasons for attendance at particular higher institutions in Minnesota indicate that the economic factor is operative in attendance at junior colleges, whereas religious influences, size of college, and reputation of its program are prominent elements in the attendance at private liberal-arts colleges.[17] The economic factor also provides a differential between attendance at junior colleges and at state colleges and universities.

In a study of the junior college in Illinois, Koos found that only 19.7 per cent of high-school graduates went on to college when there was not a free junior college in their community as against 53.5 per cent of all high-school graduates attending when the junior college was present. In the latter case, also, 46.7 per cent of the graduates of lower economic status were found to be attending the junior college.[18]

Aside from financial reasons, the choice of the local junior college by a student with a poor high-school record or with subject deficiencies is often only a choice between the alternatives of going or not going to college. Hence, junior-college students, as a group, are likely to be somewhat less motivated and less enthusiastic than those attending colleges away from home. On the other hand, as junior colleges increasingly offer special curriculums adapted to the business and industry of the community, the number of individuals attending the junior college for more positive reasons may be expected to increase.

Terminal Students and Terminal Programs. The educational plans of youth and the educational demands of employers are both highly unrealistic at times. Post-high-school education not leading to a Bachelor's degree is frequently ignored or discounted so that students are encouraged to enrol in four-year programs rather than in more appropriate terminal courses. The "white collar" complex of youth and parents also leads them to value liberal-arts and professional programs and to ignore others more suitable to their interests and abilities.

Mortality by the end of the Sophomore year in four-year colleges is 40 to 50 per cent of the entering group, and only one-third to one-half of all entering Freshman students complete degree programs. The 1955 junior-college directory lists less than half as many Sophomores (65,576) as Freshmen (144,418) enrolled in public jun-

17. *Higher Education in Minnesota*, pp. 168 and 215. Prepared by the Minnesota Commission on Higher Education, Dean M. Schweickhard (chairman). Minneapolis: University of Minnesota Press, 1950.

18. Coleman Griffith, *The Junior College in Illinois*, p. 7. Urbana, Illinois: University of Illinois Press, 1945.

ior colleges.[19] From a study of Illinois junior colleges, both private and public, Koos reported that the proportions continuing into the second year and graduating were, respectively, about three-fifths and one-third.[20] Thus, education of junior-college level is terminal for the great majority of enrollees, yet only 30 to 50 per cent of the students enter terminal programs. Even this figure is misleading because 50 to 60 per cent of the terminal-curriculum students take general cultural programs which overlap heavily the programs of students planning to transfer. From 1940 to 1952, a group of public junior colleges showed an increase of from 36 to 43 per cent of their students enrolled in terminal programs. Data from one junior college showed an increase over a twelve-year period from 4 per cent to 67 per cent. Increased enrolment in terminal programs may result from changes in the character of the group entering the junior college, but, more probably for many students it comes from increased awareness of the appropriateness of terminal education to their needs.

Reasons for Drop-outs. The reasons for drop-outs may involve any of the problem areas discussed earlier. Apathy toward study is a major factor among those students whose original motivation for college attendance was low.[21] Many of these students drop out of college even before counselors can become acquainted with them. A study made at Orange Coast College indicated that, presumably because of the efforts of counselors and instructors, the drop-out in the 17-to-20 age group decreased 15 per cent from 1949–50 to 1953–54. In the same period there was a 15 per cent increase of drop-outs in the over-25 age group, particularly among part-time enrollees.[22]

Another factor in junior-college drop-outs lies in the nature of terminal programs. As soon as the student feels he has attained the necessary degree of proficiency for a job he wants, continuance in school may well be resolved in favor of the job. Perhaps the ready assumption that discontinuance means that the student has acquired

19. C. C. Colvert and M. L. Baker, *Junior College Directory,* 1955, p. 4. Washington: American Association of Junior Colleges, 1955.

20. L. V. Koos, "The Junior College in Illinois." University of Illinois Mimeographed Report No. 8 (November, 1944), 8 p.

21. Michael F. Serene, "Motivational Counseling," *Personnel and Guidance Journal,* XXXI (February, 1953), 319–24.

22. *Educational and Occupational Needs, op. cit.,* p. 123.

little of significance needs to be revised to be applicable to junior colleges—particularly the terminal vocational programs. Many drop-outs, perhaps two-thirds of them, result from justifiable reasons, such as transfer, ill health, or permanent employment. Other drop-outs which result from indifference and poor attendance may indicate some failure on the part of the school. Such drop-outs are not explained adequately by lack of ability or by poor grades, although these certainly are involved.

The Demand for More and Varied Education

HETEROGENEITY OF THE STUDENT POPULATION

The sketches opening this chapter and the subsequent discussion of needs portray some of the differences to be taken into account in providing post-high-school education. If more such education is to be made available, there must be an increasing awareness of the tremendous variation both among and within the individuals who seek it.

Individual Variation. No matter what human characteristic one selects, wide variation is the rule among prospective college students. In contrast to the customary 18-to-24 age interval for college, the upper limit must now be regarded as 60 or 70. With reference to intelligence, an I.Q. of 110 has traditionally been regarded as the minimum for a college degree. On the other hand, a junior college which undertakes to provide education for all youth over 18 (as many of those in California now do) will enrol students with I.Q.'s well under 100. Thus, education is faced with the task of catering increasingly to individuals of more diverse abilities and interests. The same may be said of attitudes, values, personality traits, and even of previous preparation. We note that students who previously attended liberal-arts colleges and schools of agriculture, dentistry, education, engineering, law, medicine, and pharmacy, as well as students entering directly from high school, were reported as enroling in the New York State Technical Institutes.[23]

Sex differences have received only slight attention in liberal-arts education. However, for programs of education aimed at practical

23. *Report of the Temporary State Technical Institutes Board on the Experimental Institutes of Applied Arts and Sciences,* p. 13. Albany, New York: University of the State of New York, March 3, 1950.

and vocational as well as cultural benefits, the differences in occupational choices between the sexes and the differences in interests are a matter of greater concern. Boys of the late adolescent period seem to be more disturbed about physical health, safety, and money; girls are concerned about attractiveness, manners, personal philosophy, personal qualities, and home and family relationships. With adults, there is more interest among women in cultural development than among men, and the reverse is true in regard to the vocational objective.

The positive, though often small, correlation between verbal intelligence and success in college has tended to obscure the evidence on the variation among abilities and the patterns of abilities in individuals. Hull has estimated that variability within individuals is approximately 80 per cent as great as variability among individuals, and other investigators have reported figures of 75 per cent.[24] The evidence is also that variability within individuals is not related to ability level. If such intraindividual variability is regarded as applicable to artistic, mechanical, motor skill, social, clerical, verbal, and numerical aptitudes, it is apparent that individuals low in verbal facility, on which a premium is placed by most formal education, may possess other aptitudes of considerable significance.

Abilities do tend to become more specialized with age, as has been demonstrated by the decreasing intercorrelation of so-called primary mental abilities.[25] This may be partly a result of our educational program, for among persons of lower educational levels, irrespective of age, abilities appear to be less highly differentiated, and the general factor is relatively conspicuous.[26] Whatever the reason, concrete evidence of the lack of relationship is found in the very low intercorrelation of tests of verbal, numerical, spatial, musical, mechanical, and artistic ability with each other. There are several kinds of intelligence rather than one. Hahn and MacLean, for example, discuss seven: academic, scientific, mechanical, social, clerical, musical, and

24. C. L. Hull, "Variability in Amount of Different Traits Possessed by the Individual," *Journal of Educational Psychology*, XVIII (1947), 87–104.

25. Mamie P. Clark, "Changes in Primary Mental Abilities with Age," *Archives of Psychology*, No. 291. New York 27: Archives of Psychology, 1944.

26. Ann Anastasi and John P. Foley, Jr., *Differential Psychology*, p. 517. New York: Macmillan Co., 1949.

artistic.[27] In a democratic society there is no reason to place a premium on one type. All of these various abilities have their appropriate fields of endeavor and deserve careful fostering by suitable educational programs.

It must also be recognized that many of the mental and personality characteristics of an individual which affect educability are subject to some change, occasionally even to sizable change. Academic aptitude is by no means unrelated to achievement so that remedial work in reading and in basic content areas may make it possible for a person to perform types of work which were previously impossible. Individuals differ greatly in the extent to which they have had experiences relevant to the particular skills evoked by aptitude measures, and so in a limited number of cases aptitude scores may greatly underestimate the potentialities of a person. Hence, rigid classification of students on the basis of test results is not advisable.

Institutional Variation. In general, the population of a particular college tends to be more homogeneous than the total college population. There is a slight tendency for the intelligence of students to vary with their socioeconomic status, and the socioeconomic and cultural differences within any institution appear to be of lesser magnitude than the differences between total populations of different types of institutions. These differences are found also in groups of institutions. For example, the parents of students in liberal-arts colleges rank highest in the scale of occupations, those of junior-college slightly lower, and those of teachers-college groups are third in occupational status.

In a survey at Orange Coast College, 47.2 per cent of the students classified their parents as managers, proprietors, professional people, technicians, and sales representatives, whereas only 22.3 per cent of the labor force of the community was so employed. On the other hand, laborers, farmers, service workers, clerical and unskilled workers comprised 54.5 per cent of the working force of the community, but their families accounted for only 25 per cent of the students.[28]

As further evidence of the gap between parental status and youth

27. Milton E. Hahn and Malcolm S. MacLean, *General Clinical Counseling,* pp. 203–57. New York: McGraw-Hill Book Co., 1950.

28. *Educational and Occupational Needs, op. cit.,* p. 87.

goals, Weber estimated that 86 per cent of the students in his junior-college experimental-remedial classes were influenced outside of the classroom by a level of language unsuited to their occupational aspirations.[29] In the New York State Technical Institutes, two-thirds of the student body come from homes identified with the skilled and the managerial-professional occupational groups, indicating that the lower socioeconomic groups are not proportionately represented even in the Technical Institutes.[30]

Comparison of statistics from a number of institutions provides some idea of the interinstitutional variation. The median age of students in New York Technical Institutes was reported as 20.2 years, and nearly 10 per cent were found to be over 25.[31] Orange Coast College in California reported over 25 per cent of its students as being 23 years of age or older. In 1953–54, of the total student population of 338 public junior colleges, 30.4 per cent were adults, here defined as persons taking courses with no intent to graduate. In 124 institutions, adult enrolment larger than the total of Freshmen, Sophomores, and special students was reported.[32] Such proportions of older students are not, of course, common in four-year colleges.

In the matter of intelligence, the variation is even more marked. Traxler, studying the I.Q. needed for college work, found the median I.Q. for the highest college studied was 123; for the lowest college, 94. The median for four-year academic colleges was 109; for junior colleges, 105; and for teachers colleges, 105.[33]

The California junior colleges offer a dramatic picture of the wide range of abilities that may be enrolled in an institution, provided that a variety of programs is available. The following summarizing statements, based on data obtained from three different California junior colleges, illustrate this:

29. Cornelius B. Weber, "A Proposed Approach for Evolving a Course in Remedial Instruction of Junior-College Students with Deficiencies in Writing." Unpublished Doctor's Dissertation, University of California, 1952.

30. *Report of the Temporary State Technical Institutes Board of the Experimental Institute of Applied Arts and Sciences, op. cit.,* p. 15.

31. *Ibid.,* p. 14.

32. Colvert and Baker, *Junior-College Directory, 1955, op. cit.,* pp. 6–26.

33. A. E. Traxler, "What Is a Satisfactory I.Q. for Admission to College?" *School and Society,* LI (1940), 162–64.

1. Terminal students at this junior college have a median (on the American Council on Education Psychological Examination) which falls below the 18th percentile of national college norms.
2. The median A.C.E. scores of various terminal groups at this junior college range from the 24th to the 29th percentile, whereas groups planning to transfer to four-year colleges have medians ranging from the 40th to the 53rd percentile on national norms.
3. Those students aiming at a Bachelor's degree who were fully qualified for admission to the universities at high-school graduation have a mean A.C.E. score falling at the 67th percentile of the liberal-arts national norms. Those students aiming only at junior-college graduation have an A.C.E. mean of 74 falling at the 10th percentile of the liberal-arts national norms. The terminal students rank at the 23rd percentile of the twelfth-grade norms on reading and at the 13th percentile on mechanics of expression as compared with the 79th and 84th percentiles, respectively, for qualified admissions interested in acquiring a Bachelor's degree.

No doubt variation in other abilities would be just as marked, but, unfortunately, really satisfactory evidence is not available to validate the presumption.

ENROLMENT TRENDS

The prediction of college enrolments for the period up to 1970 has been undertaken by numerous individuals. As Thompson has pointed out, "there is a rather uniform agreement concerning the number of young people who will be of college age. The major point of uncertainty concerns the percentage of those of college age who will actually attend college."[34] Financial assistance, availability of appropriate education, programs of motivation and encouragement, and increase in the percentage of high-school students graduating have been listed as factors which might materially increase the percentage of students attending college.

The picture for future enrolment in the junior college is further clouded by the following considerations:

1. Since junior colleges enrol students from the immediate locality, many of whom would not and could not go to college elsewhere, the increase in junior-college enrolment will depend to a very great extent on the development of more junior colleges.
2. An increase in the percentage of high-school students undertaking

34. Ronald B. Thompson, *College-Age Population Trends, 1940–1970*, p. 8. American Association of Collegiate Registrars and Admissions Officers (Charles H. Maruth, University of Denver, Secretary), 1954.

college will probably affect junior colleges more than senior colleges simply because of the operation of the economic factor.

3. The increased emphasis on the community-service role of the junior college may result in program revisions and in the inauguration of new offerings which will greatly increase the attractiveness of junior-college curriculums.

4. As the terminal programs of two years or less in length become better known and generally accepted as appropriate training for a wide variety of jobs, youth with the encouragement of their parents are more likely to take advantage of them.

5. Four-year colleges may find enrolments so overwhelming in comparison to resources that students will be encouraged to spend their first year or two in junior colleges.

6. The demands of adults for education are, as yet, largely unfathomed. The Gallup poll reported in 1947 that 41 per cent of the adults showed interest in adult education as against 34 per cent interested in 1944. The figures for enrolment increase previously cited make no allowance for adults except as adults were included in the 1950 enrolment figures. The extent to which adults will enrol in the future depends largely on the kinds of training available to them.

As a result of these imponderables, an increase on the national level of five- or six-fold in the junior college enrolment by 1970 as compared with 1950 is entirely possible. The necessary expansion in facilities and the combination of circumstances resulting in such a development are somewhat improbable, but an increase of two- to three-fold over the same period is a reasonably safe prediction. For individual states the expectancies vary greatly, thereby emphasizing that the most meaningful surveys and predictions must be made at state and local levels and the data thus obtained used to dramatize the needs and encourage the expansion necessary to meet them. Unless this expansion does take place, the major limitation on college enrolment in 1970 will be lack of facilities to accommodate those who wish to enrol.

Summary and Implications

For long years elders have advised youth that "education is a fine investment because no one can take it away from you." Although the validity of this precept has not been accepted with equal enthusiasm throughout all social and economic strata, the trend has been steadily toward a larger percentage of youth seeking more years of education. Recently this trend has been accelerated because youth are becoming increasingly conscious that our technology and the increasing complexity of our social and political organizations have resulted in more jobs requiring more education for satisfactory performance. In an age of rapid scientific and technological development and of quick shifts from war to peace-time economy, adults often find additional education and re-education a necessity. Their experiences have emphasized the value of added education which gives the individual added flexibility in adapting to changing conditions.

Although much of the interest of individuals in additional education is related to its vocational significance, this is not the sole consideration. Both youth and adults are desirous of having some general cultural educational experiences, and adults, particularly, have a strong interest in the development of recreational or practical skills. The values attached to education and the purposes for which more education is sought depend much on motivation factors which stem from early home environment and from the expectations and plans of parents and friends. Any attempt to increase the percentage of students desiring post-high-school education or to modify the reasons for attendance must begin early.

It is clear that without any increase in the percentage or change in the type of students seeking post-high-school education, the facilities of existing institutions will be taxed by 1970 or before. The high percentage of drop-outs from existing educational programs involves a waste of talent and suggests that we have yet to develop educational programs suited to many of those who now enrol for education beyond the high-school level. Were four-year colleges and universities to reconsider their function and revise the nature of their commitment so as to include a few terminal programs, expanse and distance would limit greatly the number of individuals reached. Meeting the needs of large numbers of youth and adults who want education beyond the high-school level requires the development of a program of post-high-school education which (a) offers a wide variety of curriculums and services carefully co-ordinated with a program of testing and counseling designed to identify the particular aptitudes of the individual and to help find a curriculum and a vocation to which he is reasonably well suited; (b) demonstrates a continual alertness to changing individual and community needs; (*c*) provides for flexibility and individualization within curriculums and within courses; (*d*) emphasizes good instruction and varied instructional techniques involving an awareness of heterogeneity in the purposes and backgrounds of students and a persistent effort to give each day's work meaning related to the experience of each student; and (*e*) is inexpensive and in reasonably close proximity to the prospective student population.

It must be evident that considerations of expense, of accessibility, and of the necessity of developing a wide range of courses suited to varying abilities and yet related to the requirements of the community point strongly in the direction of a community-oriented institution, for only at that level is it possible to meet satisfactorily the demands of youth and adults for more education.

CHAPTER IV

The Role of the Public Junior College

THE YEARBOOK COMMITTEE

We have observed that society is faced with rising demands for education beyond high school. An increase of more than two-thirds in the number of college-age youth is projected between 1955 and 1970. More than this, a larger percentage of these youth than formerly are seeking post-high-school education. This pressure for additional education, as has been pointed out in earlier chapters, is in its origin both social and technological (chap. ii) and personal and individual (chap. iii).

The situation in which we find ourselves is consistent with our history. From the colonization of America and the founding of our nation to the day of jet propulsion and the hydrogen bomb, the number and percentage of youth and adults who have continued their education beyond high school has increased steadily and dramatically.

Choices Open to Society

It is folly not to recognize that taxpayers are faced with multifarious demands for public funds. They must pay the costs of two recent world wars, of waging a current "cold war," of maintaining an arsenal for the preservation of freedom, of providing security for an unprecedented number of aged, and of education for the new millions of children who are today overcrowding the classrooms of our elementary and high schools. Within the framework of these and other uses for tax monies, our citizenry will be called upon to bear the expense of appropriate extensions of public education programs beyond high school.

One alternative open to society is to ignore or reject these pressures. If this view prevails, society will refuse to expand present colleges or to establish new ones; it will hold relatively constant the present tax structure for the support of higher education; and it will withhold additional private support for higher education. As a result of such measures as these, institutions of higher learning would have to impose selective policies of admission and thus limit enrolment to students with highly superior verbal and academic ability.

The most obvious advantage of such limitations is that of financial economy. Tax monies could then be used for other purposes, and even gifts from private sources could be turned to different purposes. But there are persons who insist that education beyond high school should be highly restricted; that it should be open only to selected students of high intellectual ability. The advocates of this view believe that too many students are already going to college, that many of them are wasting their time and are diverting the facilities of higher education from the *high* ends they are intended to serve. To extend the opportunities of post-high-school education to an even larger percentage of youth would, it is contended, aggravate an already deplorable situation.

It is not difficult to find objections to this do-nothing policy for it fails to recognize the technological and social trends (noted in chap. ii) as well as the individual and personal needs (discussed in chap. iii) which can be satisfied only by more education.

In deference to its own needs and to the personal requirements of its citizens, society cannot ignore or reject the demands for more education beyond high school. How, then, can society best meet these needs?

Four-Year Colleges and Universities

Four-year colleges and universities will be called upon to multiply their staffs and to engage in unprecedented building programs—classrooms and libraries, laboratories and dormitories. These institutions may be expected to establish branches in areas where post-high-school education is not now provided. New colleges will be needed in many population centers which are now without institutions of higher learning. Extensive scholarships and government aid will be required for youth who would otherwise be unable to attend college.

The liberal-arts college and the university deservedly enjoy a respected tradition in American life. Society has a high regard for their services to the nation. Such expansion of colleges and universities as is now anticipated will further enhance their prestige and notably increase their already significant contributions to society.

The four-year college and the university can certainly provide a major part of the needed additional facilities for education beyond high school. The expansion of staff and of facilities, together with a reduction of economic barriers to college attendance (through placing colleges in the home communities of youth and through providing scholarships and government aid), can make it possible for a significantly greater number of young people to attend college.

But these institutions best serve the requirements of students who seek four or more years of higher education. The evidence (statistics of college attendance and drop-out, as well as the recognition of social, technological, and personal needs), however, indicates at least as great a need for programs of less than four years. It is, to be sure, possible for colleges and universities to offer courses of study of less than four years in length—and many do. For colleges, however, this practice is, at best, secondary rather than primary in importance. The introduction of shorter-term programs, for most colleges and universities, is but a palliative, the result of recognizing an emergency. By and large, college faculties still give major attention to four-year programs, and less to two-year curriculums—and they should probably continue to do so.

The Public Junior College

Programs of less than four years are best funished by a different type of institution—a college where the attention of faculty, administration, and board of control will be directed particularly to the needs and goals of students whose formal education is limited to one or two years beyond high school. The junior college is uniquely adapted to these ends.

Suitable building facilities and adequate staffs will make it possible for existing junior colleges to open their doors to additional tens of thousands of youth and adults. New two-year institutions can be established in communities which need them but do not have them—including population centers where existing four-year colleges and universities are not adequately meeting the local demand for programs of less than four years.

The expansion of the junior college will in no sense reduce the number of students who can complete four-year programs. On the contrary, by careful planning, many junior-college graduates can transfer to senior colleges and universities without loss of time or of credit. In fact, bringing the junior college to the home community makes possible the completion of two years of college work for many who otherwise could not enjoy that advantage. Thereafter, these students can enter a four-year college or university to continue their education.

The Concept of the Community-centered College

In recent years the terms "community-centered college" and "community college" have been widely used—by the President's Commission on Higher Education and by the Educational Policies Commission of the National Education Association, by educators and by laymen alike. These terms have appeared in the titles of several books and numerous articles. As the adjective implies, the community-centered college breaks down many barriers to college attendance by bringing education closer to the homes of youth and adults.

Typically, the community college is conceived as a two-year institution. A community-centered college need not, however, be limited to programs of less than four years. Four-year colleges and universities in Omaha and New York City, in Kansas City and Houston, in Cleveland and Denver, are essentially community colleges, since they build programs on the basis of local needs and utilize community resources (not only financial but also cultural, social, scientific, vocational, religious, and educational) in program-planning and operation.

The community-centered college is not limited by the usual college and university restrictions on courses and credits, curriculums and degrees. Its offerings and activities are geared to the purposes of the people it serves. It may provide courses, conferences, and consultant services on citrus-growing in Southern California, on fashion design in the garment-manufacturing center of New York City, on medical-secretarial work in Rochester, Minnesota, on hotel and restaurant management in Syracuse, on petroleum technology in the oil fields of Texas, on agriculture, police-training, food service, electronics, merchandising, home arts, drafting, family life, and child care in a variety of cities and regions; it may sponsor community orchestras and choruses, community forums and book festivals, community surveys and youth programs.

Although, as has been indicated, community colleges are not necessarily two-year institutions, the public junior college is particularly adapted to the concept of the community-centered college. With a really active history of less than a third of a century, the public junior college is relatively free from hampering tradition. It is usually locally controlled, as contrasted with state or absentee control. Under such control, the college is responsive to local needs and aware of community resources useful in program development and operation.

Purposes of the Public Junior College

Valid purposes of the public junior college can emerge only from the characteristics of society and the needs of individuals. These we have discussed in chapters ii and iii.

The demands of society and the needs of youth unite in requiring a post-high-school education (*a*) which prepares youth for effective living as persons, citizens, and members of a family and (*b*) which prepares them for vocations in which they can make their optimum contribution to society and, likewise, gain personal satisfaction essential in day-to-day living.

These purposes apply with equal force to the adult population. Education is a life-long process; neither general- nor vocational-education needs are ever fully satisfied at any point in life. The public junior college, because of its community orientation, is particularly well qualified to provide adults in the community with educational opportunities on a part-time basis.

The junior college serves its community through providing general education as well as vocational education. Moreover, the junior college can serve citizens who are not enrolled in any college program or course. It can assist in raising the cultural level of the community through providing varied public programs and cultural events; can aid in improving citizenship through forums and conferences, lectures, consultation services, and institute sessions. The performance of these and related functions becomes particularly important as the junior college assumes the characteristics and the role of a community-centered college.

Large numbers of young people should continue their education beyond high school—whether they wish to complete a program of general education or to prepare for entrance to one of the professions. For many of these, however, the cost of going to college away from home for several years is prohibitive. The junior college can provide two years of education for youth in their home communities and can thus make it possible for some of them to attend and complete their formal education at senior colleges and universities.

In light of the foregoing considerations, the four major purposes of the public junior college can be identified as (a) preparation for advanced study, (b) vocational education, (c) general education, and (d) community service.

Although these objectives are widely recognized and generally accepted, it is clear that each college has a responsibility for determining its own specific objectives. The degree of emphasis to be placed upon any one purpose would naturally vary from college to college in accordance with the characteristics of its particular community.

In developing its program, the junior college should consider its purposes for both terminal and transfer students, some of whom attend college full time and others part time. As the terms are used here, the transfer student is one who will continue his education at a level above the junior college; the terminal student will close his work as a full-time student sometime before or at the time of junior-college graduation.

Actually, there are two types of terminal students in junior colleges. One type is motivated by an immediate vocational objective. However, he also has a need for general education, both as an aid to occupational effectiveness and as preparation for living in such relationships as citizenship and family life. This need is often unrecognized by the student—and herein lies a difficult problem for the junior college. Also, serious problems confront the junior college in providing for terminal students of a second type, namely, those who announce their intention to transfer to an institution of higher learning, plan their programs of study accordingly, and yet fail, for one reason or another, to move on to a four-year institution. They are terminal students in a real sense, but because of changes in their plans, many of them have been unable to gain as much as they were capable of achieving in two years of junior-college work.

Although the transfer students who seriously undertake the task of preparing to enter a four-year college are in the minority in the junior college, it is usually the case that the majority of the enrollees have announced plans and intentions that classify them as transfer students. As a result, most students in a junior college pursue a curriculum which is restricted by university requirements, one which is not planned for their particular needs. This situation poses guidance and curriculum problems which, for their solution, demand senior-college and university understanding and co-operation.

PREPARATION FOR ADVANCED STUDY

A given individual's educational requirements are both general and specialized. His general needs are those which he shares with others. His specialized requirements are those which evolve out of his personal abilities, interests, background, and goals. These latter, in turn, may be grouped into those which prepare him for advanced study and those which prepare him for employment. Inevitably, these needs frequently overlap. A course in zoölogy taken for the purpose of satisfying prerequisites for medical school represents both vocational education and preparation for advanced study. The same course taken to meet the science requirement for admission to a senior college (with no plan by the student to enter a vocation in which the course would prove valuable) might simply represent preparation for advanced study. The same course taken for the purpose of understanding animal life in relation to day-to-day living would clearly be general education. Whatever the intent, the course almost certainly contributes something to both general and specialized needs.

Historically, the transfer function was the first recognized purpose of the junior college—"to offer two years of work acceptable to colleges and universities." Originally, almost every student attending a junior college did so with the intent of entering a senior college or a university. More recently, a smaller percentage of junior-college students (perhaps a third of those who entered) have continued their education beyond junior-college graduation. The transfer function is, however, far more important than might be indicated by the number of students who, at present, go on to a senior college. In the first place, many of the students who transfer are destined to assume important positions of leadership in government and the professions, in business and labor, in industry and agriculture. These students must be well prepared for their advanced specialized work. In the second place, many senior colleges and universities may have to restrict their Freshman-Sophomore enrolment in order that they may accommodate expanding numbers of upper-division, graduate, and professional students. For this reason, junior colleges will probably be called upon to educate an increasing percentage of transfer students.

VOCATIONAL EDUCATION

Incompetents who become wards of the state and a negligible number of the idle rich do not have to earn a living, but most other citizens must do so. Preparation for a vocation is clearly necessary for each of these individuals. As a matter of fact, education may well fail in its other purposes if it does not train youth to do well some kind of useful and remunerative work. Commendably, students recognize this need and seek to plan their educational programs accordingly.

The demand for vocational proficiency is not merely individual in origin; it is also social. If society is to function efficiently, it must have workers in all conceivable fields and types of employment.

The preparation of students for earning a living is a responsibility which the junior college must share with other units in American education and, indeed, with commerce, industry, agriculture, government, the trades, and the professions. The pressure for additional training beyond that offered by the high school identifies, however, an opportunity and a major obligation.

Junior-college vocational education may be of two types. One prepares the student for employment immediately upon the completion of his junior-college work. The second prepares him for advanced senior-college or university work in the profession or area of his choice. The latter type (preparation for advanced study) has been referred to above.

GENERAL EDUCATION

General education has had many and diverse definitions and descriptions. For the purpose of this yearbook, general education will be regarded as that part of education which encompasses the common knowledge, skills, and attitudes needed by each individual to be effective as a person, a member of a family, a worker, and a citizen. The complexities of contemporary life, the pressures of speed, the fears and the actualities of conflict and war, the alarming increase in problems of mental health, and the threatened breakdown of family life—these and other problems and concerns consistently revealed in surveys of youth and adults attest the demand for more general education. Herein lies an essential need, one which education and society dare not ignore.

It is very clear that the junior college does not have sole responsibility for general education. This obligation is, for example, shared with high schools, with other colleges, and with universities. It is equally clear, however, that the junior college must be responsible for contributing to the general education of a rapidly increasing number of youth and adults.

COMMUNITY SERVICE

The junior college serves its community through its offerings in general education, through its provision of preparation for advanced study, and through its program of vocational education, but this is not all.

It is natural to look to the public junior college for many and diverse types of service to groups and to individuals not enrolled in classes or courses. The junior college is a reservoir of distinctive and various talents and skills, knowledge and expertness, insights and understandings. Furthermore, the public junior college is a community-centered institution. Under these circumstances, the performance of service to the community becomes an important function of the junior college. Such service must not be limited to the meeting of requests made by citizens. The faculty has an opportunity and a responsibility to take leadership in identifying areas of community need to which the junior college can contribute.

The values of college service to the community are many and varied. They include increasing the productive efficiency of agriculture and industry, improving the functioning of communities and community organizations, contributing to the health and physical well-being of citizens, and enriching the cultural, aesthetic, and moral life of the community.

UNIQUE FUNCTIONS OF THE JUNIOR COLLEGE

The junior college has a number of characteristics which are conducive to its effectiveness in accomplishing its recognized purposes. Among these are the following:

Providing Low-Cost Post-High-School Education in Proximity to the Homes of Students. Chapters ii and iii clarify the need for youth to spend a longer period in school. To meet the requirements of youth, post-high-school education must not only be provided in or near the home community but it must also be provided at a cost which makes attendance possible. Here are areas (location near the homes of students and low cost) in which the public junior college is qualified to meet the designated needs to an unusually high degree.

Providing Guidance and Counseling. During late adolescence and early adulthood, the student is called upon to make such important decisions as choosing a life's work, selecting a mate, achieving a philosophy of values by which to guide his life. He is likewise confronted with problems attendant upon service in the armed forces as well as with the fears and uncertainties of life during a period of cold war in an atomic age. To these decisions and problems, the total educational program of a college can and should contribute. Particularly important, however, is the fact that in these complexities, students require guidance and counseling. Rarely distracted by the requirements of research and productive scholarship, junior-college faculties are in a particularly advantageous position to provide superior student personnel services. Individual attention to students is encouraged by the small size of most junior colleges.

Conclusion

Technological developments, social trends, and the needs of youth and adults unite in requiring the upward extension of post-high-school education for an increasing number of our citizens. Present educational facilities are totally inadequate to meet these demands. The public junior college is uniquely qualified to contribute to these needs, particularly through providing educational programs of less than four years located in the home communities of students. More specifically, the public junior college can contribute to the following purposes and functions: preparation for advanced study, vocational education, general education, and community services. These purposes and plans for achieving them will be discussed in chapters v through viii.

SECTION II

ACCOMPLISHING THE PURPOSES OF
THE INSTITUTION

CHAPTER V

Preparation for Advanced Study*

GRACE V. BIRD

Introduction

It is registration day on the campus of a large state university. The year is 1970. From a bench beneath an oak tree whose shade he had enjoyed when he was an undergraduate forty years before, an alumnus is watching the stream of new students flow by. It is his first visit to his college since his return from years spent in foreign service. He is struck by the mature appearance, the purposeful bearing of the students going by. Only occasionally does he see one who resembles his remembrance of the apple-cheeked Freshmen of his own day. Pricked by curiosity, he engages a passing group in conversation.

"The truth is, sir," one replies to his questions, "we *are* new students, but we are not Freshmen. We are entering the University as Juniors. We are transferring from junior colleges in our home communities." And another adds, "Most of the new students registering today are like us! We are told that only a fourth of the new entrants are Freshmen."

Scenes such as this are likely to be enacted on the campuses of senior institutions in all states in which the projected increases in student enrolments are very large. The only difference will be that

---

* In the preparation of this chapter, the author has had available, in addition to the standard professional literature on the topic, the unpublished reports of three recent surveys bearing on the junior-college function of preparing students for advanced standing in four-year institutions. One of these was made by the author herself in May and June, 1954, with replies coming in from eighty-four representative junior colleges, twenty-two state universities, eleven other four-year colleges, and five state departments of education. The second, made by Herman A. Spindt, Director of Admissions of the University of California, is based on replies from admissions officers in fifty-three state universities and land-grant colleges. The third is based on a survey made by Wayne C. Puttmann, 1953–54, in preparation for his doctoral dissertation at the University of North Dakota.

most college and university alumni, unlike our old-timer, will be familiar with the trends since the younger of them will, themselves, have been junior-college transfers, and many of the others will have lent their support and leadership to the development of strong junior colleges in their own communities. In states in which the projected increases in college enrolments will be less large, the ratio of new admissions with advanced standing to new admissions with Freshman standing will be less dramatic. There seems to be little doubt, however, that increasing ratios will be the trend wherever public junior colleges exist.

The Transfer Function in Junior-College Administration

IMPORTANCE OF THE FUNCTION

Although "preparation for advanced study" is only one of the purposes of junior-college education, it is one of the oldest of the functions and the one best known to the general public. The very term *junior college* seems to underscore the importance of this purpose. Some educators think this purpose has been underscored so heavily as to impede proper recognition of other important services such as vocational and community education. Be that as it may, of one thing we are certain. Few developments in American education have done so much to equalize opportunity for higher education as the public junior colleges. They have brought the first two years of university education to the very doorstep of the people and thus leveled financial obstacles to advanced study. Moreover, they have renewed the opportunities of study for a large group of high-school graduates who, although intellectually able, had not previously qualified themselves for immediate entrance into a four-year college or university. And they have reopened doors for adults who, today, have only to walk across the street to begin the longed-for college education which circumstances denied them in their youth. It is no longer a rare sight, for instance, to see a mother and daughter receive the associate of arts degree at the same junior-college commencement ceremony.

The community college embraces a whole range of services for the student who wishes to prepare for successful advanced study. It provides the first two years of college instruction for most of the academic schools and colleges found in universities and other four-year institutions: letters, arts, and sciences; agriculture; business administration; education; engineering; and others. It provides, also, one or two years of the preprofessional studies required for admission to most professional schools, such as dentistry, medicine, pharmacy, nursing, and law. For students who lack adequate foundation from their secondary-school experience, it offers remedial and developmental instruction to compensate for that lack. It offers rapid review instruction to adults returning to college studies after a lapse of years. And to assist the student in making wise choices from among its many opportunities, it provides extensive counseling.

The contributions which the community college will make through this function in the future are expected to be even greater than now. The factors bringing about the intensification of recent trends have already been touched on in earlier chapters. Three are of particular importance. First, more and more of the total load of the first two years of study for the Bachelor's degree is being delegated to the junior colleges as four-year institutions begin to be taxed beyond their own capacity. This is already a fact in California. Second, more and more kinds of employment require a college degree for entrance into the first job. Finally, there is unwavering American faith in the intrinsic and extrinsic values of college education.

MAGNITUDE OF THE TRANSFER FUNCTION IN JUNIOR COLLEGES

Preparation for advanced study is commonly called the "transfer function" of the junior college because it prepares students for transfer with advanced standing to four-year colleges and universities. This is the function which attracts the largest number of regular students to the local community college. In each of the twenty-one states surveyed for this chapter of the yearbook, at least 50 per cent of the students declare at entrance that their purpose in attending the public junior college is to prepare for advanced standing in four-year colleges or universities. In most states the percentage runs higher: about 66 per cent in Arizona, California, and Illinois, for example, and about 77 per cent in Colorado, Michigan, Mississippi, and Texas. In some individual junior colleges, it runs as high as 90 per cent. While the aim of many students is not always realistic, the opportunity to prepare for transfer to senior institutions remains the largest single motivating force for their entering the junior college at all.

The problem this presents to junior-college counselors is a serious one. Many students, whose personal qualifications point to far greater likelihood of success and happiness in the semiprofessions, cling tenaciously to the less attainable professional goal which they think has greater social prestige. As if *any* activity that society really needs is not honorable and socially desirable! Yet such students are often reluctant to enrol in even one course, no matter how valuable it might be to them individually, unless it is recognized for Bachelor-degree credit. One can scarcely be surprised, then, that a study such as that of Steggert[1] in Illinois found that 69 per cent of all junior college curriculums were designed for transfer and only 31 per cent were designated as terminal.

In most states only about half of those who originally declare they plan to transfer actually do continue with advanced study. In some states, such as Florida and Texas, the percentage is higher; in others, such as California, it is as low as 30 per cent. It is significant to note, however, that, while only a minority of the students who enter the thirteenth grade actually continue in higher institutions, the *majority* of the junior-college students who graduate are in transfer curriculums, and the great majority of these do continue with advanced study. In nearly every state surveyed, the percentage of the graduates transferring to senior institutions exceeds 50. In some states— Colorado, Florida, Idaho, Illinois, Michigan, Missouri, Texas, and Washington—it constitutes almost four-fifths of the total number graduating.

It is evident, therefore, that the transfer function is of major importance to the public junior college in terms of the opportunities for higher education it makes available to its community; its magnitude as an aim of junior-college students; and its vitality in holding students to graduation and in thus helping to stabilize the institution and its student population.

1. Francis X. Steggert, "Terminal and University Parallel Curricula in the Illinois Junior Colleges, 1951–52," *College and University*, XXVIII (January, 1953), 204–9.

MAGNITUDE OF TRANSFERS IN FOUR-YEAR COLLEGES AND UNIVERSITIES

In recent years, a larger and larger percentage of the new students admitted to our universities enter with advanced standing. At present, the range is from 15 per cent to 80 per cent of all new undergraduate admissions. Not all of these come from junior colleges, of course, but a large percentage of them do, and in states in which the public junior college is well developed, the number may exceed half of the entering transfer students. Other public four-year colleges reflect similar trends. This is true also of the independent colleges, but in lesser magnitude. The expected development of new public community colleges in areas not now served by them will only reinforce the trend. Happily the success generally achieved by junior-college students after transfer is reassuring to both the junior colleges and the senior institutions.

Success of Junior-College Transfers in Senior Institutions

Throughout the years, scores of studies have been made of the performance of junior-college transfers in four-year colleges and universities. Senior institutions make such studies to assist in determining and evaluating their transfer policies and standards. Junior colleges make them to appraise their strengths and weaknesses in performing the transfer function. The criterion generally used is the academic performance of the junior-college transfer in the four-year institution when compared with his previous performance in the junior college and also when compared with the academic performance of transfers from other sources and of so-called "native students," i.e., students who have done all their work in the four-year college itself. Some studies also examine the "staying power" of the transfers. A few examine other factors such as election to honor societies and persistence into graduate study.

One of the earliest comparisons of the achievement of junior-college graduates and "native students" in senior institutions was published by Mitchell and Eells[2] at Stanford University in 1928. The records of all junior-college graduates who transferred to the Upper Division from autumn, 1923, through autumn, 1927, were compared with a like-sized alphabetical sampling of native students. The trans-

2. J. P. Mitchell and W. C. Eells, "The University Records of Students from Junior Colleges," *Faculty Bulletin*, No. 13, Stanford University, June 30, 1928.

fers excelled the native students in scholastic achievement (grade-point average) for each quarter in the Upper Division except the first. The differences were statistically significant. Moreover, 43 per cent of the transfers entered graduate schools after completing their Bachelor-degree programs while only 28 per cent of the native students did so.

Other studies made at Stanford have shown somewhat similar findings, while still others have shown contrasting findings. McIntosh,[3] for example, compared 1,054 native students with 693 junior-college transfers who entered the Upper Division from 1933 to 1937. Her two groups were closely comparable on aptitude test scores. She found that on each of four counts on which she compared their achievement record, the native students excelled the transfers. A larger proportion of them received the A.B. degree. They excelled transfers in scholarship in each of the Upper Division quarters although the gaps were increasingly narrower. They earned proportionately more honors. Fewer of their drop-outs were below a "C" average. Transfers, however, had a larger percentage going on into graduate work.

In 1934 Grossman[4] reported on a study of all students entering the University of Illinois with Junior standing during a four-year period. Factors studied were scholarship averages, percentages earning degrees and earning degrees with honors, percentages on probation and dropped. He concludes:

From the facts presented in this report it may be said that without doubt junior college graduates are able to pursue advanced college courses in the junior and senior years at the University of Illinois with a degree of proficiency equal to and in some cases superior to that of students who have received their first two years of training in standard colleges and universities.

The Transfer Study Committee of the Junior College Council of the Middle Atlantic States compiled statistics from 54 colleges and universities along the Atlantic seaboard on a total of 262 junior-

3. Florine M. McIntosh, "A Comparative Study of Academic Records Made of Junior College Transfers, Native Students, and Transfers from Other Four-Year Schools." Unpublished Master's thesis, Stanford University, October, 1944.

4. D. A. Grossman, "Junior College Transfers at Illinois," *Junior College Journal*, IV (March, 1934), 297-303.

college graduates in their 1946 Senior classes. Sammartino and Burke[5] report that, on the basis of the standing in the 1946 Senior class, 37 per cent of the junior-college graduates had grades above average, 47 per cent had average grades, and 16 per cent had grades below average.

Fichtenbaum,[6] studying nearly nine hundred junior-college transfers to the University of Texas, from 1935 to 1938, found that the scholarship average of the native students excelled that of the transfers with the difference less in the Senior than the Junior year. He found that the transfers carried loads as heavy or heavier than the native student.

Three recent studies are of particular interest in reflecting current situations. French[7] reached the following conclusions from his study of the academic success of junior-college transfers at the University of Colorado from November, 1945, through the winter term, 1949: (*a*) Junior-college transfers suffered a considerable drop in grade averages after transfer to the university. Averages attained tended to rise during the second and third quarters of residence. (*b*) Junior-college transfers attained averages below the composite university all-school averages for the period. (*c*) Compared with various all-university averages, junior-college transfers attained a degree of success somewhat less than that which the majority of other studies have reported for junior-college transfers at other colleges and universities.

Martorana and Williams[8] compared a group of transfers and a group of native students at the State College of Washington. They were equated on a number of factors, such as sex, major-subject area, high school attended, and year in college. On a group basis, they were also matched on aptitude-test scores and high-school accumu-

5. P. Sammartino and A. F. Burke, "Success of Junior College Transfer in Eastern States," *Junior College Journal*, XVII (April, 1947), 307–10.

6. M. Fichtenbaum, "Junior College Graduates *vs.* Senior College Juniors," *Journal of American Association of Collegiate Registrars*, XVI (January, 1941), 144–54.

7. W. L. French, "Academic Success of Junior College Transfers at the University of Colorado." Unpublished Master's thesis, Department of Personnel Service, University of Colorado, 1949.

8. S. V. Martorana and L. L. Williams, "Academic Success of Junior College Transfers at the State College of Washington," *Junior College Journal*, XXIV (March, 1954), 402–15.

lative grade-point averages. The authors' conclusions, therefore, are of particular interest. They found that the transfers have a problem of adjustment which actually affects their academic effectiveness during the semester just after transfer. As this adjustment is made, the differences between mean grade-point averages of the transfer and non-transfer groups become negligible. When students are considered in groups, there is no significant difference between the academic success of the transfer and native student. Moreover, the junior colleges appear to be providing an avenue of admission and success in further studies to a kind of student who would otherwise miss them.

Annual studies made by the registrar of the State University of Iowa of the graduates of the colleges of liberal arts and commerce also demonstrate that junior-college transfers make approximately the same records as transfers from four-year colleges. The Iowa data serve to illustrate also the wide differences in the mean grade-point ratio attained by the transfers from different junior colleges. The average made by the transfers from one junior college, for example, will be significantly higher than the university's mean, and the average for another, significantly lower. Similar differences are noted in California, Colorado, Michigan, Texas, Washington, and other states which make periodic studies.

Perhaps no institution receives more new junior-college transfers annually than the University of California. Nearly twenty-five hundred new transfers enter one or the other of its campuses each year from the public junior colleges of the state. Annual studies of their performance are made by the Office of Relations with Schools. Two groups of transfers are noted. The first is the group whose high-school records in pattern of courses and quality of performance made them eligible for admission to the university at the time of high-school graduation[9] but who, for one reason or another, chose to go to a junior college for two years. The performance of this group in the university might be expected to be comparable to that of the

9. Admission Method 1 of the University of California bases the acceptance of new Freshman students entering from high schools on the following pattern of courses: English, 3 units; algebra, 1 unit; plane geometry, 1 unit; junior or senior laboratory science, 1 unit; United States history, 1 unit; foreign language, 2 units; and additional mathematics, science, or language, 1-2 units. The scholarship grades in these subjects taken in grades 10, 11, or 12, must average "B." The University of California has other methods of admission to Freshman standing, but the majority of Freshmen enter by Method 1.

"native" students if junior-college standards of instruction are comparable. This proves to be the case. Except for a slightly lower achievement than the "native" students in the first semester of the Junior year (a grade-point ratio of 1.44 for the transfers to a 1.60 for the "native" students), the performance in the next three successive semesters is practically identical (1.60 to 1.63; 1.67 to 1.67; 1.76 to 1.73). The drop-out rate is also the same.

The second group of transfers, which is somewhat larger than the first, was ineligible for admission to the University at the time of entrance into junior college. This group has qualified for transfer to the university on the basis of the junior-college record. It has been "salvaged," so to speak, by the junior college for further advanced study. Its performance is less strong in the junior college and also in the University than the other groups. But the important thing is that the record is satisfactory, rising from 1.1 in the first term after transfer to 1.5 in the fourth. It illustrates how successfully the junior college is reopening the doors of higher education to able students whose earlier records did not reveal their true promise.

Four general conclusions emerge from these studies and from many others like them:

1. Junior-college transfers make records approximately the same as those made by transfers from four-year colleges and by native students, sometimes excelling slightly and sometimes being slightly excelled by the other groups. They usually show a drop in their grade average in the first term after transfer but then recover that loss.
2. Junior-college transfers retain the relative scholastic standing after transfer that they held before transfer. Those who originally have high scholastic standing tend to retain such relative standing. Likewise, those with relative low standing tend to remain in the lower groups.
3. There is clear evidence that junior colleges are salvaging a large number of students for success in advanced studies who would otherwise have missed them entirely.
4. There is variation, sometimes wide, in the findings in different senior institutions and also as between junior colleges in the same institution. It should be noted, in passing, that such variations present a problem to those senior institutions who seek to maintain a uniform policy for recognition of the public junior colleges of their state. By and large, however, the performance of junior-college transfers in senior colleges has proven to be so satisfactory that doubts about the quality of junior-college preparation for advanced study no longer exist.

Problems Yet To Be Solved

Because education is a living, changing, growing thing, problems in educational relationships will continue to arise. This is true in junior college–senior college relations as elsewhere.

There are the problems that are rooted in inadequate provisions for good communication between institutions: the lag in keeping junior colleges informed of changes in programs and policies of senior colleges; the slow transmittal to the teaching faculty of knowledge of agreements reached on the administrative level; the too-little exchange of meaningful data on the characteristics of students in the two types of institutions.

There are still unsolved problems in curriculum relationships. Some junior colleges feel that the rigidity of requirements in the senior college hampers the development of their own programs. Still others feel that a more generous recognition of credits earned in community-centered courses is warranted. They feel, moreover, that such recognition would contribute more than a little toward the solution of the junior-college problem mentioned earlier of counseling students who are overconscious of the "prestige" value of transfer courses. Meantime, senior colleges show some concern over an apparent, although probably not real, conflict between junior-college vocational or community-directed courses and upper-division courses of similar title, such as courses in advertising, electronics, child development, and others. A better understanding of the comprehensive purposes of the community college and of the differing nature of the programs it has would reduce such concern.

And there are the problems already referred to which arise from differences in grading standards between institutions. This matter, not particularly serious in itself, introduces difficulties when students are being appraised for admission to such highly selective programs as medicine or law or dentistry.

But perhaps few matters call for closer co-ordination in junior college–senior college relationships than that of achieving the most desirable balance between general and specialized education in the total program of the individual student.

It is of the first importance, therefore, that sound principles underlie the educational planning of junior colleges and senior institutions, alike, if the transfer function is to continue to be carried on with mutual confidence and with proper gain to the individual and society.

Some Basic Principles of Sound Institutional Relations

MUTUAL UNDERSTANDING OF PURPOSES AND CHARACTERISTICS OF
JUNIOR COLLEGES AND SENIOR INSTITUTIONS

Junior-College Understanding of Senior Colleges. If junior colleges are to understand clearly the purposes and characteristics of universities and four-year colleges, each of these senior institutions must accept the responsibility of describing clearly and fully its educational purposes and the programs of study it requires in terms of such goals. Junior colleges need to know about the breadth of such programs, the depth needed for later specialization, the level at which the student will be expected to perform, and other important characteristics of their nature. Moreover, the senior institution needs also to define the kinds of students it feels it must have if it is to fulfil its purposes.

Most senior institutions try to meet these obligations. In his recent survey of co-operative programs between selected state universities and public junior colleges, Puttmann[10] found that, in three-fourths of the cases, curriculums are so co-ordinated as to provide ease of transfer between institutions. However, junior colleges are asking for further refinements in senior-college definitions. They want to know, for example, the characteristics of the students already in the senior colleges to which they send transfers. They also want to understand clearly any specialized functions the senior institution serves in its state or region.

For their part, the senior institutions hope the junior colleges remain aware of the time schedule of degree programs. Any lag on the part of the junior college in advancing its potential transfers toward senior-college goals *on bases comparable to those of the senior institution* delays the process unduly, both for the student and for society.

The implications are clear. The junior college serves as a selective institution for the senior institution, both in its guidance procedures and in the nature of its instruction. It encourages students with proper qualifications to continue with advanced study. It screens students in terms of the differing needs of the various senior institutions. It diverts some students into other channels of activity.

10. W. C. Puttmann, "A Survey of Co-operative Programs between Selected State Universities and Public Junior Colleges." Unpublished Doctor's Dissertation, University of North Dakota, 1954.

Senior-College Understanding of Junior Colleges. Emphasis has thus far been placed on junior-college understanding of the four-year institutions. Equal emphasis belongs on the senior institutions' understanding of the junior college as a community college. All are partners in the post-high-school education of the people of their region. Any senior institution which understands well the wide range of functions performed by the community college will do more than develop good procedures with reference to the transfer function. It will recognize the worth of the other purposes of the junior college and the other kinds of students it serves. It will guard against closing the door on experimentation in teaching that has promise in terms of senior-college goals as well as community-college goals. Recognizing the wide variety of institutions to which junior-college students transfer, the appreciative senior college will encourage and even co-operate with the junior colleges in such experimentation in order to reduce oversplintering of the junior-college effort.

MUTUAL UNDERSTANDING OF PATHS TO GOALS

It is generally agreed that there is more than one way to fulfil a purpose, to reach a goal. It is also agreed that some ways may prove quicker or better than others. Many of the revisions that have taken place in programs of higher education over the years have been designed as improved paths to long-established goals. While some have not proved out, many others have. It is the possibility of success that invites further experimentation.

What shall be meant, then, by "the kind and quality of education" that advances the transfer student properly toward the four-year college goals which are his ultimate aim? Shall it mean strict course-for-course parallels in the junior college and the lower divisions of senior colleges? Not necessarily, although some four-year colleges require such parallelism in transfer courses. The thing that does seem necessary is that the junior-college programs of study for transfer students shall be equivalent in educational value to the programs in the senior colleges in terms of the senior-college purposes. Thus, for example, if high proficiency in quantitative thinking, logical inference, hypothesis, and synthesis are goals of the four-year institution, the junior college will need to develop in its transfers levels of proficiency in these intellectual skills which are comparable to those expected in the senior institution of students with similar advanced standing. Likewise, if breadth of experience or depth of understanding in some particular field of learning is essential to the achievement of success in advanced study in that major, the junior college will seek to supply that breadth or depth in the quality and to the degree expected. But it need not be imitative. This principle of "equivalence" as contrasted to strict parallelism is the one now accepted and practiced in many institutions.

CO-OPERATION IN DETERMINING TRANSFER POLICIES

In the eyes of the four-year colleges and universities, good transfer policies are those which insure the acceptance of the number and kinds of students they need to fulfil their particular purposes and which screen out those not likely to succeed. Junior colleges agree that these are proper criteria. But they think there is a third criterion deserving recognition. In their eyes, good transfer policies are those in which the selective factors will be kept flexible enough to permit experimental recognition of exceptions to the rules. In the words of one junior-college president, "We hope to see experimental recognition of exceptional performance in fields other than the traditionally recognized ones." It appears highly desirable, therefore, for junior and senior colleges to meet in joint conferences and to engage in joint studies as bases for determining transfer policies. Puttmann's study,[11] however, shows that in less than half the cases is the co-operative determining of transfer criteria or requirements at present practiced.

MAINTAINING GOOD MACHINERY FOR CONTINUING CO-ORDINATION

Because education is subject to growth and change, it is important to provide for continuing interinstitutional liaison. In regions where such provision does not exist, more problems in junior college–senior college relationships are reported as existing. In areas in which good provision for long-range co-ordination is established, both types of institutions report misunderstandings and problems to be at a minimum.

Brief descriptions of some of the existing evidences of good planning and strong liaison may serve as touchstones.

11. *Ibid.*

Examples of Good Practices

ORGANIZED MACHINERY FOR CO-ORDINATION IN CALIFORNIA

The program of public higher education in California embraces the University of California and its eight campuses, the ten state colleges, and the sixty public junior colleges. Good and comprehensive machinery for co-ordination has been developed among all three. On the highest policy level, there is a liaison committee of the Board of Regents (responsible for the University of California) and the State Board of Education (responsible for the state colleges and the junior colleges). On the institutional level, and functioning within the accepted top policies, there are standing committees on co-ordination between the university and the state colleges, the university and the junior colleges, and the junior colleges and state colleges. All matters of relationships, including transfer requirements and policies, are studied jointly. These over-all co-ordinating committees meet twice a year. Their work is supplemented by the activities of subcommittees in subject fields which also meet semiannually, or oftener if circumstances make it desirable. In university–junior college relations there are nine such subcommittees which bring together university and junior-college teachers and officers in each of the following fields: agriculture, architecture, business administration, engineering, home economics, letters and science, physical education, student personnel work, and university extension. The State Department of Education and the University's Office of Relations with Schools have ex officio membership on all such liaison committees. Similarly organized machinery exists for junior college–state college relations, although there are at present fewer subcommittees. Thus far no formally organized machinery has been developed for relations with the independent colleges.

Regional conferences constitute another major aspect of California's efforts at co-ordination. Their purpose is to extend the joint activities to wider representation from the faculties. Thus, Fresno State College, for example, may be host to all the colleges of its geographic region to discuss the curriculum for elementary education or for business education or for some other field in order to improve articulation and transfer therein. Or, the University or a junior college may serve as the host institution for similar regional meetings.

UNIVERSITY OF COLORADO ANNUAL JUNIOR-COLLEGE CONFERENCE

Annual conferences for junior colleges are held on the campus of the University of Colorado. The program has three major parts: (*a*) a general session for the discussion of a topic of special interest to all, such as general education and professional curriculums; (*b*) group discussion of articulation problems in such specific subject areas as fine arts, music, prenursing requirements, and others; (*c*) individual conferences between junior-college representatives and their former students now enrolled in the university. Teachers and administrators of junior colleges and the university take part. A Colorado junior-college executive writes: "Success in effecting good transfer comes from concerted effort on the part of both types of institutions to establish adequate transfer bases."

TYPES OF CO-ORDINATING PROCEDURE

The University of Michigan has an annual junior-college conference somewhat similar to that at the University of Colorado. During its first part, transfer students are interviewed by their former junior-college deans. These meetings are then followed by joint conferences of university advisers and junior-college deans. Michigan also sponsors an annual conference on higher education to consider major issues in higher education. All the colleges, including junior colleges, take part.

The University of Missouri Committee on Accredited Schools and Colleges meets regularly once a year, sometimes oftener, with the Missouri Association of Junior Colleges. Conferences are called periodically at Florida State University to discuss articulation matters. The junior colleges meet with the Council of Deans. In the words of one of the junior-college presidents, "These meetings have accomplished much toward increasing understanding from both viewpoints." Junior colleges in Minnesota meet semiannually with university committees. They also co-sponsor with other educational groups an annual workshop for junior-college teachers at the University of Minnesota.

Many other good illustrations could be cited: Idaho's semiannual meetings of higher institutions, the Utah Conference on Higher Education, the meetings of the Association of Texas Colleges, the Mississippi Association of Colleges, and others. There is general testimony to the great value of the activities of these groups in improving articulation and enlarging mutual understanding and confidence.

SPECIAL CONTRIBUTIONS TO GOOD COMMUNICATION

In addition to official catalogues and bulletins, some senior institutions issue supplementary publications to assist junior colleges in keeping abreast of new developments. The state universities in Oklahoma and Washington issue newsletters. The University of Southern California prepares a special handbook for junior-college counselors. The University of California distributes semiannually a sixty-page bulletin called *California Notes* reporting changes and new developments in curriculums, student housing, library services, counseling, and other aspects of operation on its several campuses. All these devices improve articulation.

FORMAL OFFICES OF INSTITUTIONAL RELATIONS

Many senior institutions maintain offices of school relations or standing committees charged with interinstitutional affairs. The University of Minnesota has a senate committee on institutional relationships; the University of Michigan, a committee on college relations; the University of Kansas, a committee on junior colleges. Other states provide similar illustrations.

SPECIALISTS IN JUNIOR-COLLEGE EDUCATION

Both Texas and California have professors of junior-college education on the staffs of their state universities. A few state departments of education maintain a division of junior colleges. Minnesota, for instance, has a director of junior colleges in its State Department of Education, and Washington has a supervisor of junior-college education. Such specialists contribute significantly to the maintenance of strong junior-college programs of preparation for advanced study as well as to the other functions of the community college.

Summary and Recommendations

The junior-college function of preparing students for advanced study in four-year colleges and universities is of increasing importance to the senior institutions, the junior colleges, and the youth and

adults of the communities served. The junior colleges have long fulfilled this function with credit and continue to do so. Moreover,
they have greatly increased the numbers of students profiting from
higher education.

While the major problems in junior college–senior college relations have been solved, a few others persist and sometimes new ones
arise with new educational developments. Where sound educational
policies exist as bases for co-ordination, and where well-planned machinery for liaison operates, good relations have become the rule.
This is quite as true in states in which junior colleges are wholly independent of the university or state colleges as it is in states where
they are extension centers of the four-year institutions.

Good machinery, however, does not exist everywhere, nor have
policies reached full enlightenment. Improvements can still be made
which will continue to strengthen the junior-college transfer function without influencing unduly the development of other community-college curriculums and services. And senior institutions can
improve their provision for the rapid assimilation of the transfer student once he is enrolled.

The following procedures are recommended:

1. Adequate provisions should be insured for the clearest and fullest possible mutual understanding in junior college and senior college of
similarities and differences in their functions, similarities and differences in the *nature* of their instruction, and similarities and differences in the characteristics of their students.
2. Policies governing transfer and the acceptability of transfer credit
should be jointly developed. Senior colleges can well risk the recognition of a few experimental courses if these will enable junior colleges to improve quality of instruction through reduction of excess in
variety of courses offered to parallel the work of several institutions.
3. Continuing organized machinery for co-ordination should exist, even
in states where there are few junior colleges, for the improvement of
relationships and, indirectly, the improvement of the over-all programs of education and guidance. The machinery should provide for
the participation of teachers, counselors, and administrators.
4. Junior colleges should make periodic evaluations of their success in
performing the transfer function. Senior colleges should evaluate their
success in assimilating transfers. Not only the performance of the students but the students, themselves, should be a party to the evaluation.

CHAPTER VI

Vocational Education

LAWRENCE L. BETHEL

Introduction

Chapters ii, iii, and iv have made reference to the importance of earning a living as an educational purpose and its relevance to the junior-college program. Previous chapters have indicated that a high percentage of junior-college enrollees register in university parallel or transfer curriculums, but the fact remains that the junior college is terminal for 70 to 75 per cent of all enrollees. We are here concerned with this group and particularly with their preparation for realizing their ambitions for economic betterment.

Vocational education in the public junior college does not follow a universal pattern. Rather, it follows numerous patterns as the junior college adjusts its program to the needs of individuals within the community and to the general sociological and technological demands of the community. Whatever its form, the program of vocational education in the junior college is very different from vocational programs in the high school and those of the senior college or university. For example, the teaching of vocational courses, even skill subjects such as typing, accounting, merchandising, or tool-design, should be distinguishable in the junior college from the same subjects in the high school in the same way as are the physics, chemistry, basic communications, and languages taught in other types of institutions. The greater maturity and increased background of the junior-college student make it possible to approach each subject with a broader base in understanding and with increased speed of learning. This is so because learning is facilitated to the degree that we are able to associate new experiences with previous experiences. Therefore, the greater the wealth of properly integrated experience in education, the greater the facility for learning.

It is to be noted, however, that this factor of added facility for learning is frequently overlooked in collegiate instruction.[1] A study sponsored by the Ford Foundation in co-operation with a group of universities and preparatory schools revealed that, generally speaking, a student who had certain specific courses, such as physics or chemistry, in preparatory school did not do as well in the first courses in physics and chemistry in college as did the student who had never experienced the courses in preparatory school. The implications drawn from these findings are that needless repetition in college of what has gone before in preparatory school results in diminished motivation with resulting carelessness and lack of application.

The approach to learning in the broader curriculum pattern of many junior colleges takes cognizance of the fact that high-school graduates are capable of dealing with entirely new fields of study. For example, the study of tool-design in the junior college, in contrast with the study of the same subject in high school, utilizes added learning in mathematics and the sciences that will enable the student to progress faster and to deal with more intricate problems related to tool-design. The junior-college vocational program should have characteristics distinctly its own that make it different from either the high school, on the one hand, or the upper division or graduate school, on the other.

Succeeding divisions of this chapter will be devoted to some of the major points to be considered in the present and probable future development of junior-college vocational programs. Specifically, the chapter is designed: (a) to report trends and conditions which influence junior-college preparation for vocations; (b) to report illustrative practices in public junior-college vocational education; (c) to propose requirements for a vocational-education program in a community-centered junior college; (d) to identify problems in junior-college vocational education; and (e) to recommend directions for further development of public-junior-college vocational education.

1. *General Education in School and College.* A committee report by members of the faculties of Andover, Exeter, Lawrenceville, Harvard, Princeton, and Yale. Alan R. Blackmer, Chairman. Cambridge, Massachusetts: Harvard University Press, 1952.

Trends and Conditions Which Influence Junior-College Preparation for Vocations

TECHNICAL TRENDS, CREATING NEW QUALIFICATIONS FOR JOBS

Chapter ii discussed a trend toward mechanization and automation of production and distribution with the resulting reclassification of jobs and the actual reduction in the number of workers required on certain types of operations. These technological developments have a real meaning for vocational education in the junior college. They call for a de-emphasis on certain types of technical training and for the creation of a category of new positions that can be served best by the junior college.

These new jobs created by the trend toward mechanization and automation are to be found not only in the field of manufacturing but also in distribution and in the service industries. Benjamin F. Fairless, in a talk at the annual dinner of the Greater Johnstown Chamber of Commerce, Johnstown, Pennsylvania, February 11, 1955, made the following statement:

> As mechanization has enlarged the output and the purchasing power of our people, it has also multiplied enormously the demand for services. . . . Employment in the service industries alone has risen by more than two million during these fourteen years. And that is a jump of 65 per cent. The same thing has happened, too, in the general field of trade. As the volume of production has increased, it has taken more workers to sell and to handle these goods.[2]

THE SOCIOECONOMIC MORES OF THE COMMUNITY

A statement has been made in chapter iii that perhaps two-thirds of the youth who do not go to college lack the motivation to do so. Reference was made to a contention by Hurst and Rogers that motivation is closely related to social status and that the social patterns of the lower class lead these youth to ignore college or to consider it as unrelated to their aspirations and beyond their means. Therefore, we may assume that socioeconomic status of a community will dictate to a high degree the number of youth who will want to pursue a program of college studies. In a community of very high socio-

2. Copies of Mr. Fairless' talk may be obtained from the United States Steel Corporation, 71 Broadway, New York 6, New York.

economic standing, we may find that a large number of people, perhaps a majority of youth, will seek to attend a senior college or university. Some of them may take the university parallel program in the junior college and then look toward transferring to the senior college. In contrast, in another community with a lower socioeconomic status, a smaller proportion of youth will seek to attend the senior college or university, an equal or larger proportion will take the vocational programs of the junior college, and a large group will not go beyond high school. Such a community will require increased emphasis upon the vocational program by both the high school and the junior college.

THE VOCATIONAL LIFE OF THE COMMUNITY

We find occupational differences not only among rural, semirural, and urban communities but also among different geographic regions of the country. For example, an industrial area of Connecticut may differ greatly from an industrial area in Texas. In Connecticut, manufacturing is confined principally to metal-working plants. Here one will find producers of machine tools, aircraft engines, military weapons, locks, electrical appliances, electrical meters, and various other types of mechanical and electrical equipment. Accordingly, the community-centered junior college will need to emphasize mechanical and electrical technology as well as business administration and industrial administration. In Texas, however, there are areas with a concentration of oil companies. Here the community-centered junior college will stress industrial chemical technology and petroleum technology as well as business administration and industrial administration. Just as much variation will be found between rural sections of different parts of the country. For example, a dairy-farming section such as New York State would vary in its needs from those of a grain-farming area or a citrus-fruit area.

AVAILABILITY OF OTHER EDUCATIONAL
FACILITIES IN THE COMMUNITY

Any urban community, such as New York City, Chicago, or Los Angeles, contains a multitude of educational facilities on all levels. In New York City, for example, there are located the third, fourth, and fifth largest universities in the United States. (Only the University of California and the State University of New York are larger.) These three large institutions—New York University, Columbia University, and City College of New York—provide a wide range of advanced vocational offerings and programs for practically every professional undertaking. On the other hand, the vocational programs of the community junior colleges in New York City provide instruction for positions of a type not offered by the universities, principally in the various technologies such as chemical, electrical, mechanical, and food service, and in certain highly specialized occupations such as apparel design, textile design, and apparel management and production.

Contrast this situation, however, with a community such as Orange County, New York, only seventy miles from New York City, where there are no facilities for public higher education other than the Orange County Community College. Here the community college becomes the center for higher learning. In this capacity the community college organizes many programs of instruction to serve the needs of the community. These may be at an elementary or a very advanced level. President Miner has stated that the college is endeavoring to meet the obvious and expressed needs of many segments of the community. To this end, courses have, at times, been introduced at the request of government agencies, engineers, insurance groups, banking groups, social workers, librarian and library trustees, state hospital personnel, and others.

Types of Junior-College Vocational Programs

In analyzing the junior-college vocational programs in operation one will observe that they vary also according to (a) the timing of intended use of vocational preparation, and (b) the occupational areas served. It makes considerable difference in the planning of a vocational program whether the student plans to enter employment immediately following the junior-college program, whether there will be opportunities for him to continue at least part-time studies following graduation from the junior college, whether there is opportunity for on-the-job training in some of the essential skills after he enters employment, or whether the full-time junior-college program is to be the end of his vocational preparation.

Most urban junior colleges offer programs of vocational preparation for full-time students ranging all the way from a few weeks to two years in duration. These programs prepare the individual for his probable first job and provide him with sufficient breadth of background that he can add to his preparation later through part-time studies or through on-the-job training. Most public junior colleges also provide programs of part-time studies for workers currently on jobs who seek to be upgraded with the necessary skills and understandings essential to higher positions. These programs are usually arranged in co-operation with committees of employers.

Then there are refresher programs, often at a very advanced level, for office managers, engineers, accountants, social workers, and junior executives. These refresher programs and the upgrading programs are usually conducted in the late afternoon or evening and may continue a few weeks or three or four years.

In the planning of vocational programs, therefore, the junior college recognizes that it cannot be all things to all people within a period of two years. It considers instead that the three stages of pre-employment preparation, part-time upgrading, and advanced refresher education should all become a part of a total plan of service to individuals of the community and should be planned concurrently.

Jesse P. Bogue, Executive Secretary of the American Association of Junior Colleges, reported in 1952 a survey of the frequency of offerings of certain terminal and semiprofessional curriculums among 560 junior colleges.[3] A portion of the results of this survey is given in Table 1. Only those subjects which are offered by 5 per cent or more of the junior colleges are included in this extract. Thirty-six other subject specializations offered by less than 5 per cent of the colleges are reported in Bogue's survey. Many of these were highly specialized, as they should be, to serve the particular needs of a specific community.

We are interested here, however, in the pattern of the common

---

3. Jesse P. Bogue, *American Junior Colleges*. Washington: American Council on Education, 1952.

types of vocational training. The report indicates that secretarial and general business rank one and two, respectively, in the list. These are programs that prepare people for work in offices, retail stores, and the general business activities of communities. Contrast these pro-

TABLE 1

FREQUENCY OF OFFERING OF CERTAIN TERMINAL AND SEMIPROFES-
SIONAL CURRICULUMS AMONG 560 JUNIOR COLLEGES
LISTED IN *American Junior Colleges*

Curriculum	Frequency of Mention	Numerical Rank	Percentage of Colleges Offering
Business, Secretarial	260	1	46.4
Business, General	232	2	41.4
General Cultural	202	3	36.1
Music	170	4	30.4
Art	153	5	27.3
Home Economics	136	6	24.3
Journalism	121	7	21.6
Physical Education	112	8	20.0
Agriculture, General	101	9	18.0
Auto Mechanics	97	10.5	17.3
Drafting	97	10.5	17.3
Business, Salesmanship	95	12	17.0
Teaching, Elementary	94	13	16.8
Nursing	92	14	16.4
Medical Secretarial	91	15	16.3
Building Trades	80	16	14.3
Engineering, General	77	17	13.8
Woodwork	71	18	12.7
Architecture	59	19	10.5
Metal Work	58	20	10.4
Electronics	57	21	10.2
Agriculture, Forestry	52	22	9.3
Recreational Leadership	47	23	8.4
Engineering, Mechanical	45	24	8.0
Librarianship	42	25	7.5
Social Service	41	26	7.3
Engineering, Electrical	39	27	7.0
Business, Merchandising	34	28	6.1
Engineering, Civil	33	29	5.9
Aviation, Flight	31	30.5	5.5
Mechanical Technology	31	30.5	5.5

* Jesse P. Bogue, *American Junior Colleges*. Washington: American Council on Education, 1952.

grams with the frequency of those in engineering, electronics, and mechanical technology, which rank seventeen, twenty-one, and thirty, respectively. While engineering is limited largely to the in-dustrial urban centers, the need for business programs exists in a much larger number of communities. It is possible, however, that junior colleges have not given sufficient attention to the need for preparation of engineering technicians.

Perhaps the most interesting aspect of this tabulation is the wide range of subjects included in the terminal programs. Note the high frequency of the programs in general culture, music, art, home economics, and journalism. The prevalence of such programs indicates that junior colleges not only provide for business and engineering courses in connection with terminal programs but also include many cultural and creative pursuits in which people engage in their respective communities.

Illustrations of Community-Centered Junior-College Vocational Programs

Since vocational programs should vary greatly in accordance with community needs, it is perhaps appropriate to consider specifically how some of these programs develop and operate. The following illustrations have been selected to typify variations and the influence of the community needs on shaping the programs.

MOHAWK VALLEY TECHNICAL INSTITUTE, UTICA, NEW YORK

Utica, New York, is an important business, industrial, and agricultural center in a mid-state rural area. It is a city with a population of over 100,000, located in the western portion of the Mohawk Valley, and is the county seat of Oneida County. It is a railroad-junction point on the main lines of the New York Central Railroad. The Mohawk Valley Technical Institute is a division of the State University of New York and is a two-year community-centered college offering programs in technical and general education. The technical programs include electrical technology, mechanical technology, retail business management, and, until 1953, textile technology.

The elimination of the textile program is an interesting example of how the changes within a community result in changes in a local junior college. Utica was at one time a center of textile activity. With the movement of the textile industry to the South, the demand for vocational training in textiles declined. In 1954 the Institute decided to eliminate its program in textiles and to transfer its laboratory equipment to the Fashion Institute of Technology in New York City, another State University institution located near the headquarters offices and sales and engineering departments of many of the large textile organizations in the state. On the other hand, a new industry has developed in the electrical and mechanical fields in the Utica area, and the community has continued to grow as a merchandising center. Consequently, Mohawk Valley Institute is placing emphasis on program development in new and expanding areas of need.

The purpose of the Institute is to train young men and women as technicans for business and industry and for better lives as individuals, parents, and citizens. The Institute defines technical occupations as those which usually require a high degree of specialized knowledge, a broad understanding of operational procedures, and the ability to supervise the work of others. Usually the term is applied to that new stratum of a profession which lies between the skilled worker and the engineer. In order to move freely up the job ladder, the technician must be familiar with the entire field rather than especially skilled in any one job. Thus, the programs attempt to combine theory and skill-training for entry jobs and familiarity with those operations which will be essential to the student when he begins to climb up the ladder.

DEL MAR COLLEGE

Del Mar College is a community college located at Corpus Christi, Texas. It was organized as a junior college in 1935 by the Board of Education for the purpose of furnishing educational advantages to the youth and adults of the region. The Del Mar catalogue states the functions of the college as, first, to provide fully accredited academic and semiprofessional courses leading to college degrees; second, to train terminal students for immediate employment and homemaking; third, to offer the adults of the community opportunities for more general education or job training; and fourth, to serve the city of Corpus Christi through specially sponsored organizations, such as the Fine Arts Colony.

It is no wonder that Del Mar College is spoken of by the townspeople as "our community college." From seven each morning until ten each night, five days of the week, its doors are open to serve the citizens of the community.

High on the list of special interests of the college is that of health in the community. Without the aid of the college it would be difficult, if not impossible, to maintain the two nursing programs now in progress. The first of these programs is the three-year professional nursing program. While the student nurses have the hospital as their home base, they attend the college for such basic prenursing subjects as chemistry, biology, foods, and histology.

Then there is the program of practical nursing. In this program the college plays an even more important role. The classroom and nursing laboratory are on the college campus. The students are taught foods and home management by two college instructors. The remainder of the subjects are taught by nursing instructors. Since the program consists of only one year of training, it must be intensive. It is divided into two parts called the preclinical and the clinical periods. During the preclinical period (the first fourth months) the students remain at the college and attend classes there. The clinical period, or last eight months, is spent in the affiliated hospitals. In this program may be found women from seventeen years to forty-five years of age. They must have had two years of high school and be in good health both mentally and physically. For the older woman, practical nursing may well represent the extraordinary opportunity which enables her at last to realize her ambition to become a nurse.

The college also offers vocational programs of study in such fields as secretarial work, general business, music, auto mechanics, woodworking, electrical technology, dental technology, industrial supervision, petroleum technology, police training, and agriculture.

One of the very interesting programs is a two-year program for students who are actually engaged in farming. In order to register for the program, a student is required to have a farm under his control—by renting, by farming on shares, or by ownership. Courses offered include the following: animal husbandry, poultry (home poultry flock); dairying for home milk supply; operation, care, and maintenance of farm machinery; farm shop; home garden; farm health and safety; home orchard; farm crop; soil management; food preservation.

Here, obviously, is a junior college that is analyzing the needs of its geographic community and establishing programs to serve those needs, just as the Mohawk Valley Technical Institute at Utica is building a curriculum based on the needs of its community.

Representative of a city-wide development of two-year (or shorter) vocational programs are the offerings of the seven junior colleges which serve the Los Angeles City Junior-College District, an area of 826 square miles with a population of 2,500,000.

During the development of junior colleges in Los Angeles, it was suggested that in order to provide equal opportunity for all residents of the metropolitan area, the city must establish either a system of specialized colleges or a system of regional colleges, each serving a particular geographical section. Actually, however, neither a system of specialized colleges nor one of regional colleges has developed. Rather, Los Angeles has a group of colleges that are both specialized and regional.

Each junior college has a limited number of programs which the other colleges do not offer. These programs could not be duplicated in all sections of the city on a sound economic basis—nor would there be sufficient placement opportunities for the graduates of most of these programs if they were offered in all seven junior colleges. Examples of these special offerings are petroleum-refining technology at Harbor Junior College; beef production at Pierce Junior College; cosmetology at Trade-Technical Junior College; paint technology at Los Angeles City College; Los Angeles General Hospital Co-operative Vocational Nursing at East Los Angeles Junior College; and merchandising at Los Angeles Junior College of Business. The vocational offerings of Los Angeles Junior Colleges include such varied fields as dairying, butter and ice cream manufacturing, subtropical horticulture, aviation technology, garment manufacturing, lithography, training for dental assistants, ceramic and clay-production technology, plumbing technology, food trades, household service, instrumentation, real estate and insurance, police training, and transportation technology.

In addition to the specialized programs offered in single junior colleges, a number of vocational curriculums are provided by several colleges. Basic business subjects, such as accounting and secretarial education, are offered by six of the seven junior colleges; graphic arts by three; basic electronic subjects by six; and engineering-technician training by four.

The high-school graduate ordinarily needs to travel but a short distance from his home to attend junior college. If, however, he wishes to work in a specialized curriculum, he is free to select the junior college which offers that particular program.

Apprentices who are regularly indentured under the California Apprenticeship Law may attend one of the Los Angeles junior colleges to secure related or supplemental instruction. They may earn regular college credits toward an Associate in Arts degree, both for the related classwork and for the practical instruction received on the job from a journeyman. To earn the Associate in Arts degree, the apprentice meets the requirements shown in the accompanying tabulation.

Work experience: Credit is granted on the basis of evaluation of the applicant's performance in trade tests administered by the chairman of the trade department concerned. All such testing takes place during the last two years of apprenticeship.   Maximum units allowed.   20

Related and supplemental instruction   Units allowable.   14

Electives   Units.   14

General education   Minimum units.   12
  English
  American history
  American political institutions .
  Health education
  Physical education   Total units.   60

The most important question to be answered in establishing any new vocational program is, "Is there a genuine community need for this curriculum?" In answering this question and in developing new vocational programs, the junior colleges of Los Angeles engage in extensive co-operative planning with advisory committees, the members of which represent the areas under consideration. These committees are consulted, not only regarding curriculum content but also regarding equipment, housing, qualifications of instructors, placement of trainees, and financial costs.[4]

THE FASHION INSTITUTE OF TECHNOLOGY

New York City, being one of the largest cities in the world, is at the extreme in terms of breadth of vocational opportunity and also in terms of the kinds of educational opportunities which are available.

Two public community colleges of the State University of New York are located in New York City: One is the New York City Community College in Brooklyn; the other is the Fashion Institute of Technology. The New York City Community College is devoted to the preparation of technicians for electrical, mechanical, and construction industry, and for the preparation of the various professional technicians. The Fashion Institute of Technology is devoted exclusively to the preparation of people for entrance into the apparel and allied industries as designers, merchandisers, and industrial administration specialists. The apparel industry is the largest industry in the state and city of New York and the second largest in the nation. New York City is the capital of this industry. Over 65 per cent of all the clothes made in the United States are made in New York City. Most of the headquarters offices and salesrooms of the larger apparel companies are located there. Since this industry is so predominant in the life of the city, the Fashion Institute of Technology has been organized as a public community college specifically to prepare students for entrance into this industry.

The Fashion Institute of Technology is one of the ten community colleges under the program of the State University of New York. It is devoted exclusively to education in the arts and sciences related to the apparel and allied industries. To fulfil its purposes it offers programs in apparel design, in textile design, and in management. Each of these programs contains approximately 40 per cent general education and 60 per cent technical education. Graduates of the college enter immediately into positions as designers, assistant designers, buyers or assistant buyers, plant engineers or assistant engineers, assistant plant managers or specialists in various management control

4. J. Douglas Wilson, "Junior College and Apprentice Curriculum Construction through Advisory Committees," *Junior College Journal*, XXI (December, 1950), 207-11; "More about Advisory Committees," *Industrial Arts and Vocational Education*, LXII (November, 1953), 291-94.

functions. Accompanying is a tabulation of positions which members of the class of 1954 went to immediately following graduation.

PLACEMENT OF GRADUATES OF FASHION INSTITUTE OF TECHNOLOGY
CLASS OF 1954

Apparel Design—Total 212

Designer	96	Asst. Production	2
Asst. Designer	51	Demonstrator	1
Asst. in Design Room	3	Exec. trainee	1
Sketcher	20	Salesgirl	1
Sketcher Model	1	Asst. Buyer	1
Model	1	Fashion Copywriter	1
Samplehand	16	Fashion Reporter	3
Model Maker	1	Teacher in Fashion School	1
Draper	1	Showroom & Office Asst.	1
Fitter	1	Clerical Asst.—Buyer's Office	1
Grader	1	Custom Dressmaker	1
Asst. Patternmaker	1	Patternmaker	5

Industrial Management—Total 20

Asst. Production Mgr.	7	Costing Analyst	1
Engineer	4	Assistant Foreman	1
Management Trainee	1	Asst. Department Head	1
Production Exec. Trainee	1	Asst. in Production Control Department	1
Exec. Assistant	1		
Time & Motion Analyst	1	Production Records Asst.	1

Textile Design—Total 15

Assistant Designer	2	Colorist	11
Textile Artist	2		

Millinery Design—Total 11

Designer	1	Textile Artist	1
Asst. in Design Room	4	Merchandise Trainee	1
Asst. in Sample Room	1	Clerical Asst. in Specialty Department	1
Paster	1		
Fashion Reporter	1		

Persons applying for admission to the Fashion Institute of Technology are screened by the college to determine whether or not they possess the specific aptitudes which have been found essential for entrance into the design, merchandising, or industrial administration fields in the apparel industries.

The Institute is a community college in a large metropolitan area that is devoting itself to preparation for distinctly upper-level jobs in a family of industries. This training, at the moment, represents the greatest need of the industry. It is planned within the next two years to initiate a technician program as the second phase of development of vocational education for the apparel and allied industries. This program will be for the purpose of training students for jobs as assistants in the upper-level positions. They will not secure the breadth of education necessary to enter into the upper-level positions, nor will they need to have the high degree of specialized aptitudes required in the present programs of the college. Nevertheless, it is recognized that the work of technicians in the apparel industries is exceedingly important and that training should be provided through proper preparation as soon as possible.

Some Basic Requirements for Developing a Community-Centered Vocational-Education Program

A community-centered program does not come about through mere accident or chance. Furthermore, such a program involves considerably more than effort and thoughtfulness on the part of one or two people. Many factors are to be taken into consideration regarding the characteristics of the community in question, the "climate" or attitude of faculty and staff, and the general organization and procedures for appropriate development of the program in a given community. We call attention here to seven requirements which appear to be fundamental to planning in most communities.

THERE MUST BE A NEED FOR VOCATIONAL EDUCATION

It is quite possible that in a given community a junior-college vocational program would be not only unnecessary but inadvisable. Let us assume, for example, that there is a suburban community adjoining a large city, 90 per cent of whose residents are in the upper income brackets. There is very little business life in the community. The people are employed in the adjoining city, a very large urban center. Really the only business activities are grocery stores and drug stores. No part of the community is zoned for industrial activity. Parents in this community are ambitious for their sons and daughters to receive a good general education at the collegiate level. The public junior college in such a community can provide general-education and university-parallel programs. Students, who are qualified, go on to major colleges and universities, either immediately after high school or after graduation from the junior college. Those who are not qualified for admission to the major universities find opportunities to enter "finishing schools" or other private institutions that provide facilities for continuing education of a general nature. Others go to work in their fathers' businesses or in firms in the city which offer the training necessary. Many of these people take positions that do not really require specific vocational training of more than a few days or a few weeks.

Here is a case in which it would be exceedingly difficult to organize a vocational program that would serve the wide range of vocational activities engaged in by a limited number of people. One would not expect to be able to attract more than fifty or seventy-five people at most into any one vocational program. Obviously, this would necessitate limitations in the variety of offerings. The result is that the vocational needs of youth and adults in this community can be best served by vocational training on the job where employed or in specialized institutions in the large city near which they live.

THERE MUST BE INTEREST AND DESIRE

There must be an interest and desire on the part of the residents of the community for the establishment of a vocational-education program. We have mentioned that in Community A the people want their children to pursue collegiate education of a general nature rather than education that is specifically vocational. We may argue that these residents are misinformed, or that they are not cognizant of the basic educational values possible through a good program of vocational education. Even if this is true, and even though we are willing to initiate efforts to bring about a more realistic understanding on the part of the citizenry regarding vocational education, we must await the time when the effectiveness of such an effort establishes a general attitude that will make them want to co-operate in the development of a community-centered vocational-education program.

It is the job of the professional educator to lead; but his first task must be to work with the citizens of the community to bring about a common agreement regarding the kind of program that should be developed. Premature development may lead to resentment and obstruction that will in fact postpone future programs. It must be remembered that people are "copyists" in education. There is often a feeling that the programs of the largest and the oldest institutions must, by virtue of their size and age, be the best. Most parents desire for their children the best for which they are capable; and many of them are reluctant to accept the evidence of limitations in capabilities. Therefore, we find a strong tendency to perpetuate in education that which is prevalent or conventional.

THERE MUST BE A FEELING OF CONFIDENCE BETWEEN THE COLLEGE AND THE BUSINESS AND INDUSTRIAL LIFE OF THE COMMUNITY

Confidence is essential to frank and open discussion of community needs and opportunities. Experience has shown that problems of employment policies and vocational training may be explored by the community college with greater freedom and success than between school authorities and industry on a state-wide level. This is true, however, only if close personal relationships have been established between the administration and faculty of the junior college and the business and labor leaders of the community.

Mutual confidence often comes about through participation in various civic and social activities. Members of the college faculty and representatives of business and labor serve on various social welfare committees; they may bowl together, play golf together, and engage in church activities until they feel that they really know each other. If they then meet for discussion of employment policies, as these policies might relate to the opportunities and the needs for collegiate vocational education in the business of the community, it is possible to reach an understanding of the real facts of the situation and to come to an agreement regarding the vocational programs to be maintained for youth and adults attending classes at the community college.

THERE SHOULD BE A COMMON COMMUNITY INTEREST IN TERMS OF MONEY AND EFFORT

The community obviously has a "stake" in the program in terms of money and effort. The question has been asked many times: What are the distinguishing characteristics of a community which sends the majority of its high-school graduates to the local community college? There is reason to believe that the community that has engaged in a strong organizational effort to establish a public junior college will value its college most highly. It appears also that if the local community, either by local taxation or by individual subscription, contributes to the financial support of the junior college, it will manifest great interest in the future development of the facilities and programs that will improve the services of the college.

The New York State pattern of organizing community colleges has taken cognizance of these characteristics and has included in its pattern several requirements intended to stimulate such community participation. First of all, it is required that there be a local "sponsor." The sponsor may be the board of education, a county board of supervisors, or any other official public body of the community. The sponsor *must* initiate the proposal to organize the college and support subsequent developments and improvements in the college. Furthermore, the local community must be responsible for half of the capital expenditures and for two-thirds of the operating costs. Some of the New York community colleges have set up separate foundations to which individuals and groups within the community may contribute funds for new projects, scholarships, and loan funds. Such contributions are designed to supplement appropriations from tax funds, which are sometimes difficult to secure for experimental projects.

THERE MUST BE AN OPPORTUNITY FOR THE COMMUNITY
TO EVALUATE THE EXISTING PROGRAMS

There should be opportunity for the community to become familiar with the existing programs of the community and to assess their value. Dr. Samuel P. Capen, Chancellor Emeritus of the University of Buffalo, in commenting on the administration of an urban university calls attention to the fact that it "sits in the midst of its constituency."[5] Because of its proximity to the community, it cannot enjoy the privacy of the national institution. The same situation exists in the case of the community-centered junior college. In the true spirit of the community college, however, this should be considered an asset and an advantage to be used to the fullest. Ways must be found for the community to know about the institution, its strengths and its needs.

5. Samuel P. Capen, *The Management of Universities,* p. 33. Buffalo, New York: Foster & Stuart Publishing Corp., 1953.

THERE MUST BE OPPORTUNITY FOR THE COLLEGE TO
DEVIATE FROM ESTABLISHED PRACTICE

There must be opportunity for the junior college to vary from "standards" in terms of content of vocational programs and procedures utilized in these programs. So-called standards that may have been established by the city, the state, or some accrediting organization frequently are based on programs typically found in university parallel programs or in the specialized divisions of senior colleges and universities. Most state and regional accrediting agencies have now adopted the philosophy that a program is to be judged in terms of the fulfilment of its stated purposes, thus providing opportunity for necessary variations. (See chap. xii.) However, a community must be ready to stand firm on its right to define its own purposes for vocational education and its right to experiment with new content and procedures that appear to be most appropriate for its particular purposes. Only in this way can we develop truly community-centered vocational-education programs.

THERE SHOULD BE A SPECIALLY ASSIGNED COLLEGE
STAFF TO WORK WITH THE COMMUNITY

A competent group of faculty members should work with the community in assessing needs, in the continuous revision of existing programs, and in the development of new ones. New Haven College at New Haven, Connecticut, found during the period following World War II that all of its vocational programs went through at least one basic change every two years. These changes were brought about as the administration and faculty of the college obtained new information that caused them to rethink their educational programs and as business and industry changed their methods of operation and the nature of their products and services.

Let us consider for a moment the kinds of new information that a faculty may obtain through contact with business and industry. When some of the New Haven College faculty visited a large manufacturing organization, representatives of the industrial personnel department asked where they could best secure employees for the various phases of their industrial accounting activities. It was suggested that an analysis of these activities be made as a basis for making recommendations. A joint committee of faculty and industrial representatives undertook the project and considered not only this one company but other industrial organizations of the city. The results of this analysis showed that very little of the content of traditional accounting programs was actually essential in most of the industrial accounting activities and that other types of subject-matter content that are essential were not included in the usual accounting programs. This study led to the introduction of a completely revised program of accounting instruction. The new program included only two basic two-semester courses in accounting but did include courses in industrial organization and management, mechanical processes, engineering materials, work simplification, statistics, quality control, and fundamentals of supervision, in addition to the usual general-education courses.

The changes which occur as the activities and needs of a community develop require the time of certain members of the staff and require at least that some one person be given the major responsibility for co-ordination of plans with business and industry. It is also necessary that other members of the staff be assigned to work in these activities. There must be broad participation involving many members of the faculty, depending upon the type of industrial activities involved. Furthermore, the community-centered junior college must have teachers who are capable of working with business and industry in these analyses and interpretations, who are sufficiently qualified technically to command the respect of accountants, engineers, and managers, and who are thoroughly competent as professional educators so that their interpretations may be acceptable.

Problems and Issues in Junior-College Vocational Education

THE TIMING OF VOCATIONAL EDUCATION

The timing of vocational education raises the question as to how much vocational preparation can be given effectively prior to actual work experience, and how much might better be postponed for on-the-job training, for part-time collegiate education, or for a later return for full-time periods of study. If we are to give greater attention to the general-education phases of our vocational-education programs, as is recommended in this yearbook, perhaps it will be possible for us to rethink the vocational or technical offerings and postpone some of these offerings until after the individual has entered employment. This would mean that the two years of full-time junior-college vocational education would be composed of a good framework of general education plus an introduction to the technical phases of a specific vocational field of activity. This introductory technical instruction should include the fundamental principles and techniques essential to the first few jobs of the usual sequence in given technical fields. This could then be followed by a part-time up-grading program for further specialized instruction.

DIVISIONS OF RESPONSIBILITY BETWEEN BUSINESS AND COLLEGE

There is a serious question relating to what best can be learned in college and what best can be learned on the job. This problem is of particular significance where skills are involved in the job. Business and professions will vary in their demands in different communities. Nevertheless, the administration and faculty of the junior college should assume responsibility for the analysis of the jobs in question and for recommendations. It is recognized that if these recommendations are not accepted by the community, the junior college must abide by the requirements of employment practices.

Consider for a moment just one program, namely, retail sales. Should the college attempt to teach students of this program how to wrap packages, how to make out a sales slip, how to keep a stock inventory, how to handle returned sales and cash refunds? These activities vary in practice in different stores and possibly could be learned in a very short period of time on the job. If they were taught in the college, they would take a proportionately longer period of time. Even if these techniques were learned in college, there would be a certain amount of forgetting prior to entering employment merely because the techniques had not been continued in practice while the student was still in college.

EMPLOYMENT POLICY VERSUS EMPLOYMENT PRACTICE

It is a well-known characteristic of business enterprise that employment policies may vary from actual employment practices. This divergence was revealed most significantly in a survey conducted and reported by *Fortune* in April, 1953. In response to frequently repeated demands by industrial executives for less specialization and greater breadth of preparation for young men seeking to enter industry, *Fortune* surveyed fifty colleges and universities to analyze curriculum offerings and placement requests. *Fortune* found, however, that in actual practice the recruiters from companies ask to interview those who are graduating from specialized programs. Only an extremely small minority of company interviewers even mentioned possibilities for liberal-arts graduates.[6]

This situation leads us to wonder if the "upper" hand knows what the "under" hand is doing. Perhaps community colleges can make effective contributions to the clarification of this confusion through stimulating top management of companies to audit policy and practices in recruiting and to help plan instructional programs consistent with realities. If companies want graduates with broad preparation, they must agree to give them preference at the time of recruitment. If they want specialists, the programs must be constructed to develop specialists.

COST OF VOCATIONAL EDUCATION

The cost of some specialized vocational education is admittedly high and has become a topic of considerable concern in communities planning the expansion of their junior colleges. Many programs require highly specialized laboratories. Frequently it is not possible to get as high a percentage of utilization of these laboratories as is found in more general programs of the junior college. Some people contend that this highly specialized training for jobs is rightfully an expense of the employer rather than of the community at large. Others recognize the importance of employment to a community and feel that specialized preparation is an appropriate form of encouraging business to stay in the community and of encouraging new business to enter the community.

Some states and local communities are considering the possibility of regional planning of specialized programs such as are now found in Los Angeles. This would suggest that a highly specialized program located in one community might also serve the needs of adjoining communities. By appropriate location of these different programs, each community would be better served by a superior program and at less expense than if each community attempted to offer all programs. However, this kind of planning is only in the embryo stage and is yet subject to many uncertainties.

6. "Should a Businessman Be Educated?" *Fortune*, XLVII (April, 1953), 113.

STUDENT RETENTION

Higher institutions of learning at all levels have been much concerned in recent years with the high percentage of drop-outs prior to graduation. It is significant, too, that many junior colleges report a high drop-out in vocational programs because of high employment opportunities, even before the individual has completed his vocational preparation.

There is some difference of opinion among junior-college educators regarding this problem. Some feel that an injustice is being done to the individual if he is induced to accept a position and to leave college before he is thoroughly prepared for work in the field of his choice. There are other educators, however, who contend that since the objective is to place the student in a job, the quicker he is placed the better for both the student and the institution. Perhaps this is a question that requires study by joint committees of employers and faculty to determine length and content of specific vocational programs as well as the employment policies and practices to be followed. Certainly the first concern of the junior college should be for the individual—his present and future opportunities. It is of foremost concern that his preparation shall at least be adequate in terms of general breadth and specific skills.

DETERMINING VOCATIONAL OFFERINGS APPROPRIATE TO THE JUNIOR COLLEGE

What is a semiprofessional job? What is the work of a technician as distinguished from that of an engineer? What categories of jobs in the nursing profession can be taught in the junior college? These are questions on which there is wide difference of opinion. Certainly we know that in most instances the old classifications of pre-World War II are no longer applicable. Jobs have changed and preparation for the jobs should undergo corresponding changes. What institutions are most appropriate for serving these new classifications of positions? This is a subject worthy of joint consideration by representatives of employers, the professions, and by authorities in high schools, junior colleges, and senior colleges.

TEACHER PREPARATION

Perhaps one of the greatest difficulties confronting junior colleges in the development of vocational programs is that of securing adequately prepared instructors. In many vocations it is considered essential that instructors acquire practical experience plus the usual educational requirements of at least a Master's degree. Is there any logical way in which we can combine practical experience with teacher education on a co-operative basis? Perhaps one alternative is to develop extensive in-service training programs for instructors who possess practical experience but who do not meet the teacher-education requirements or vice versa. On the other hand, it may be that we need to establish an entirely new set of standards for vocational instructors with respect to essential experience, necessary basic education, and essential teacher education.

Conclusions and Recommendations

Vocational education now looms as a rapidly growing feature of community junior colleges. This is a natural result of rapid developments in mechanization and new ways of living. With increased mechanization comes the need for new and higher skills. We live in an age when all men and women are expected to make productive contributions to our total society. They must have preparation for this productivity.

The junior college may well be identified as the institution to plan the types of vocational programs that are most appropriate to specific communities. Some students will enrol in full-time programs of vocational education immediately following their graduation from high school. Others will enter junior-college vocational programs after completion of liberal-arts programs in the junior college or elsewhere. Still others will come to the junior-college for part-time upgrading in refresher courses after entering employment.

This may well be a period that will provide the best opportunity in the history of higher education for the development of realistic and practical programs of instruction geared to the needs and desires of the people of each community. If such is to be accomplished, it will not be through "armchair philosophizing," but will be through the joining together of representatives of the community in organized planning of distinctive vocational programs. Here is the opportunity for the development of functionally distinctive community-centered post-high-school education.

CHAPTER VII

General Education

JAMES W. THORNTON, JR.

Nature and Scope of General Education

DEFINITION OF GENERAL EDUCATION

General education refers to programs of education specifically designed to afford young people more effective preparation for the responsibilities which they share in common as citizens in a free society and for wholesome and creative participation in a wide range of life activities. Proponents of general education recognize that students differ and that a wide variety of specialized educational programs is required to accommodate these differences. At the same time, these proponents are keenly aware that students are also alike in many ways. They know that likenesses beget common needs, just as differences beget divergent needs. They have chosen for themselves the task of analyzing these common needs and of organizing educational experiences so that college graduates will be prepared to satisfy them.

There have been many statements, by individuals and by groups and by commissions, of the common purposes which must be met by the general portion of a student's education. Nearly all the statements begin by recognizing that people are individuals, members of families, members of society, and workers; that, because of these universal aspects of civilized life, certain educational goals are shared by all students; and that the college bears a responsibility for serving these purposes.

At this point the analysts begin to diverge more widely, both in their philosophy of the nature and extent of collegiate responsibility and in their statements of the educational consequences of the common needs. One such statement of the goals of general education has been developed by a junior-college group as follows:

The general education program aims to help each student increase his competence in

1. Exercising the privileges and responsibilities of democratic citizenship.
2. Developing a set of sound moral and spiritual values by which he guides his life.
3. Expressing his thoughts clearly in speaking and writing and in reading and listening with understanding.
4. Using the basic mathematical and mechanical skills necessary in everyday life.
5. Using methods of critical thinking for the solution of problems and for the discrimination among values.
6. Understanding his cultural heritage so that he may gain a perspective of his time and place in the world.
7. Understanding his interaction with his biological and physical environment so that he may better adjust to and improve that environment.
8. Maintaining good mental and physical health for himself, his family, and his community.
9. Developing a balanced personal and social adjustment.
10. Sharing in the development of a satisfactory home and family life.
11. Achieving a satisfactory vocational adjustment.
12. Taking part in some form of satisfying creative activity and in appreciating the creative activities of others.[1]

It is fully apparent that the commonly accepted goals of general education are not newly recognized aims of education; on the contrary, these goals, stated in various ways, have been recognized throughout the recent history of American education. The current emphasis on general education developed partly as a reaction (a) against excessive vocationalism and other specialization; (b) against the tendency for colleges to teach introductory courses as if all students were preparing for advanced work in the field; and (c) against an overemphasis on subject matter at the expense of student growth. The goals stated above may, therefore, be amplified by several additional considerations as follows:

1. That general education is not an attempt to achieve new purposes; rather, it is an attempt to achieve accepted purposes directly and effectively.
2. That education should be useful to the student, effecting improvements in his behavior.

1. B. Lamar Johnson, *General Education in Action*, pp. 21-22. Washington: American Council on Education, 1952.

3. That these concepts of utility and of changed behavior lead to a consideration of social and individual needs, and to selection of instructional materials calculated to help students satisfy their needs and the needs of society.

4. That because of concern about students, about improved behavior, and about meeting needs, those interested in general education are led inescapably to a consideration of course organization, of teaching method, and of appropriate selection of materials. In some cases, the logic of their analysis causes them to depart from traditional subject organization in favor of a more functional organization of educational experiences drawn from many disciplines but contributing harmoniously to student growth.

UNITY AND VARIETY OF GENERAL EDUCATION

Though the purposes of general education are widely accepted, there is sharp difference of opinion and of practice in methods of achieving them. It is the variety of these approaches which so often confuses new students of educational policy and arouses the hostility of both traditionalists and practical educators. Yet there exists a very real unity beneath these many approaches to general education. All who are concerned about general education realize that too often in the past graduates have not achieved the stated purposes of the college. The single object of the "general educator" is to find means to lessen this gap between the goal and its realization. It is not surprising, nor is it to be deplored, that general educators have attempted to reach this objective by widely differing paths.

Liberal-Arts Approach. Some colleges emphasize the fact that general education is not new and that almost every department and almost every course can make a real contribution to the general education of students. As they see it, the problem in the past has consisted in allowing students to specialize too narrowly. Most of them have adopted the oldest and still the most common approach to general education, which may be called the "liberal-arts" approach. They require students to select, usually during their first two years of college, one or more introductory courses from each of several fields of knowledge. Thus, typically, a student may be expected to complete courses in (*a*) natural sciences and mathematics, (*b*) social sciences, including American history, (*c*) personal relations (or psychology), (*d*) health and physical education, (*e*) philosophy and the arts, and (f) English composition and literature and also, perhaps, in a foreign language.

Survey-Course Approach. Still other colleges emphasize that courses must be explicitly designed to meet the common needs of students. Several types of course organization may derive from this point of view. The "survey course" avoids the compartmentalization of the liberal-arts approach. Instead of having the student select an introductory course from a single field of science, the college develops and requires broad courses which cut across departmental lines. These courses are designed to afford the student an introductory acquaintance with the several subareas within a broad field. It is not uncommon to find survey courses in the fields of social studies, natural science, and the humanities.

Functional-Course Approach. Still other colleges object that both the liberal-arts approach and the survey-course approach focus too much on subject matter, not sufficiently on the student. These colleges adopt the "functional" approach, beginning with thorough analysis of the activities of people in a given society and of the characteristics of the students in a given college. Courses are then designed afresh to prepare students to perform better those activities in which they will be engaged in any case. In functional courses traditional titles are abandoned, and materials are drawn from any disciplines which contribute to the growth of the students toward the course objectives. Among usual courses of this nature may be found such titles as "Family Life," "Personal Adjustment," and "The Citizen and His Government."

THE RELATION BETWEEN SPECIALIZED EDUCATION AND GENERAL EDUCATION

One of the continually perplexing problems in American education is that of the proper relationship between the specialized education which prepares the student to earn a living and the general education which enables him to profit from his life in other ways. The rapid increase in scientific and technological knowledge has demanded the expansion of specialized training for work at all levels of abstraction. The very same developments, however, have freed more and more of man's time from labor and have underscored his need for an education broader than the vocational. The result of these economic trends too often has been that general and specialized education have seemed to be in opposition to each other, that their proponents have engaged in unseemly contest for larger portions of the student's time.

Such contention betrays a lack of true awareness of the purpose of all education. Both general education and specialized education serve students and serve society. Each portion of the student's education complements and enriches the others. The two types are concurrent, sometimes intermingled, often even indistinguishable. There is not time enough to teach any student all that it would be good for him to know, either for vocational or for general purposes. The necessity of selection is a basic and inescapable part of human life; the establishment of the proper proportions of special and general training in the education of the individual demands wholehearted and mutually respectful co-operation on the part of all educators. As the President's Commission on Higher Education has stated, "The ends of democratic education in the United States will not be adequately served until we achieve a unification of our educational objectives and processes. American education must be so organized and conducted that it will provide, at appropriate levels, proper combinations of general and special education for students of varying abilities and occupational objectives."[2]

Importance of General Education in the Junior College

MEETING THE NEEDS OF STUDENTS

In chapter iii, Dressel has pointed out the differences among student bodies in public junior colleges. No previous collegiate institution has been faced so sharply with the task of providing so broad a program of education—preparing some students for further study in almost all university fields and others for immediate employment in a wide variety of occupational fields. Whatever human quality we wish to assess, it appears that the range among students in public junior colleges is greater than that among other collegiate groups. The development of extensive programs of adult education resulting

2. *Higher Education for American Democracy.* A Report of the President's Commission on Higher Education, Vol. I: *Establishing the Goals,* pp. 62–63. New York: Harper & Bros., 1947.

from fundamental social changes has extended the age-range of students upward into the 60's and 70's. The availability of the public junior college, coupled with the demands of employers for greater maturity and training in their employees, has attracted students of lower academic intelligence, and narrower educational purpose than were formerly acceptable for admission to college. The public junior college is becoming truly "the people's college" and "the community college."

This expansion of the clientele of higher education requires the junior college to become especially effective, even more so than institutions with more homogeneous student groups, in designing college programs to provide a common, unifying, enriching education for all of its students.

There is evidence that a number of public junior colleges have accepted this obligation. For instance, a few public junior colleges began their existence as strictly vocational institutes, dedicated to the task of providing thorough training in the skills of an occupational field and in the related technical information. Almost invariably, however, these colleges quickly came to the realization that such narrowness of scope was a disservice to their students and began to expand their programs so as to offer a complete education for effective living. Such a development may be traced, for example, in the Clarence A. Pierce School of Agriculture, which opened in September, 1947, as an agricultural junior college and added a liberal-arts curriculum in 1950.[3] In the same way, Los Angeles Metropolitan Junior College has broadened its curriculum in order that the Associate in Arts degree might be granted.[4] These developments in the junior-college curriculum have been paralleled in the technical institutes of New York State.[5]

The demand for general education, of course, is not limited to the vocational and technical student; there are other classes of junior-college students whose needs for appropriate general education are equally compelling. At present, each student who plans to continue his education beyond junior college is practically forced to accept the definition of general education prescribed by the university he

3. Jesse P. Bogue, *American Junior Colleges*, pp. 90–91. Washington: American Council on Education, 1952 (third edition).

4. *Ibid.*, p. 107.   5. *Ibid.*, pp. 351–75.

hopes to attend. The breadth of exposure commonly included in the lower division requirements is certainly a very important element in a well-planned program of general education. Yet the public junior college, obliged to afford "transfer" students the opportunity to meet the general-education requirements of representative higher institutions, may tend to neglect appropriate general education for other groups of its students. It is quite likely that many "transfer" students may have progressed further toward general education while they were in high school than did average "nontransfer" or "terminal" students. This fact does not lessen the responsibility of the public junior college toward either group of its students; but it certainly increases the difficulty of discharging the obligation.[6]

Moreover, the regularly enrolled full-time day student, whether terminal or transfer, is not the only one who should have and wants a general-education program. As MacLean and Dodson point out in chapter ii, the techniques of civilization and the problems of citizenship change so rapidly and so inexorably that education must be considered a life-long process. Analysis of junior-college enrolments indicates that this point of view is increasingly accepted by the adult population. In 1953–54, of the 553,000 students enrolled in public junior colleges, 264,000 (47.5 per cent) were adults.[7] There is a growing need for the development of broad and carefully planned programs suited to the special purposes of this large group, composed mostly of older, employed, part-time students.

The foregoing paragraphs seem to assume that any student will either complete junior college and continue his education in the university or complete junior college and return year by year for more education. This assumption is, of course, inaccurate. For a majority of the students who enrol each fall in the public junior colleges, the current period of enrolment will be their last organized instructional experience.

According to the *Junior College Directory*, Freshman enrolments in 1953–54 were 144,000 (26.2 per cent of all), but Sophomore enrolments amounted to only 66,000 (11.9 per cent of all enrolments).

6. *Infra*, p. 126.

7. C. C. Colvert and M. L. Baker, *Junior College Directory, 1955*, p. 4. Washington: American Association of Junior Colleges, 1955.

Less than half of the Freshmen return to the junior college for the second year![8] This fact adds increased urgency to the obligation of the junior college to provide attractive, meaningful, effective, comprehensive offerings in general education for all categories of its student body.

ITS GROWING IMPORTANCE IN THE FUTURE

The present responsibility of the public junior college for the general education of its present student bodies is clear. It is possible to speculate, moreover, that the public junior college will play an increasing, and perhaps even a dominant, part in the total organization for higher education in America. In support of this point of view, facts discussed at length elsewhere in this yearbook may be stated summarily here:

1. Unless educational opportunity is to be severely restricted, the growth in numbers of college-age youth will require the establishment of new educational institutions.[9]
2. Financial considerations, for the student and for the commonwealth, suggest that a large part of the increased enrolment should be cared for in public junior colleges.[10]
3. The junior college, with major emphasis on instruction, is in a position to undertake independent planning of programs of general education to serve the purposes of full-time and part-time, terminal and transfer, college-age and adult students.

In the light of their present status and certain future development, the public junior colleges of America have an inescapable obligation to work boldly and imaginatively in the field of general education— in the definition of purposes, the selection and organization of materials, and the development of evaluation, so that they make their optimum contribution to students and to society.

---

8. *Ibid.*, p. 4.

9. *Call for Action*, especially p. 9. Washington: American Council on Education, 1954.

10. *A Restudy of the Needs of California in Higher Education*, chap. iii, pp. 1a–18. Mimeographed draft prepared for the Liaison Committee of the Regents of the University of California and the State Board of Education. Sacramento: State Board of Education, February, 1955.

*Conditions Affecting Provisions for General Education
in Public Junior Colleges*

DETERRENTS AND DIFFICULTIES

Drop-out Rate. Many conditions inherent in the very nature of
the public junior college make it difficult to develop effective programs of general education. One of the most puzzling of these difficulties emerges from the high drop-out rate of students in the public junior college. If the college is to offer educational opportunity
to almost every high-school graduate of the community, it will inevitably attract significant numbers of students whose high-school
achievement has been minimal. Because of poor study habits, poor
finances, low motivation, comparatively low academic ability, and
outside responsibilities, many of these students will become discouraged and withdraw during or at the end of their first term.
Others will withdraw because they are offered jobs. Nevertheless,
their need for general education is undeniable and should be met as
far as their limited period of enrolment allows. On the other hand,
the requirement during their first semester of a high proportion of
general courses may discourage them and cause even more drop-outs.
The combined difficulty of developing courses of real value to these
students and of keeping them enrolled until the value becomes apparent to them is so great as to seem almost insurmountable. Yet,
these are the persons who are least likely to attain general-education
objectives independently of organized instruction, and every effort
should be made to reach them while they are enrolled.

Diversity of Student Background. The heterogeneity of the junior-
college population adds another dimension of difficulty to the problems confronting the curriculum-maker. General education intends
to satisfy common needs; yet students differ so greatly in their past
achievement and other qualities that a single course seems unlikely
to stimulate the interest and expand the understandings of all. On
the other hand, it is not always possible to develop several programs
leading to the same objective by varying paths—whether the limitation be in finances or in the ingenuity of the faculty.

Four-Year College Requirements. Difficulty is increased, too, because of the different prescriptions by four-year colleges and universities respecting lower-division requirements. A single public jun-

ior college may well have graduates attending fifty or more different colleges, each with its own pattern of lower-division requirements. There is very real hope, as Bird has suggested in chapter v, that receiving institutions will come to be more interested in a high quality of performance than in the completion of specific courses; yet the very necessity to develop courses which parallel university offerings tends to discourage junior colleges from experimenting with additional nonparallel courses for their students.[11]

Vocational Education. A second major function of the junior college, vocational education, begets an additional obstacle to experimentation in general education. Some students feel pressure to achieve marketable skill as rapidly as possible and tend to resist recommendations or requirements of nonvocational study. At the same time, it is not uncommon for instructors in business or in trade subjects to feel that more and more of the student's time should be devoted to learning the skills of his specialty. This pressure arises from a commendable interest of the instructor in his subject and in his students; and it persists in spite of accumulating evidence that personal qualities (outcomes of general education) play as large a part in job satisfaction and progress as do specific vocational skills.

In this connection, a study conducted by the writer at Orange Coast College is pertinent. In an effort to determine the degree of acceptance of general-education courses by terminal students as compared to transfer students, a "Course Rating Scale" was developed and administered to 380 first-semester students in "Introductory Psychology"—a course required of all full-time regular students who intend to graduate. The scale afforded ten separate ratings, with four points on each item. A score of 1 was most favorable, with 4 least favorable; a total score of 10 would indicate perfect acceptance of the course by the student; and a score of 40 would indicate complete and uncompromising rejection.

On this scale 213 transfer students rate "Introductory Psychology" at an average of 18.07 points. At the same time, 167 terminal students rated the course at an average of 18.50 points. The range of ratings in both groups was from 10 to 31. This result seems to indicate that the vocational student does not always reject general-

11. James W. Reynolds, "The Adequacy of the General Education Program of Local Public Junior Colleges," p. 220. Unpublished Doctor's Dissertation, Department of Education, University of Chicago, 1945.

education courses, especially if the purpose of a course is understood by the student and if the course is well taught.

Faculty Inertia. Perhaps more difficult to overcome than the narrow objectives of the student may be the apathy and resentment of the instructor in traditional subjects. Too often he has been trained as a scholar and a specialist; he has found textbooks and methods for his traditional courses with which he feels comfortable; he is too much aware of the diversity and uncertainty of general-education offerings; he distrusts his ability to be as broad and creative as the development of a good general-education course demands. For these reasons he takes refuge in a spirited defense of the values of his own limited specialty and in attacks on the "superficiality" and "lack of respectability" of the courses in general education which have been organized by others.

Lack of Funds. A final deterrent to the development of general-education courses is a shortage of funds. Experience shows that only the finest instructors can successfully develop and teach and revise experimental courses and that such instructors must be assigned adequate time to devise and carry out experimentation. Under pressure of rising enrolments and inadequate income, however, most junior-college administrators are apt to assign such instructors full teaching loads, thereby limiting their opportunities for developing new courses and improved course organization.

FACTORS FAVORING DEVELOPMENT OF GENERAL
EDUCATION IN THE JUNIOR COLLEGE

General education in the junior college, then, shares in many of the difficulties which beset the development of such programs in any other institution of higher learning. Nevertheless, there are other characteristics of the public junior college which favor experimentation.

New Institutions. The expected growth in numbers of junior colleges is in itself a hopeful factor. Newly established institutions, free from accumulated traditions, vested faculty interests, and alumni pressures, can select faculty and design their offerings from the outset in complete harmony with their educational philosophy. If such new institutions accept the logic of the general-education movement, they will be able before many years to present concrete evidence (rather than reasoned theory) about the effectiveness of their approaches to general education.

Emphasis on Instruction. Another characteristic of the junior college is its opportunity to concentrate on instruction. Selection and promotion of faculty may be based solely on teaching ability. Extending the frontiers of knowledge and writing for publication, traditionally a part of the responsibility of university faculties, are minor elements in faculty success at the junior-college level. The junior-college student-body, unselected and heterogeneous, becomes discouraged by pedestrian teaching but makes satisfactory progress with good instruction. For this reason, exceptional instruction must become a primary responsibility and a major distinctive quality of every junior college.

Community-College Conditions. The development of general education in the junior college is favored still more by the better conditions for teaching which characterize the institution. Classes in the junior college are frequently smaller than those in four-year colleges and universities; the public junior college is uniquely a part of its community, responsive to the nature and the needs of that community; it is easy for the local junior college to draw upon all kinds of community resources—business, industry, government, institutions, persons—to illuminate and vitalize classroom instruction. Emerging social conditions and the primary characteristics of the junior college afford it unprecedented opportunity to develop bold and realistic educational programs to meet the new challenges of higher education for significant proportions of relatively unselected young people and adults.

General-Education Practices in Public Junior Colleges

There is wide diversity in general-education practices among the public junior colleges of the nation. Some colleges have attempted to improve their curriculum mainly through the in-service training of the faculty. Others have worked through committees to develop one or another course as student-need or the enthusiasm of faculty members has dictated. Again, programs vary in accordance with the age of the institution; administratively, it is much simpler to institute a program in a newly organized college than to revise a curriculum in a college with a longer history. A further source of difference lies in the decision on the question of electives versus requirements: whether to attempt to adapt programs to individual attainments by offering general-education electives under guidance or to emphasize the "common" aspect of general-education goals and require certain courses of every student. From this diversity, sample programs will be summarized briefly.

A STATE-WIDE PROGRAM OF STUDY

For several years the public junior colleges of California have carried on state-wide studies of general education. In 1950, the American Council on Education secured funds from the Carnegie Foundation for the Advancement of Teaching for the "California Study of General Education in the Junior College." Several positive results of this fourteen-month study may be identified:

1. The development, through faculty participation in summer workshops and in conferences, of state-wide interest in general education on the part of instructors and administrators.
2. The publication of the report of the study, *General Education in Action.*[12]
3. Annual meetings of instructors from each of the junior colleges in California, at which developments in the general-education program of each college are described and plans laid for the further encouragement of general education in the colleges.
4. The development of a plan for a series of studies of instructional method in several fields of general education, for which sponsorship is now being sought by the Committee on General Education of the California Junior College Association.

The "California Study" is an excellent example of the effectiveness of state-wide co-operation in the study of curricular problems.

COLLEGE PROGRAMS OF GENERAL EDUCATION

Eastern Oklahoma Agricultural and Mechanical College, a junior college situated at Wilburton, offers an excellent example of a consistent college-wide program of general education, including an accepted philosophical statement, required courses, and emphasis on general education in all aspects of the college program. The program

12. Johnson, *op. cit.*

is described at length in a letter to the writer from President E. T. Dunlap:[13]

From the educational philosophy of the college stem the objectives of its general education program and from these objectives the functional program of the college is derived.

The philosophy of the college is stated as follows:

All people have both individual and common needs. It is the responsibility of the college to help each student identify these needs. The educational program in all of its aspects should contribute directly to satisfying these needs in order that the student may effectively fill his place as a citizen in a democratic society. The faculty recognizes the importance of using all the activities of the campus, both class and out-of-class, to help the student achieve his goals. The sum total of a student's experiences in and out of the classroom constitutes the college program or curriculum.

Purpose number one of the college, as adopted by the faculty, is "To provide a general education for all students which enables them to develop the attitudes, knowledge, qualities and skills necessary for them to be effective as a person, a worker, a family member, a citizen. . . ."

The formal courses set up as a minimum of studies in general education are: Communications, General Biology and General Physical Science, American History and Government, Orientation, Health and Physical Education, Introduction to Literature, and Music Appreciation. The general objectives of these courses are understanding and appreciation of the fields, with experience in the knowledges and skills, plus development of attitudes.

Each year the college Curriculum Committee surveys the courses and the activities provided for the students, and determines the extent to which its educational objectives are being implemented. The results of these surveys form a basis for meeting general-education objectives to a greater degree in the total college program.

During the last year a survey of the extent to which general-education objectives are recognized in planning courses of study and are utilized in in-class and extra-class instructional activities, was made. In 21 classes with 425 students and in 36 extra-class activities with 950 students, the objective "developing a balanced personal and social adjustment" was operative in the classes and the activity experiences. Also, there was indication of significant achievement in the other nine objectives listed under Purpose No. 1 of the college, relating to general education, and referred to earlier in this letter.

13. See *Catalog Announcements of Eastern Oklahoma Agricultural and Mechanical College, Bulletin of 1954-55.* Wilburton, Oklahoma: 1954. Quotations in President Dunlap's letter are from pp. 16 and 25.

The Technical Institutes of New York have adopted, by action of the Board of Regents, a standard program in general education which has been described as follows:[14]

Technical institutes and community colleges should offer a well-balanced, functional program in general education, including both curricular and extracurricular activities for every student enrolled in a full-time day curriculum.

The kind, amount, and quality of general education should be adequate to enrich the lives of the young men and women graduating from these institutions.

In considering a general program of studies for all students, we must establish a minimum standard in terms of the number of semester hours or the number of courses to be offered. The standard set recently by the Board of Regents of the State of New York specifies that all students enrolled in a two-year program must earn 20 credit hours in the areas of communication (English), social studies, and the mathematics-science combination. The common practice in our institutes is two 1-semester, 3-hour courses in communication arts and skills, two in the social science field, and the remainder of the 20 hours in mathematics and science.

Dr. Lawrence L. Bethel, president of the Fashion Institute of Technology, has commented on these requirements in an inter-office memorandum as follows:

A brief analysis of the programs at the Fashion Institute of Technology, New York City Community College, and Farmingdale [State University Agricultural and Technical Institute] indicates that from 30 to 35 per cent of the content of these programs is devoted to the study of sociology, psychology, English, History, economics, mathematics, and basic science. Comparing this with senior colleges, I find that approximately 30 per cent of the Massachusetts Institute of Technology program is devoted to this area. . . . The State University of New York School of Forestry shows only about 23 per cent. . . . By comparison . . . , therefore, the community colleges of the State University appear to measure up rather well with all the senior specialized institutions.

The Chicago City Junior College also has adopted a "Basic General Curriculum" which is required of all students.[15] The prescribed

14. Francis E. Almstead, "A Design for General Education in Technical Institutes," *Technical Education News*, XIV, No. 1, (Special Issue, 1954), 9.

15. *The Chicago City Junior College Bulletin*, 1954–55, p. 20. Chicago: Board of Education, 1954. See also: Peter Masiko, Jr., "The Program of General Education at Wright Junior College," chap. xxi in W. Hugh Stickler, *Organization and Administration of General Education*. Dubuque, Iowa: William C. Brown Co., 1951.

courses include English (Communications), Social Science, Biology, Physical Science, Humanities, and Physical Education. Other introductory liberal-arts courses are taught so as to emphasize the attainment of general-education values. In addition, remedial courses in reading, speech, and composition, based on need demonstrated by tests, are offered at the Wright Branch.

An interesting effort in curriculum revision, involving an entire faculty, was that undertaken at Bakersfield College. First, the faculty agreed to adopt the goals of general education as stated in the report of the California Study of General Education in the Junior College, *General Education in Action*.[16] Next, through painstaking committee work, a detailed analysis was made of specific means by which each goal might be attained. Then each instructor rated the extent of contribution of each of his courses to these specific aims. This evaluation, finally, became the foundation for intensive faculty study of curriculum, including recommendations for new courses and the revision of almost every course in the college. Although the study did not result immediately in a new pattern of course requirements, it has stimulated the development of several new general-education courses. The Bakersfield survey particularly emphasized the contribution of every course to the goals of general education. It seems also to have increased the concern of every instructor to teach so that students would attain the accepted goals of general education.[17]

EXAMPLES OF SPECIFIC GENERAL-EDUCATION COURSES

Single courses have been developed to meet general-education objectives in almost every field of instruction; in some colleges such courses are a part of a required pattern; in others they are offered as electives. Some half-dozen examples will demonstrate approaches in several instructional fields.

1. San Bernardino Valley College (California) has extended its graduation requirements to include six units of related arts. This requirement may be met through a course in history of western civilization; through selection from among twenty-two listed courses in

16. Johnson, *op. cit.*, pp. 21–22.

17. "Opportunities in General Education at Bakersfield College, 1951–52." Bakersfield, California: Bakersfield College, 1952 (mimeographed). See also: Thomas B. Merson, "A Faculty Study of General Education," *Junior College Journal*, XXIV (January, 1954), 260–67.

art, English, music, and philosophy; or through a specially developed six-unit course entitled "Humanities."

The humanities course is intended to provide the student with some insight into the interrelatedness of knowledge, to increase his understanding of his culture, and to help him think more critically; it centers on a synthesis of concepts basic to art, music, literature, and philosophy. Instruction is shared by four staff members, one from each of the four areas; all four attend every class meeting. Presentations are animated by the conviction that general education must utilize forms of communication that are more than words about words. Methods include lecture-discussions, panel discussions, art displays, musical performances, field trips, and student projects in photography, drama, and singing.

Other newly developed courses which satisfy the related-arts requirement at San Bernardino include a two-semester course in home planning, a one-semester course in philosophy entitled "Basic Ideas in Modern Life," and a one-semester course in "Applied Sociology."

2. Orange Coast College includes two graduation requirements beyond the basic instruction in English, American history, hygiene, and physical education required by state law in all California junior colleges. One is the introductory course in psychology, based on a standard text but emphasizing the understanding of individual differences, adjustment, mental hygiene, and test interpretation. A valuable feature of this offering is that the psychology instructor is also the counselor for students in his classes. One interview with the counselor, for interpretation of tests administered in the class, is a requirement of the course. All students, of course, have other interviews for registration, and perhaps personal counseling interviews as well.

The second added requirement is in the field of mathematics. In 1949 a faculty committee began the development of a college-level test in basic arithmetic as needed in every-day adult life. After two years of experimentation and refinement of the test, standards were developed, based on test scores of entering students. Those students who scored below the fiftieth percentile on the "Applied Mathematics Test" were advised to complete a one-unit course in applied mathematics. It is recognized that many students have had no instruction in arithmetic (although possibly in algebra and geometry) since the eighth grade; so it reviews the very beginning steps of arithmetic and progresses to fractions, decimals, interest, and mensuration. Since 1954, students have been required to pass either the test, on its first administration to them, or the applied mathematics course, before graduation.

3. In an attempt to achieve more directly the goal of training students for more effective citizenship, Mohawk Valley Technical Institute at Utica, New York, has developed four courses in the social sciences which are required of all students. Departing from the more traditional requirements in history and political science, Mohawk Valley requires one course in "Citizen and His Government," emphasizing responsibilities and privileges of citizenship; politics in government; pressure groups; trends of centralization and integration; and the relation of local, state, federal, and international governments.

A companion course, "Citizen and His Community," studies the various communities of which the student is and will be a part. Topics include ecology of the city, state, and region; marriage and the family; development of culture; racial discrimination; ethnocentrism; individual adjustment.

In addition to the two courses described, Mohawk Valley Technical Institute also requires, in the social-science field, a course in economics and another in industrial and labor relations.

The programs and courses referred to above are presented only as illustrations of junior-college practices. For more extensive accounts of general-education developments, the reader is referred to the report of the California Study of General Education in the Junior College.[18] The major part of this volume is given over to accounts of general-education practices in the junior colleges of California.

Deficiencies in Junior-College General Education

The examples cited indicate that some junior colleges are developing fresh and creative approaches to the problems of course organization and presentation. On the other hand, there is ample evidence to indicate that too often the programs of general education

18. Johnson, *op. cit.*

offered in the junior colleges are partial or nonexistent; that the content and organization is uncritically imitative; that only a minority of the students are exposed to general-education courses; and that evaluation is inadequate.

Thus in 1952, after almost two years of intensive study, Johnson stated:

> As one examines the graduation requirements of California junior colleges with the goals of general education in mind, he is impressed (1) by diversity of practice, (2) by the spotty and limited recognition given some of the general education objectives, and (3) by the apparent failure as yet to make any provision for some of the others. These impressions are further confirmed by an examination of recommended programs listed in junior college catalogs.[19]

Reynolds, in an extensive study of the adequacy of junior-college general-education programs, came to similar conclusions. Reynolds first developed a comprehensive list of specific objectives of general education, and then compared course objectives with this list. He found that in five public junior-college curriculums the percentage of general-education objectives recognized was 8.5.[20] Yet he found that there was a trend to increase the proportion of total credit hours assigned to courses in vocational education and to decrease the relative number of credit hours assigned to electives. He concluded that while "evidence exists . . . that junior colleges are making progress in broadening the scope of their general-education programs," it is still possible to "doubt that junior colleges have well-defined policies governing their provisions for the general-education needs of their students."[21] At a later point, Reynolds comments, "While senior colleges have dictated policies of preparatory education, and occupational competence has led to the adoption of comprehensive programs of vocational education, the area of general education in most local public junior colleges has received little or no attention."[22]

Another deficiency in general-education programs seems to lie in the quality of instruction offered. Dressel and Mayhew note that in the four-year colleges involved in the Co-operative Study of Evaluation in General Education (and presumably in junior colleges as well), "General-education classes are not well planned to make the

19. Johnson, *op. cit.*, p. 49.   21. *Ibid.*, pp. 176–77.
20. Reynolds, *op. cit.*, p. 59.   22. *Ibid.*, p. 220.

most economical use of time, of teaching aids, or of student motivation and interest. This is not to say that general-education instruction is bad, rather, that it has not, in the large, met the challenge involved in general-education objectives."[23]

A further deficiency is found in the failure to evaluate the degree of attainment of the goals set for general education. Because evaluation is costly in time and in money, it is not surprising that few public junior colleges have gone beyond course examinations in their attempts to evaluate. For this reason, it may become necessary for the junior colleges to join together in an extensive study of the purposes and methods of evaluation in general education. As Dressel points out, "Good instruction requires a constant awareness of the effect on each individual student of the totality of experiences which that student is undergoing; it requires adaptation of the experiences to the needs and background of each student; and it requires that each student be provided with evidence so that he can discern his own strengths and weaknesses and be motivated to further improvement with regard to general-education goals. Since evaluation is the means to each of these requirements, it follows that good instruction and evaluation are not only complementary but actually almost indistinguishable."[24]

Finally, the large enrolment of adults in public junior colleges indicates that growing interest in lifelong learning is coupled with increasing opportunity to study. Yet the adult programs of junior colleges concentrate most heavily on vocational and avocational skills, with little planned opportunity for adults to increase their general background. If there is validity to the philosophy of general education, it seems very probable that well-conceived, carefully planned, imaginatively taught general-education courses would merit enthusiastic reception by large numbers of adults.

Recommendations

In the field of general education, the fundamental recommendation must be that the junior colleges realize that they have attained adulthood in the family of American higher education and begin to ac-

23. Paul L. Dressel and Lewis B. Mayhew, *General Education: Explorations in Evaluation*, p. 256. Washington: American Council on Education, 1954.

24. Paul L. Dressel, *Evaluation in General Education*, p. 333. Dubuque, Iowa: William C. Brown Co., 1954.

cept the responsibilities for leadership that their stature implies. As America moves into a period of very rapid growth in numbers of college-age youth and, at the same time, into a period when increasing proportions of youth need a post-secondary education, the junior colleges will inevitably exhibit very rapid expansion. At the same time, they must realize that they have emerged into full partnership with the "senior" institutions; they must cease to be so largely imitative and begin to make decisions for themselves about the nature and the quality of the education they provide for their several clienteles.

If the junior colleges are to achieve this basic and all-inclusive recommendation, several types of co-operative, and perhaps sponsored, study and endeavor will be required. In the first place, now is the time when junior colleges throughout the nation must analyze with great care the areas of demand in which increased enrolments are likely to occur. If, as seems very possible, completion of the fourteenth grade is to be as common as completion of the twelfth grade has become, the junior colleges must begin now to prepare to care for new types of students. Too often, during its meteoric rise toward the ideal of free public education for every child, the American school system has been overwhelmed by numbers. Under the pressure of finding buildings and teachers, educational practice has developed out of unadorned expediency. Thereafter, principles have been elaborated to justify existing practice. The junior college has now an all-too-brief forewarning of its impending problem; it has an opportunity to establish principles and to experiment with appropriate practices before the period of most rapid growth sets in.

A second field for co-operative endeavor is that of instructional materials and organization. Instructors willingly accept the need for the improvement of instruction which is basic to general education but find that they lack the time, the imagination, and the administrative support to bring about fundamental changes in their practices. Studies such as the California Study of General Education point the way to effective methods of joint endeavor toward the solution of problems. The next step, however, must be to search for more effective means of instruction to achieve each of the goals of general education. Most instructors will welcome such help. They realize that general education requires superior teachers, and many are eager to become superior teachers. If master teachers could be identified and freed to demonstrate their methods to ordinary teachers of good will, the number of superior teachers could be markedly increased very quickly.

A third recommendation may perhaps be characterized as "evangelistic." In the third section of the present chapter it has been pointed out that apathy and resistance on the part of the majority of the faculty to the needs and the challenges of general education are a major obstacle to the effective education of college youth. For this reason, studies must be carried on to discover means of training college teachers so that faculties in the years to come may understand the full scope of their dual responsibility—to their scholarly endeavor and to the students entrusted to their care. Because of the educational lag involved in this suggestion, however, junior colleges in their associations and through their administrators need to study and to carry out effective in-service methods of broadening the vision and stimulating the pedagogic inventiveness of their faculties.

Finally, far more effective means must be developed to make use of the experience, insight, and concern of the junior-college student —adult, terminal, transfer—in developing all of the programs of education of the junior college. Industry has found consumer research essential to the development of acceptable products. It has been demonstrated also that student participation is more likely and learning more lasting if students have participated in the planning of their activities. The problem, then, is one of making the most efficient use of the common concern and varying abilities of the student, the adult citizen, the faculty member, and the administrator, in devising a program of general education which will truly serve both social and individual needs.

CHAPTER **VIII**

Community Services

JAMES W. REYNOLDS

Introduction

The educational significance of a program of community services in community colleges, as we now know them, may be inferred from the recognized goals of these colleges. That the interests and motives underlying present-day objectives of collegiate education represent a striking departure from the college-community concept of early American colleges is commonly understood. Two excerpts from the writings of a notable American educator of the nineteenth century give expression to the older concept of the place of the college in American life.

Let any reflecting man think for a moment of the kind of education which society furnishes to a great extent in this country. . . . Let him reflect on the trickery of business, the jobbery of politicians, the slang of newspapers, the vulgarity of fashion, the sensationalism of popular books, the shallowness and cant that dishonor the pulpit and defile worship, and he may reasonably rejoice that there is one community which for a considerable period takes into keeping many of the most susceptible and most promising of our youth, to give them better tastes, higher aims, and above all to teach them to despise all sorts of intellectual and moral shams.[1]

The college community is emphatically an *isolated community* more completely separated and further removed than almost any other from the ordinary and almost universally pervading influences of family and social life. When the student leaves his home to enter college, it is true that in a most important sense he leaves it forever.[2]

These statements appeared in the *New Englander* in 1869. The author was Noah Porter, who at the time of their publication was professor of moral philosophy and metaphysics at Yale College and,

1. Noah Porter, "The American College and the American Public," *New Englander*, XXVIII (1869), 501.

2. *Ibid.*, p. 490.

two years later, president of this institution. The point of view exemplified by the statements was a popular one at the time of their publication. They are presented in this chapter as a means of bringing into sharp focus the contrast between the old and the new.

There is no disposition to criticize Porter's comment on college-community relationships for the times in which he was writing. There is a possibility that, in this period immediately following the American Civil War, the nature of the social environment justified withdrawal by those who wished to pursue an intellectual life in an uncontaminated atmosphere. It is superfluous to observe that the times as well as individuals have changed in the past eighty-seven years. The nature and extent of some of the changes have been described in chapters ii and iii of this yearbook. Today, the concept of the college as a thoroughly isolated community is as unacceptable as it is impracticable.

One of the innovations appearing in the eighty-seven-year period since Professor Porter's series of articles appeared in the *New Englander* is the public junior college. This institution has moved further away than any other institution of college rank from the ideal which Porter described. The products of these adaptations have been identified in preceding chapters as preparation for advanced study, general education, and vocational education.

The junior college, however, has not confined the changes in its educational program to serving the needs of full-time students only. As with other educational institutions, it has looked beyond its classrooms and campus and found educational needs in the community of which it is an integral part. The attempt to satisfy these needs has led to the development of community services.

Definition of Community Services

In another connection the writer has characterized the community college as a "two-way street with traffic of services moving in both directions." That is, the community-college idea presupposes "an increase of services from the community to the college to correspond with the increase of services from the college to the community."[3] With this idea in mind, community services may be defined

3. James W. Reynolds, "Another Job for Your Community," *Junior College Journal*, XXIII (October, 1954), 61.

as involving both college and community resources and conducted for the purpose of meeting specified educational needs of individuals or enterprises within the college or the community. From this viewpoint, community services are provided through an extension of the regular school program in terms of the traditional school day, the traditional locations of the instructional activities, the traditional curriculum, and the traditional concept of students. Community services, moreover, often transcend the traditional definition of education in the sense of teacher-student relationships. In many instances this relationship is entirely absent. A consideration of some examples of community services will make this observation more clear.

1. Local office managers recognize a need to improve their skills. The college is called on to conduct a clinic in which the participants are regularly employed office workers and the observers are the managers. Following the clinic, a period for questions and answers is provided. Significant procedures are emphasized by the faculty member who conducts the clinic.

2. Small high schools in the same area of the state as a junior college are unable to afford the cost of a vocational-guidance program. Representatives of the junior college who are prepared in this field administer vocational-preference inventories and then counsel with the students who otherwise would not receive the benefit of such service.

3. A chemistry teacher in the junior college serves as a consultant to a city water department.

4. The college either independently or co-operatively provides for the presentation of a series of fine arts exhibits for the community.

5. College faculty members and students co-operate in various enterprises intended to improve social affairs in the community, e.g., community night, a community chorus, the little theater.

6. A speaker's bureau consisting primarily of college faculty members is organized, and a listing of available speakers and subjects is provided to program chairmen of various clubs.

7. The college baseball diamond is made available during the summer for the American Legion baseball competition; the college gymnasium, for the county basketball tournament; the college cafeteria is used by local civic clubs for regular meetings.

8. Surveys are conducted to secure pertinent information concerning such questions as population trends, incidence of occupations and annual replacement needs, the nature of a needed industrial-education program.

9. A special class is set up for the purpose of helping individuals fill out their income tax blanks correctly.
10. A "great books" class is organized for adults and taught by a member of the college faculty.

These examples of community services indicate the marked departure from tradition on which comment was made. Also, the examples represent college activities which are in sharp contrast to the concept of a college found in the description which Noah Porter presented.

An analysis of the list of examples will reveal two characteristics which are common in these activities: (*a*) Each activity was provided to help satisfy a genuine educational need in the community and (*b*) the chief beneficiaries of each of the activities were adults. Since these are also characteristics of adult education, as the term is customarily used, the question naturally arises, "What is the basic difference between community services and adult education?"

In answering this question, one would be reluctant to regard the terms as synonymous. On the other hand, any attempt to separate the two by mutually exclusive definitions would reveal that the two types of educational enterprise are so intertwined as to make a complete distinction virtually impossible. Moreover, there is no uniform agreement as to the meaning of these terms by those who contribute to the literature of education.

No attempt will be made in this chapter to answer the question as to the difference between community services and adult education. In developing a description of community services, adult education is treated as such a service. Purists who have a reverent regard for one term or the other will doubtless be offended. It is believed, however, that no real violence will be done to either term but that considering adult education as a part of community services will be advantageous in avoiding the confusion that would inevitably result from making artificial distinctions.

Before considering the range of community services, it is desirable to clarify one other aspect of the definition. By implication, the services illustrated have been those which are limited pretty much to adults. If this were universally and necessarily true, it would rule out any consideration of the educational service which is provided for the full-time students in junior colleges whose age range is that normally associated with this level of formal schooling. It is obvious that such an inference is not intended since this chapter will deal with only that phase of community service which is provided primarily for adults.

Types of Community Service

The diverse nature of community services makes it desirable that efforts to describe them be organized under a few major categories. While this procedure suffers because it cannot be exhaustive, yet in a field in which the only limiting factor is the power of individuals to project themselves beyond the confines of tradition, the provision of an exhaustive listing would be an endless task. Organization under major categories permits some indication of the broad scope of the field of services without the monotony which would occur sooner or later in a complete and detailed elaboration.

The categories of community services used in this chapter have been adapted from a recent publication by H. Curtis Mial.[4] Additional categories were added to Mial's list, and those finally adopted include the following: mutual aid for meeting college-community needs; community-experience programs; community study and research problems; public-affairs education; specialized community services including the subcategories of economic conditions, public education, health, cultural and recreational activities, and conservation; community development; community participation and leadership-training; use of mass media of communication; public-relations programs; community use of school plant; and formal adult-education programs.

The description of most of these categories of community services is supplemented by reference to specific practices reported by junior colleges. The writer acknowledges his indebtedness to two studies as sources of these junior-college reports: *Junior College–Community Co-operation*,[5] which Mary E. Blair prepared as her thesis for the Master's degree at the University of Texas; and a study made by the Southern California Junior College Association under the direction of Robert E. Swenson of Fullerton Junior College. Mrs.

4. H. Curtis Mial, *College-Community Relationships in New York State*. Albany: New York State Citizen's Council, Inc., 1953.

5. Mary E. Blair, "Junior College–Community Co-operation." Unpublished Master's thesis, University of Texas, 1954.

Blair's study was based on questionnaire returns from several sections of the country; Swenson's, on returns from junior colleges in southern California.

MUTUAL AID FOR MEETING COLLEGE-COMMUNITY NEEDS

Activities listed under this category involve participation by representatives of both the college and the noncollege population in services which are of benefit to both the college and the community. Some idea of the nature of such services can be obtained from the following list of activities reported by the junior colleges included in the Blair and Swenson studies: promotion of a historical society and museum; establishment of a community center; making an occupational survey of the community; improvement of local fire department; organization of a nursing-education program in connection with a local hospital; co-operation with community health department in organizing mental-health clinic; operation by college of the local weather station located on college campus; college-conducted course for church ushers; co-operation with community to improve program of state employment service; provision of an upgrading program for both the police and fire departments; printing a directory of welfare organizations; co-operation with safety council and committees; participation in blood-donor programs, United Fund Campaign, and parent-teachers association; co-operation in organizing a civic symphony orchestra.

The concept of college-community needs embodied in these activities is in direct contrast to the ideas advanced by Noah Porter. Boundary lines between the college community and the geographical community in which the college is located have been obliterated completely. The idea of the college as an *isolated community* has been abandoned. Each unit of the community recognizes its interdependence with the other in suffering the detrimental effects of unsolved problems. On this basis, the college and the community join together in attacking these problems.

It should be observed that, with many of the examples of mutual aid in meeting common problems, the contribution of the college transcends the ordinary definition of an educational service. Thus, the college acknowledges its functional identification with community life; both college and community recognize the peculiar competence of a college faculty, administration, and student body in attacking certain community problems; and representatives of both units accept an obligation in seeking a solution to these problems.

COMMUNITY-EXPERIENCE PROGRAMS

Community-experience programs include three essential elements: (*a*) the college regards the broader community as an instructional laboratory in which more efficient learning can occur through direct experience; (*b*) the instructional program of the college is planned so that frequent use may be made of this instructional laboratory; and (*c*) persons in the noncollege community understand the significance of use by the college of the instructional laboratory and co-operate in the enterprise.

In this instance, the contribution of service comes from the non-college community. The success of the undertaking, however, depends on the freeing of the faculty and the administration from the practice of restricting instructional activities to the college campus and on the broadening of the arena of instructional facilities.

This broadened concept of instructional facilities already prevails in many junior colleges. Evidence of this may be seen in a representative list of activities reported by the junior colleges included in the Blair and Swenson studies: attendance at churches and temples of different faiths by student groups; visitation of industries and businesses; organization of interfaith council with special religious groups working together; encouragement of students and help in securing part-time or summer jobs in occupations similar to those in which they expect to make a lifetime career; story-telling at children's hospital; field trips to art museums, radio and television stations, and industrial plants; assistance provided by local square-dance instructors to college classes in square dancing to show students procedures used in public square dancing; field trips by elementary-school pupils to college greenhouse for student-directed activities; demonstrations and talks presented by science students for elementary schools; help given by college students working in recreation programs for younger children during recess periods and after school; services performed by college students in summer camps; and "A-Community-Goes-to-College Day," pointing up welfare services available in the community.

COMMUNITY STUDY AND RESEARCH PROBLEMS

It has been established in preceding chapters that socioeconomic conditions have changed sharply in American communities since the 1880's. Moreover, it may be observed that the period of change is not finished—society in this country is undergoing continuous alteration. In the face of this phenomenon, there is a constant need for facts, for information that is current, to serve as a basis for realistic planning of community enterprises and educational programs. These facts, this information, can be obtained most satisfactorily by frequent studies and research.

The specialized competence of the faculty and administration of most colleges provides a valuable reservoir from which personnel can be drawn to make or direct such needed studies. The provision of this personnel, thus, becomes a desirable community service.

The services of faculty personnel in making or directing studies and research in community problems is enhanced, furthermore, by the participation of college students in such activities. When the study includes personnel from the noncollege community as well as faculty and students in the college, the resources available are usually adequate for most studies that would be undertaken.

The variety of community problems that might be studied is virtually limitless. Some idea of the range of problems may be secured from the following list of actual studies reported by junior colleges: participation in a five-county survey to discover the needs of industrial-education program, conducting an incorporation-need survey for community, cost-of-living survey for communities of comparable size in the state, community occupational survey, analysis of student spending in community, analysis of selling techniques in the community, studies of community population trends and distribution as to economic and racial status, a land-use survey, investigation of the needs of the older people in the community, survey of problems of small businesses, and an inquiry among business executives to learn what skills are deemed necessary for stenographers.

PUBLIC-AFFAIRS EDUCATION

The term, "public affairs," as used in this analysis of community service is difficult to define because of the broad scope of activities it includes. Like the term "citizenship," its definition ultimately depends on the individual or group using the term. In this instance, the term will be limited arbitrarily to the political aspects of any individual's personality.

The use of the term "public affairs" in relation to community services presents an additional problem of distinguishing between public-affairs education carried on as a regular part of the classroom program and public-affairs education which is peculiarly a community service. Any attempt to set up an acceptable line of demarcation between the two activities encounters many elements of serious overlap. To disentangle these elements is virtually impossible. This situation, it is believed, justifies a second recourse to arbitrary definition. Accordingly, public-affairs education as a community service will be regarded as limited to the noncollege segment of the population.

The urgent need for public-affairs education as a community service stems, in part, from the changed role of the individual citizen in this country. Socioeconomic changes occurring in this country have removed restrictions previously imposed on the average citizen's relationship with the agencies of government. At the time that Professor Porter was attacking the "jobbery of politicians," the average citizen had little familiarity with government agencies beyond his local community. Today, this same citizen has broadened his scope of personal concern to include not only the state and federal government but international political organizations as well. This situation has created a need for a greatly enlarged concept of public-affairs education.

The need for increased public-affairs education is further stressed by the threat which hostile political and economic ideologies pose for the basic principles of democracy. The danger to democracy presented by fascism and communism is a real one. Elimination of this danger depends to no small degree on public-affairs education.

Junior colleges, as well as other educational institutions, are active in their efforts to meet this need. While the list of activities carried on by all junior colleges would be almost endless, the following indicate some idea of what is being done: speeches by faculty and students before service clubs; maintenance of a speakers' bureau for a variety of community meetings; film discussion groups; conducting community public affairs forums; dinner meetings held at student union to discuss community advisory problems, with faculty members participating; co-operation with local bar association in a series of lectures on "Law Everyone Should Know"; series of in-service-education meetings for teachers in local public schools; student-service forum operating in elementary and secondary schools to inform pupils from minority groups about further education; co-operation with local civil defense organization in educational program.

SPECIALIZED COMMUNITY SERVICES

The subcategories considered under this heading are more restricted in their implications than those in the preceding categories or those which follow. The restrictions, in the main, refer to the characteristic of subject matter. The subcategories here used pertain to five specific aspects of community life: (*a*) economic conditions, (*b*) public education, (*c*) health, (*d*) cultural and recreational activities, and (*e*) conservation.

Economic Conditions. Community services considered under this title are, for the most part, those dealing with various aspects of business life. Many of these services are similar to those which the junior colleges include in their programs of vocational education. Other services, however, meet the previously enunciated criterion of applying primarily to the noncollege segment of the population of the community.

A survey of the practices of junior colleges in this field of specialized community service shows a wide range of activities. Included under this heading will be found the following: community placement bureau; management clinics; investment seminar; national course for life-insurance underwriters; industrial-management program; job-relations training for department heads; tie-in program with accountants of the region who have become specialists in tax matters; co-operative program with engineers; course in community resources; short unit course in how to make out income tax report; participation in labor-management committees.

Public Education. The host of professional, financial, and social problems associated with the public schools constitute the basis for community services under this heading. The comprehensiveness of the community-service activities of junior colleges is indicated by the following examples: special recruitment drive for elementary- and secondary-school teachers; county-wide vocational-guidance service for high-school students; professional courses on the senior-college level conducted by junior-college faculty through the extension service of the state university; courses for parents of preschool children; use of junior-college evening-school students in the instruction of crippled children, as assistants to a teaching principal both in classroom and office, and as helpers in the visual-aids department; remedial-reading instruction for elementary-school pupils by junior-college students; community teacher-education program through junior-college credit courses and senior-college and graduate extension courses; provision of extension programs so people unable to attend high school can complete their high-school requirements; high-school evaluation programs projecting county-school needs; committees for recommending school locations and planning facilities; and political science examinations to meet constitutional requirements for teaching credentials.

Health. As in the other areas of specialized services, health services require professional preparation at a level higher than that usually required of teachers in a junior college. Thus, it will be found that junior-college faculty members, administrators, and members of the student body contribute their services to the community through a co-operative arrangement in which the specialized personnel needed is secured from the noncollege part of the population of the community. This recognition of a need for personnel with training not usually provided by the junior college in no way detracts from the value of the service. A consideration of the following list of services will make this observation clear: courses for practical nurses taught by local physicians through arrangements made by the junior college; co-operation with local physicians in giving the chemistry, biology, and physiology courses needed by laboratory technicians; co-operation with the county health service, county tuberculosis unit, Red Cross, chest X-ray program, and cancer drive; child-development classes for adults; co-operation with civil defense organization on chemical and radiological defense and first aid; college-sponsored medical forum conducted by leading physicians of the community on eight specific diseases; student co-operation through first-aid and health classes with the community health center; city-county health unit on college campus; maintenance of mental-health clinic and provision of academic program for two hospitals; service by members of faculty on community health committees; courses conducted for training hotel and restaurant workers in sanitation and health measures.

Cultural and Recreational Activities. Socioeconomic changes noted in previous chapters have increased materially the amount of leisure time. This increase has, in turn, resulted in greater opportunity for participation in cultural and recreational activities. Collegiate institutions have a peculiar advantage in providing this opportunity through their programs of fine arts and recreation.

The variety of community services reported by junior colleges under the heading of cultural and recreational activities is evidence of the consideration being given them by junior-college leaders. Probably the best method of indicating the range of activities will be found in listing the practices reported: community lyceum series; water carnival; great-books-classics and films-classics programs for adults; art exhibits featuring the work of local artists; co-operation of college choir and community church in presenting local artists; co-operation of college choir and community church in presenting Christmas and Easter programs; a series of dramas presented by means of records with commentary by junior-college instructors; musical entertainment provided for local civic clubs; weekly half-hour organ concerts broadcast from college over local radio station; weekly book review conducted in college auditorium and supervised primarily by members of college staff; service of college instructor as conductor of local symphony orchestra; provision by college of space and facilities for an area music festival each Spring; series of chamber-music concerts presented each year by outstanding groups; sponsorship by college of annual fiesta; class in women's choral work offered for women of community; college sponsorship of little-theater organization; children's annual book festival; a weekly sacred-music workshop; college faculty directors of choral groups for men and for women.

Conservation. The importance of conserving natural resources has long been recognized as a valid concern of the community. On this basis, conservation education has found its way into educational programs from the elementary level through the graduate school. The translation of this sort of education into action projects, however, often requires a species of community service not customarily associated with the traditional curriculum of educational institutions.

The needed service often consists of arousing community groups to action in a field in which the dangers of wasting natural resources are not immediately apparent. A second service for which there is a need is that of guiding the progress of action programs when sufficient public support has been aroused. Junior colleges have contributed help in line with each of these types of service. The nature of their contributions may be observed from the following practices carried on in individual junior colleges: adult classes in conservation; field trips jointly conducted by the college and governmental agencies; numerous short courses for various farm groups held annually; arrangement for speakers from forest service department or from game and fish commission to address session of night-school classes; a soils-testing laboratory operated by college; faculty participation in county conservation program; weekly radio program by head of biology department; faculty participation in state conservation program; faculty service as officers in state Audubon Society and in wild life federation; weekly radio program by college students; college campus used in state reforestation program.

COMMUNITY DEVELOPMENT

Community development bears the same relationship to specialized community services as does general education to specialized education. Practices considered under this category are characterized by a consideration of the community as a whole. In most instances, this approach to community development will result in the identification of specific problems for attack since such a procedure lends itself best to problem-solving. The comprehensive view of the community, however, as an approach to problem-identification probably provides a sense of perspective that would otherwise be lacking.

Junior-college personnel are involved in activities intended to consider the community as a whole. The number of instances reported was not as great as in many of the other categories. While this condition may indicate that the field of community development should be expanded, there is also the fact that the very breadth of the approach automatically reduces the variety of practices as compared with a category based on a more specialized attack on problems. Indicative of what is being done in the community by junior colleges is the following list of practices: participation of college faculty in community-development forums, in a citizens' council for a better community, and in various other community-improvement groups; faculty service on co-ordinating council meetings in two areas; services of president of the college on committees for home-and-community-improvement contests.

COMMUNITY PARTICIPATION AND LEADERSHIP TRAINING

The procedures employed in leadership training are designed to include more and more citizens of the community in active participation in community affairs. Leadership training is an integral part of this undertaking. The service, if performed satisfactorily, will mean that a large number of people gain the skills needed in group participation and will discover and develop an increased number of leaders. Although the concept of community participation as a desirable type of community service is comparatively new, yet it has been in existence a sufficient length of time to have gone beyond the experimental stage. Successful practice and a modest amount of literature attest the maturity of the idea.

There are several practices being carried on by junior colleges which may be correctly classified as examples of community participation and leadership training. One gets the impression, however, that the field is one in which those who plan the junior-college program of community services will find ample opportunities for expansion, especially in working with informal neighborhood groups. The practices reported by the junior colleges include the following: community-leadership workshop to supply leadership training for persons carrying local leadership responsibilities of various kinds, citizenship clearing-house of availability of well-informed citizens, community-materials project which has as its function the development of visual and discussion materials needed by leadership-training projects, training program in vocational education with outstanding leadership brought in for a special-day observance, citizenship-education project for unnaturalized citizens, and classes for study of English language.

USE OF MASS MEDIA OF COMMUNICATION

The field of mass media of communication is one in which educational institutions find unusual opportunities to furnish community services directly related to other services mentioned in this chapter. The emphasis is placed on methods of use rather than on the topics communicated. Most junior colleges are making some use of the mass media, although only a few have approached a realization of the great potentiality for community service which these media make possible. Among the methods being employed will be found: production on the campus for rebroadcast; a weekly radio program to inform the community of the activities of the departments of the college; a journalism course in which each student is assigned to work for a period of time with a newspaper or radio station; distribution of the college yearbook annually to professional offices; wide distribution of the college newspaper in the community; weekly television program; weekly radio program; co-operative film library for twenty-six independent school districts; community use of visual-aids department of the college.

PUBLIC-RELATIONS PROGRAMS

The concept of public relations associated with the community services of a junior college may be described simply as an effort to bring about a mutual understanding between the college and the community in which it is located. The methods used are those which will negate the idea of the college as an *isolated community*. Every effort will be made to insure (*a*) that all people in the community understand the purposes and program of the college and (*b*) that all personnel in the college understand the basic mores of the community. Success in these efforts will effect a complete disappearance of any barriers to satisfactory communications between the college and community.

Leaders of the junior colleges have recognized the importance of this type of community service. The demand for more information about successful practices is great. Some of the activities reported are: annual visitors' day at the college; press service of the college made available to the community for local drives or services of a similar nature; citizens serve on public-relations advisory committees to the college; parents' night program held each year; active alumnae association; service clubs hold annual program on campus to become better acquainted with the college; service to public schools in academic counseling; appearance by college faculty and students on programs of local civic, cultural, religious, and community groups as well as local high schools; annual Christmas party for children of minority groups; testing and placement center administered by the college; observance of business-industry-education days.

COMMUNITY USE OF SCHOOL PLANT

The limited utilization of the physical plant of public schools has been regarded for a long time as undesirable. Because of this, boards of control have approved policies leading toward use of the plant during times when these plants are not needed in the regular school program. Furthermore, school architects have recognized this policy in their designing of school buildings. Many junior colleges make provisions for opening parts of the building for community services. These developments represent an application of this policy of more efficient utilization of the plants and facilities.

The following list of practices gives some idea of the types of community services contributed by junior colleges in making their facilities available for use by the community: facilities used for conferences; college library opened to the public; laboratory equipment available for community needs; college sponsors county track meet; auditorium available for public meetings of various community groups; swimming pool used for water-safety programs and for training local lifeguards; classrooms used for courses conducted by insurance associations, bankers associations, Boy Scout officials, and others; use of college cafeteria by community organizations and general public; provide facilities for stock-judging contests; free use of tennis courts by community; maintain a free county library in addition to college library.

ADULT EDUCATION

Enrolment in adult-education programs in junior college has increased rapidly since the end of World War II. The *1955 Junior College Directory*[6] reports a total of 263,305 persons registered in adult-education programs in public junior colleges in the United States. This represents an increase of 120 per cent in adult-education enrolments in junior colleges over the number enrolled in 1949.

Another evidence of the rapid growth may be seen in the in-

6. C. C. Colvert and M. L. Baker, *Junior College Directory, 1955*. Washington: American Association of Junior Colleges, 1955.

creased number of public junior colleges in the United States which reported adult-education enrolments. The *1949 Directory* listed 157 such junior colleges, representing approximately 48 per cent of the public junior colleges reporting. By 1955, the number had increased to 77 per cent.

Junior colleges, in the main, confine their adult-education programs to evening schools. There is some tendency, however, in the direction of absorbing the evening school into the regular college program through the adoption of an extended-day policy. In the extended-day program, teaching assignments are usually within the framework of a school day beginning at the regular time in the morning and extending to the time of the closing of the last class at night.

The variety of courses offered in junior-college adult-education programs makes it impossible to present a representative listing of them. Moreover, the courses run the gamut from very short units to semester or year sequences; from credit courses to noncredit courses; from vocational education to hobby education. There can be no questioning of the value of junior-college adult-education programs from the point of view of the needs of the adult populations of their communities. They provide a stimulating example of a genuine community service.

Initiating a Program of Community Service

Imagine a typical American city of 15,000 population, having the customary complement of wealth and poverty represented among its citizenry. Suppose it is the location of Washington Junior College, a publicly controlled institution which has been in operation for twenty years. It is obvious that the people of this community are not particularly proud of the college, nor are they ashamed of it. The truth is that a majority of them know little more about the college than that it exists.

At the time the story begins, this junior college would be classified as a safe and sane institution. Its program was an exact replica of the first two years of the liberal-arts college of which the first administrative head was a graduate. The standards were very high, and the instruction met every criterion of academic respectability defined in the narrowest sense. There was no program for terminal students, no guidance program, and no program for adults. Graduates who transferred to four-year colleges, however, received full credit for work done in the junior college and experienced no difficulty in doing satisfactory work at the higher institution.

The chief administrative officer at Washington Junior College was the president. The first president saw the college through its first nineteen years of existence and was proudest of the fact that during his administration he had been able to secure accreditation by the regional accrediting agency. While many of his eighteen faculty members were happy with the program of the institution, some of the younger ones who had joined the staff within the last four or five years of the first president's tenure were not satisfied with the narrow curriculum. When at the end of the nineteenth year of service the president retired, the Board selected a man with a broader vision of the program of the college. Out of this background, a program of community services might have evolved in the following manner.

The new president spent the first year in getting thoroughly acquainted with the college and the community. He recognized that, as successor to an administrator who had spent a long time with the college, he would need to build a firm base if he were to expand the work of the institution. Board members concurred in this policy and accordingly were satisfied with the progress made by the new president.

The first year was not entirely unproductive, however, and in addition to building the strong foundation needed for an expanded program, President Wye talked informally with the Board at the regular meetings about the possible direction the expansion should take. His talk was of a curriculum for terminal students and a community-service program including adult education. He talked of the importance of guidance and counseling for both the regularly enrolled students and the adults enrolled for part-time instruction. He was careful to point out that an expanded program would require additional staff members since the present staff could not perform all the contemplated services. He talked in terms of better utilization of the college plant and of the necessary improvements that would have to be made in plant and facilities. He answered questions which Board members raised and was careful to curb his enthusiasm sufficiently to limit his descriptions to a modest program. By the end of the year the Board members were satisfactorily informed about the possibilities of expanding the college program.

Near the end of the first year, President Wye began making references to the enlarged program in his conversations with faculty members. While this occurred most frequently with the younger faculty members who had been dissatisfied with the narrow curriculum of the college, at the same time care was exercised to avoid any possibility of creating a division of the faculty over the topics. By the end of the year, President Wye could count on the sympathetic understanding of the Board for plans for extending the curriculum and for some progress in orienting the faculty toward such an understanding.

During the summer intervening between the first and second years of his administration, a modest program of community services was developed by the President and two of the faculty members who were employed to assist him during the summer vacation. The plan was highly tentative, with many optional possibilities. It did provide, however, for an evening school, a series of public forums, and a series of weekly radio programs. Furthermore, President Wye had previously arranged with the Board to pay the faculty to return a week early in the Fall for a preschool planning conference.

The program of community services was the theme of the conference. Faculty members discussed the program in full and made recommendations at the end of the conference concerning the proposals which seemed feasible of adoption. Even the more conservative of the faculty members had advanced during the week from a position of open hostility to one of "we're willing to try it." It was the decision of the faculty to try out the program with the opening of the second semester.

At this point, advisory committees were organized in the community, one for each of the three phases of the program of community services. Invitations to serve on the committees went out from the Board, the function of the committees being clearly explained so as to prevent any committee member from assuming that the Board was abdicating its responsibility. Care was exercised to select committee personnel representative of the different economic and social levels in the city.

Once the committee members became familiar with their functions, they were of value to the development of the program in two distinct ways. In the first place, committee members brought to planning sessions the viewpoint of the lay citizen, thus providing a broader base on which to make plans. In the second place, the members served as an excellent medium through which the general public could gain a better understanding of the nature of the program being developed.

Faculty and advisory committees of citizens completed their work by the first of November, and President Wye presented the committee report to the Board with his comments. The Board reviewed the reports carefully and made such modifications as seemed desirable in line with over-all college policy. The final plan was approved just before the Thanksgiving holidays. Immediately after approval of the plans, steps were initiated to implement them. While the time intervening before the opening of the second semester was short, it was possible to complete the details of implementation within the time limit.

The evening school was started with a modest program of classes in typing, shorthand, art, public speaking, and conversational Spanish. The publicity given was effective, and the enrolments were adequate to justify each of the classes. The weekly radio program proved more difficult than had been anticipated because the teacher in charge of its preparation insisted that scholastic standards should be kept high. The public forums started slowly, both on the basis of attendance and participation of the audience. Great care had been taken, though, in selecting a moderator and, because it had been possible to secure an effective person for this job, the popularity of the forums increased steadily.

Part of the original plans for the undertaking had been given over to a comprehensive program of evaluation. In this program it was hoped that evidence could be obtained to justify a conclusion of success or failure in regard to the various aspects of the program and also that evidence could be obtained to indicate the need for changes in the original plans. By the end of the semester it was possible, on the basis of this evidence, to conclude that the three parts of the program were, in the main, desirable of continuation but that certain practices and procedures were in need of change.

Summary

Socioeconomic changes of the past hundred years have created new educational needs from the standpoint of the individual person and of the social order. The junior college that develops a program consistent with educational needs must take into account the many alterations in the socioeconomic environment. These changes have implications for the general-, preparatory-, and vocational-education programs, and also in the comparatively new field of community services.

While space limitations prevent an exhaustive listing of all community services, some idea of their nature can be obtained from an examination of the major categories under which these services may be classified. Actual practices reported by junior colleges serve to make more graphic the description of each of these categories.

Since a program of community services entails a departure from the traditional concept of the functions of a college, certain essential factors must be recognized. The college personnel must have a sympathetic understanding of the importance of such a program. Moreover, the community to be served must have an understanding of what is being done by the college. It should be realized from the outset that an expansion of the educational program into the field of community services will require additional staff members, facilities, and expense. When these factors have received adequate attention, the success of the program rests on a sound basis. In order to maintain a feasible course of direction, constant evaluation is highly desirable. Given a college and a community in which these matters receive the needed attention, one has the basis for predicting success in the provision of a program of community service.

SECTION **III**

IMPROVING THE INSTITUTION

CHAPTER IX

The Program Defined and Implemented

RALPH R. FIELDS

Introduction

To visualize the task of defining junior-college programs, recall for a moment the institutions described in chapter i. The program of "Tech Institute" immediately causes one to envision laboratories with complicated electronics equipment; a workshop for planning and blue-printing construction activities, another for testing building materials, and sufficient space for constructing different types of building; extensive chemistry laboratories dedicated to special petroleum work, and in all likelihood a co-operative-work experience program with the near-by oil-drilling and oil-refining industries; a food-preparation room which appears more like a hotel kitchen than a college classroom, with perhaps a display of delicacies as aromatic as fondest childhood remembrances of the neighborhood bakery.

Compare these mental images with those brought forth by the description of Moulton College. To fulfil its purposes, Moulton would probably have a fairly typical college program, with classrooms suitable for group work in English, social studies, and foreign languages; a science laboratory or two; and a secretarial-science workroom.

How were these programs developed and how are they changed as conditions change? How would the president-elect of a recently voted public junior college go about the task of building an appropriate program? How does the faculty of a modern metropolitan community college work for curriculum improvement? How are the results assayed? What role should citizens play? These and many similar questions regarding program development are the focus of attention for this chapter.

Sections I and II of the yearbook have set the stage for this consideration. The changes in the demands of present-day society analyzed in chapter ii affect the *how* of curriculum development as well as the *what* of the program that evolves. The speed with which conceptions of educational needs change must be matched by an equal speed in the method of translating needs into program provisions. The study of students as reported in chapter iii implies, in addition to what it means for the program itself, that *students* themselves must be brought into the process of curriculum-planning. The statement of the purposes of the public junior college as suggested in chapter iv furnish the script, so to speak, for considering how such program demands can be met.

This task is a complicated one. The literature abounds with reports describing how junior colleges have developed curriculums, specific programs, or particular courses. But the author's impression resulting from visit after visit to the campuses of junior colleges in all sections of the United States has been that much more is going on than busy workers have had time to write about. Accordingly, a letter was written to some forty junior-college administrators, asking each to dictate a brief description of how he worked on the task of improving his program, utilizing a specific example if he thought that to be desirable. Further, he was requested to list points which might be of help to other administrators. For a generous response to this request, the writer expresses sincere appreciation. Practically every person responded with descriptions and observations. Many of these illustrations and comments are noted in succeeding sections of this chapter.

The general plan of the chapter will be to examine briefly the problem of defining the junior-college program, to consider more fully the approaches utilized in initiating and improving programs, and then to identify guiding principles which emerge from these considerations.

Defining the Program

Many forces affect program definition. Section I of this yearbook provides a helpful analysis of the forces which affect the role of the public junior college. These forces influence the way in which a specific college defines its program, and our purpose here is to look briefly at this process.

PROGRAMS EMERGE FROM PURPOSES

In chapter iv, the major purposes of the public junior college have been set forth as (*a*) preparation for advanced study, (*b*) vocational education, (*c*) general education, and (*d*) community services. Bearing in mind the concepts underlying these purposes as discussed in that chapter, one immediately visualizes programs that are defined in a radically different fashion from that which characterized the typical college program of the past. Reports received from the junior-college administrators queried evince a conviction on their part that the college programs have to emerge from clearly defined purposes. For example, one reported that "much attention has been given to the development of a basic philosophy of education and a set of educational objectives. This was the first major task to which our staff turned its attention when it first came together four years ago." Another wrote: "In the first place, improvement of program involves a thorough appraisal of the objectives of that program as these relate to the stated purposes of the college."

Specific institutions quite appropriately stress different purposes. For instance, while both are public community colleges and would be expected to stress certain common purposes, the Fashion Institute of Technology in New York City and the Clarence W. Pierce School of Agriculture in the San Fernando Valley in California formulate their purposes quite differently. The common purposes could be expected to account for some program similarities, and there are some; the differing purposes could be expected to result in wide differences in program, and they do. Programs must emerge from clearly conceived purposes.

PROGRAMS REFLECT COMMUNITY LIFE

As the public junior-college movement develops in the direction of community service so forcefully indicated in Sections I and II, the program should be defined in terms of community living and community needs. In colleges where community service is stressed, it would be natural to expect an effort to identify specific community needs as a part of the process of defining a program. Many such examples were reported in the letters from administrators, and one is cited as illustrating this practice.

San Jose Evening Junior College, San Jose, California, has a unique method of defining and improving its program. There, the Adult Education Senate is "the advisory council of the department of Adult Education, which develops the curriculum, governs the use of student funds, plans Vagabond tours, builds the visual slide collection, and manages student property."[1] The curriculum efforts of this senate are implemented at registration, not by faculty members but by a Community Counseling and Registration Committee. "Members of this committee are experienced and trained student advisers in the various Centers and are prepared to assist registrants in making the best use of the resources of the Department of Adult Education."[2] David L. MacKaye, the responsible director, described the inception of this plan in a letter as follows:

Our first step was to organize a committee of volunteer counselors. A group of four or five women prominent in social leadership, and all with college degrees, was selected to make a selection of thirty-five other women who they believed had some capacity for educational counseling work. Such a list was submitted and the school thereupon wrote to each, explaining the project and what was hoped for it and asking them if they would take a ten-weeks course in the problems and discussions of possible solutions. Thirty accepted, and this committee of thirty served for ten years before it was necessary to train other counselors. Since then, the system of selection has been changed a little, and women who have served their term on the Student Senate automatically go to the Counseling Committee.

Other examples of institutions which work with community groups will be cited later in this chapter as we look at the problem of initiating and improving programs. Here the purpose is to note that community groups play a part in the process of defining programs.

The normal working procedure within modern society is for the individual to operate through group membership. Political, recreational, and neighborhood groups, social clubs, employment councils, unions, and service clubs in various communities work on different problems and with varying effects. The list of different groups attached to programs is as long as that of our cultural groups: There are art groups, music organizations, young men's athletic leagues, lapidary clubs, photography clubs, and clubs of book lovers, creative

1. *Adult Education, 1954–55.* San Jose, California: San Jose Unified School District, Department of Adult Education, p. 3.
2. *Ibid.*

writers, hikers—to name just a few. And through their very existence, their requests, their support, and their pressures, these organizations help define the community-college program. To the extent that the communities served by junior colleges are similar, there would be justification for expecting similarities of program. These cultural similarities are at least one element in the cement of our national structure, and public junior colleges share with other levels of the American public school system the task of inducting youth into our society.

To the extent that differences exist among our American communities, differences in junior-college programs should likewise be expected. And in truth, the variety to be found among junior-college programs is a significant characteristic which will warrant further attention as the fourth point of this section.

PROGRAMS REFLECT STAFF BELIEFS

Clearly, the college staff must wield a major influence in program development. Among four-year colleges we have many examples of on-going staff efforts at program definition and improvement. In addition to the colleges of leading universities in the country, Antioch in its thirty years of efforts at implementing and improving the utilization of co-operative work-experience, Hiram with its intensive study plan, Sarah Lawrence with its continuous self-improvement planning, California Polytechnic College with its "upside-down" curriculum, St. John's with its "Great Books" program—all of these and the hundred of others which could be cited—illustrate the impact of the teaching staff on the college program.

The experiences of a few junior colleges serve to illustrate the way faculties define the institutional programs.[3] For over thirty years the practical agricultural program at the Long Island Agricultural and Technical Institute at Farmingdale, New York, has been evolving. In 1946, along with its sister agricultural and mechanical institutes, the Institute at Farmingdale was included in a state-wide

3. Paul L. Essert, in *Creative Leadership of Adult Education* (New York: Prentice-Hall, Inc., 1951), pp. 228–29, describes procedures at Denver's Opportunity School; Roy Ivan Johnson, in *Explorations in General Education* (New York: Harper & Bros., 1947), reports efforts at Stephens College; and John Sexson and John Harbeson, in *The New American College* (New York: Harper & Bros., 1946), recount faculty activities in defining the program of Pasadena Junior College.

effort to introduce technical-education opportunities. A complete, new division had to be created, a faculty for it recruited, a program developed, facilities secured. Under this intensive stimulation, within a short period of time programs have been developed in fifteen technical areas and are now housed in a functionally designed building.[4]

The first program for the new-born Orange County Community College at Middletown, New York, in 1950 was necessarily formulated by a special committee. The present program still contains that part of the first offering which has proved to be based on actual needs, but the program as a whole has been constantly defined and redefined as the staff has continued to work at the task of building a *community college*. Some of the unusual aspects of the program which reflect contributions of the *college* itself include courses at the near-by Mitchell Air Base; a center created to serve the residents of Newburgh, some twenty-four miles away; emphasis on nursing education represented by co-operation with two hospital schools as well as a completely college-controlled, experimental two-year program which leads to licensure as a registered nurse; college-organized refresher courses for medical practitioners in the area, staffed by the best experts in the metropolitan area of New York City; in-service courses for teachers in the county; a general-education program developed around student and community problems and needs; and a technical-vocational program carefully matured through exploration, study, experimentation, and evaluation.

Another example, illustrating the way in which a college staff defined its program, is that of the Henry Ford Community College at Dearborn, Michigan. A college planning committee worked for about two years, produced reports extending to hundreds of pages, and estimated enrolments for the present and proposed offerings of the college. While the selected programs represent to some degree the uniqueness of the region served, they also represent hard work, imagination, and practical ideas on the part of the faculty and administration of the college. Courses are provided in the following areas: college parallel programs, co-operative secretarial, co-operative general business, accounting, nursing, industrial drafting, com-

4. For a pictorial presentation of the nature of the program at this unusual institution, see *The Farmingdale Way*, a 16-mm. movie produced by members of the faculty.

mercial art, metallurgical technology, metal production and design, automotive technology, chemistry technology, electricity, electronics.

CURRENT PROGRAMS VARY GREATLY

Present junior-college programs vary widely. An unpublished study conducted under the auspices of the Curriculum Committee of the American Association of Junior Colleges revealed a great range in the subjects found in 115 junior colleges. Alphabetically, these ran from *accounting* to *zoölogy;* in between were such subjects as ornithology, embryology, histology, short-story writing, jewelry design, Greek, anthropology, paleontology, solfeggio, practical home-nursing, modern philosophers, atomic physics, criminology, and the Far East—Ancient and Modern. In all, some 295 courses were listed by this committee.

Three comments regarding the range of courses seem pertinent. One reason for the number of subjects offered is the attempt to provide courses similar to the offering within four-year colleges and universities, so that students at the conclusion of one or two years in a junior college are able to transfer without loss of time or credit to a four-year institution. As four-year colleges have expanded their offerings, the junior colleges have kept pace.

The second comment relates to general education. Junior colleges have not been at the forefront of this movement. Perhaps this is accounted for partly by the tremendous emphasis upon developing "terminal" courses and partly by the fear that conservative four-year colleges would not accept work in general-education courses for transfer credit. Reynolds, as a result of his study of junior-college programs in general education in 1945, reported that they were seriously inadequate in all areas[5] and that only recently had a wide-scale attempt to improve general-education curriculums emerged among junior colleges.[6] The very lack of a commonly followed pattern of general education means a greater variety of courses.

A third observation may be made to the effect that the heaviest contribution to the great breadth of the junior-college offerings has

5. James W. Reynolds, "The Adequacy of the General Education Program of Local Public Junior Colleges," *Journal of Educational Research*, XXXIX (December, 1945), 272–80, (See also series in *Junior College Journal* in 1946.)

6. B. Lamar Johnson, *General Education in Action*. Washington: American Council on Education, 1952.

come from the attempt to provide technical-vocational training for the variety of careers which seem to call for more than high-school education but less than a baccalaureate degree. One of the primary characteristics of vocational education, whether at the semiskilled, skilled, technical, or professional level, is that it prepares the trainee to perform identified tasks. As junior colleges developed an increasing vocational emphasis, it is not surprising that such efforts have taken the form of specific courses.[7] As a consequence, the junior-college vocational offerings, as discussed in chapter vi, show tremendous variation from college to college. When one considers the numerous ways different colleges are serving the needs of adults for continuing education, it is not surprising that the current junior-college program is differently defined from institution to institution.

Initiating and Improving Junior-College Programs

The inquiry directed to junior-college officials throughout the country revealed that among these colleges the effort is continually made to initiate new programs and to improve existing programs.

While administrators report many specific examples of ways of initiating new programs and a great number of ways of working to improve existing programs, analysis failed to reveal significant differences in the methods of working on these two aspects of curriculum improvement. Consequently, this discussion has not been divided between initiating and improving but is centered around the *way* the problem has been approached. Four approaches seemed to stand out: (*a*) surveys of student and community needs, (*b*) faculty-centered efforts, (*c*) lay participation, and (*d*) research and experimentation. Yet a word regarding the interrelatedness of all improvement efforts is necessary. In almost every case the administrator's letter revealed some use being made of more than one of the four approaches, but the relative emphasis varied a great deal from college to college.

THE NEEDS SURVEY

Community Needs. Organized surveys have usually been regarded as essential to intelligent curriculum-planning, but as late as 1947

---

7. Note, as one example, the wide variety of curriculums listed in the pamphlet entitled *Careers for Youth*, published by the New York State Institute of Applied Arts and Sciences in New York City.

Phebe Ward reported that there is very little material written about
the survey from the point of view of its use by junior colleges and
that most junior colleges have no written record of their surveys.[8]
More recently there have appeared reports of a number of surveys,
both formal and informal, made for the purposes of discovering the
nature and extent of educational needs, collecting information that
would aid in the formulation of programs, or identifying ways of
improving existing programs.

One of the most thorough surveys of educational need was made
by the state of New York to find the answers to three questions:

1. For what occupations is there need for pre-employment education
on a technical level?

2. In what geographic areas might institutes be established to offer
educational programs meeting the occupational needs of their areas?

3. For how many students should provision be made in each program?[9]

State-wide surveys give social and occupational information regarding the need or demand for junior colleges; but it usually takes
local studies to ascertain specific community needs. For instance, in
addition to the information available through the various state-wide
and regional studies, the president of a community college felt it advisable to carry through a detailed study of his county in order to
plan the improvement of the program in his institution.[10] After the
transition from technical institute to community college had been
achieved and the survey results utilized in various ways, Martin
wrote regarding their worth: "A comprehensive community survey
is of inestimable value in establishing community-college programs
and provides a background for testing the pertinency of the curricular offerings."

Another study of the potential for a community college in Rockland County, New York, demonstrated the use of census data, state
reports, and formulas for projecting enrolment. The investigator in

8. Phebe Ward, *Terminal Education in the Junior College*, p. 144. New
York: Harper & Bros., 1947.

9. C. Kenneth Beach and Associates, *Technical Occupations in the State of
New York*, Part I, pp. ii–3. Albany, New York: University of the State of
New York, March 30, 1946 (mimeographed).

10. Philip C. Martin, *The Potential Ability of the Westchester-Rockland
Area of New York State To Support Two-Year Community Colleges, 1953*.
Ithaca, New York: Cornell University, 1953.

this case also utilized estimates of jobs by employers and high-school counselors as a basis for establishing program potentials.[11]

One junior-college faculty analyzed the need in this fashion:

Prior to starting instruction in September, 1948, Orange Coast College completed a survey of the educational and occupational needs of Orange County. Information gathered was used as a guide in building instructional curricula. Since 1948, there have been many changes in Orange County: the population has greatly increased, business and industry have grown, and the number and types of business and industrial firms have changed. Therefore, there is need to make a new survey of educational and occupational needs. The instructional offerings of Coast College should be evaluated in terms of present needs.

The major purposes or objectives in making the educational and occupational needs survey are these:

1. To determine fields or areas in which Orange Coast College should provide training, now and in the future, which will lead toward occupational competence;

2. To evaluate the total program of education now offered by Orange Coast College;

3. To forecast the growth of Orange Coast College and the area in which it is located;

4. To determine whether or not Orange Coast College is meeting the needs of its students and of business and industry.[12]

Supplementing formal surveys organized on a geographic basis, two other types have been found of great assistance in assaying the demand for programs, as well as in instituting and improving them. One of these was labeled by the junior-college terminal-education study as the "single-curriculum survey." It involved:

Organizing the survey, conducting the field work, summarizing the findings, making the survey information available for the report, planning recommendations for the administration on a basis of the findings, and providing for the continuation of the survey. The findings that resulted from these continuous surveys were interpreted with the assistance of an advisory group and were used in planning the curriculum, in administering and supervising it, and in evaluating and

11. Lester E. Rounds, *A Plan for Meeting the Post-High-School Educational Needs of Older Youth in Rockland County.* New York: Teachers College, Columbia University, 1954.

12. *Educational and Occupational Needs,* pp. 4–5. A Self Survey Made by Orange Coast College. Costa Mesa, California: Orange Coast College, 1954. See also: B. H. Peterson, "A Self Appraisal of Educational and Occupational Needs of the Coastal Area of Orange County," *Junior College Journal,* XXV (March, 1955), 385–91.

revising it. Thus, the survey technique was employed not only as a basis for establishing the curriculum but also as a means for developing it.[13]

The second type might be called "systematic but informal surveys." This represents the efforts of one instructor or a small group of teachers to keep in systematic contact with an industry, trade, or business for the purpose of implementing and improving the program. D. W. Adamson designated this method as "Personal," and pointed out that, in addition to the direct informational results, there are certain *accrued* values such as becoming acquainted with management and with labor leaders, collecting supplementary information for other teachers and counselors, keeping up with technological changes.[14]

Student Needs. Since the middle thirties, emphasis upon student needs as one approach to curriculum-planning has been heavy and insistent both at the college level and at the elementary and secondary levels. One of the earlier attempts to translate information regarding students and their needs into program provisions was reported in 1937 by Heaton and Koopman,[15] and an impressive list of colleges have considered it essential to college data on student needs for planning programs—Minnesota's General College, Stephens College, Sarah Lawrence, Bennington, Antioch. Except for Stephens, few junior colleges reported studies in the early years. Many were, however, providing offerings adapted to student needs. Public junior colleges in several states and localities were a part of the secondary-school system which was giving intensive attention to the "Imperative Needs of Youth." The strength of this impact is indicated by the designation of *community institute* as a part of the American city educational system in *Education for All American Youth.*[16]

So many colleges are attempting various specific curriculum provisions in order to translate student needs into desirable learning re-

13. Reported in Ward, *op. cit.,* pp. 144–45.

14. D. W. Adamson, "Food Technology at Pre-professional and Terminal Levels: Personal Survey Techniques in Curriculum Building," *Junior College Journal,* XXIII (October, 1952), 68–74.

15. Kenneth L. Heaton and Robert Koopman, *A College Curriculum Based on the Functional Needs of Students.* Chicago: University of Chicago Press, 1936.

16. Educational Policies Commission, *Education for All American Youth.* Washington: National Education Association, 1944.

sults that it is impossible here to mention all of these efforts. However, three or four problems which are perhaps peculiar, at least accented, at the junior-college level merit mention.

1. The possibility of having community-college students participate in community affairs is only recently claiming the attention it deserves. Recently launched projects in California and Texas appear promising.[17]

2. The need for appropriate preparation for marriage and home membership is widespread and keenly felt among junior-college students and should warrant appropriate instruction. In adult life, moreover, family living looms as an almost continuously recurring problem area: premarriage concerns, prenatal worries of mothers and fathers, child care and management, family feeding, family finances, family-group recreation, home repairs, home decorating, furniture upholstering. This list is, indeed, extensive, and many junior colleges are doing much along this line.

3. A steadily increasing number of colleges are discovering that the most effective way to insure the meeting of student needs is to have students themselves help to plan the curriculum, not just through selecting courses from among those available, but through participation in curriculum-planning committees and in co-operative student-faculty data-gathering projects.

4. It is essential that more care be formally exercised in identifying fundamental needs. Helpful suggestions have been brought together by Homer Kempfer[18] in a bulletin of the Office of Education. David MacKaye, in his letter to the author, made some significant observations regarding the problem of identifying fundamental needs of adults:

> With respect to adult motivation, we found shortly that the expressed desire of an adult for work did not always correspond to his need, e.g., many would request a class in high-school English because "I didn't do well in that in school," or because "I didn't go to high school, and maybe that would help me now." It frequently appeared that English was no solution, that the individual reported for registration because of conflicts at home, because of loneliness, or for other

17. B. Lamar Johnson and W. H. Harless, "Implications of the Citizenship-Education Project for the Junior College," *Junior College Journal*, XXV (March, 1955), 369–75.

18. *Identifying Educational Needs of Adults*. United States Office of Education Circular No. 330, 1951. Washington: Government Printing Office, 1951.

reasons. In one typing class six elderly women admitted that they enrolled because they were lonely and "typing was the easiest course to think of," as one put it.

With respect to social purpose, we found in the literature many suggestions for ready-made purposes in which a "knowledge of United States history," or "better citizenship," or "a citizenship better informed on national and international problems" and so on, were emphasized. But in practice we found in San Jose that history, literature, and science, among the "solids" of formal education, had no attraction for adults.

MacKaye then goes on to tell in detail how he and his colleagues at San Jose gradually built up an atmosphere, a program, a corps of teachers, and a community understanding that has put "the cultural subjects in the curriculum."

FACULTY-CENTERED EFFORTS

Faculty Committees. While the ultimate approval of courses offered in the case of public junior colleges resides with the board of education or board of trustees, the role of the faculty in the determination of the offering is crucial. Almost all of the administrators in describing the way programs were improved mentioned faculty committees. Excerpts from several letters will reveal the important functions fulfilled by such groups.

We have three standing committees with membership appointed on a rotating basis and including at least one student (usually a Sophomore), appointed on an annual basis. . . . In brief, these committees enter into the development of our educational program. . . . All programs, whether they be individual courses or curriculums, must be approved by the campus Curriculum Committee before a recommendation is made to our Board of Directors for the inclusion of them in our program. . . .

In the period 1946–53 a joint committee of teachers and administrators representing the three branches of Chicago City Junior College studied students, community, and curriculum and recommended many modifications of curriculum and procedure. . . .

In Long Beach, where the City College and the School for Adults are part of the city school system, three curriculum committees are functioning, one each for the Liberal-Arts Division, the Business and Technology Division, and the Adult School. These groups have representative membership on the General Committee on the Curriculum for the entire system. A sample of the minutes of a meeting of the Adult School Committee revealed that students and lay representatives participated actively along with faculty members and that the committees approved suggested courses and exercised leadership in assessing general program needs.

In addition to regular or standing faculty committees, most colleges report the use of *ad hoc* or special faculty committees for specific fields. Several reports illustrate the important functions such committees discharge.

In the development of a number of courses, particularly general courses in such fields as the social sciences and the humanities, we have used inter-area committees. In other words, instead of having a group of social scientists plan our general course in that field by themselves, there have been representatives from a number of other areas sitting in with them to help plan the course. . . .

In 1952, the Sacramento Assistant Superintendent of Schools appointed a committee of junior-college officials and instructors to study the need for a vocational nursing program in Sacramento, to advise the City Superintendent of Schools regarding the setting up of this program, taking into account the personnel and facilities needed and hospital affiliation where students might acquire clinical experience. . . .

About five years ago people teaching our Freshman English decided that something ought to be done about the content and procedures in the Freshman English course. A committee composed of all the Freshman English Teachers first surveyed what was being done in other colleges in regard to this program. . . . Upon resumption of our college classes in the fall the English Department seriously set about revising our Freshman English Course in outline. The matter was thoroughly discussed in the Curriculum Committee and finally presented to the faculty. All of the ideas were not accepted by all of the faculty, but the plan was put into operation the next fall. . . .

These examples would seem to justify the observation that junior-college faculty committees are exercising leadership in the development and improvement of program offerings.

Informal Program Ventures. In past years considerable faith was put in the "uniform-front" approach: A new curriculum was planned, produced, and installed. Gradually, from experience and through follow-up results came the realization that new curriculums are not *installed* but have to be *home-grown*. In place of the uniform-front approach a different concept evolved, that of a single teacher or a small group of teachers getting an idea, trying it out, changing it, improving it, trying it again. Others observed or learned about the idea, tried it out, changed it further. Thus, the theory of the broken-front and grass-roots approach has evolved.

Many signs attest the fact that this is happening: new courses in catalogues, the reports of new methods attempted in classrooms, the proposal of improved curricular arrangements within teaching fields. Witness, for example, the titles of a few articles in a late issue of the *Junior College Journal:* "Educational Theatre in Texas Junior Colleges," "A Successful Experiment in Religious Education," "Can Creative Writing Be Taught?" In November, 1953, this same magazine put out a "Special Issue on Teaching" which contained articles dealing with foreign-language study, use of information bulletins as part of an in-service program for instructors, the library as the "heart of the college," teaching procedures with classes in remedial writing, junior-college assembly programs, the selection and utilization of texts, and measuring communication skills.

Witness also the proposals of new ways of teaching or plans for reorganized programs indicated by representative titles of new-type doctoral studies pursued in just one university in a period of a few years. These are not primarily *research* studies, but represent carefully thought-out proposals for program improvement.

"A Study of the Phoenix Evening College Program for Adults with Recommendations for Improving Their Expansion, Including Special Reference to Business Education."

"An Evaluation and Recommendation for the Administration of the Technical Program of the Evening and Extension Division of the Institute of Applied Arts and Sciences at New York City."

"Formulation of a Program of Music for the Wenatchee Junior College."

"Health Instruction in Biology (The Development of a Teaching Program for Dealing with Community Health Problems in the Second Ward High School and Carver College of Charlotte, North Carolina)."

"The Organization, Installation, Implementation and Administration of a Course in Physical Science Designed for General Education."

"A Proposed Program of Music for Yakima Valley Junior College and Recommendations for the Junior Colleges of Washington State."

"A Plan for a Program of Physical Education for Penn Hall Junior College."

"A Proposed Plan for the Improvement of Physical Education at Mary Baldwin College."

"A Plan for Training Southern Mountain Junior-College Coeds as Lay Workers or 'Yeomen' for Church and Community."

"Co-operative Development of the English Program by Members of the English Staff in a Community Junior College."

LAY PARTICIPATION

A relatively new development in education generally, the participation of lay persons in improving programs in the public schools has become increasingly common. Such informal participation has led citizens to think more and more of the schools as instruments for the common good, an essential concept if education in a democracy is to fulfil its highest purpose.[19]

Community colleges benefit in much the same way, and there is evidence that college after college is utilizing lay advice and help. If the author of the present chapter had any doubts regarding the commonness of this practice, the letters he received from junior-college administrators would have dispelled such doubts. Practically every respondent mentioned lay participation and many wrote several pages describing the results of such co-operative work. A few excerpts will illustrate the importance placed upon lay contributions by these college leaders.

Long Beach, California, reports:

In our Business and Technology Division we have approximately 50 advisory committees made up largely of lay members. There is an advisory committee for each training area within our Business and Technology Division. These committees are not rubber-stamp committees but deal with such basic matters as the original lay-out of buildings, the selection and location of equipment in the buildings, curriculum planning, and the placement of students in job situations. These advisory committees have been given great freedom in developing the instructional program within their respective areas. The Business and Technology Curriculum Committee co-ordinates its activities and develops a unified instructional program for the division.

From Sacramento:

The purpose of advisory committees is to provide a link between the school and the community through which their activities may be co-ordinated. Their function is to counsel with and advise the school with respect to improving the program. These committees have no administrative or legislative authority. Such authority rests with the Board of Education, the Superintendent of Schools, and his staff.

19. *Citizen Co-operation for Better Public Schools.* Fifty-third Yearbook of the National Society for the Study of Education, Part I. Chicago: Distributed by University of Chicago Press, 1954.

Our committees are organized and appointed for a one-year term. Their personnel, however, may be reappointed from year to year. All action and recommendations of the committee should be carried out if possible. If not, or if the situation should change, which would make the recommendation of questionable value, the reasons for a change in plans and procedure should be made to the committee at its next meeting.

These committees are helpful in surveys, procurement of equipment, placement of students, and bond elections but, above all, in helping to make a program functional.

At Westchester Community College:

An Advisory Committee exists for each curriculum or technology in addition to a General Advisory Committee made up of the chairman of each of the Curriculum Advisory Committees. These committees have been especially helpful in assisting with the evaluation of the relevancy of curriculum content. . . . Advisory Committees offer new ideas for inclusion in existing curriculum offerings. In addition, Advisory Committees assist in promoting the educational program, the placement of graduates, securing co-operative work assignments, and form a most effective public relations group."

From Corpus Christie, Texas:

New programs are developed through inviting leaders in various interested groups to meet with us as consulting committees. These have been very helpful . . . for any program to succeed in the offerings of a community college it must meet a local need. Consulting committees of local representatives of interested groups from the citizenry will generally prevent the College from offering programs not in real need in the community.

Brief sentences from a number of letters confirm the conclusion that lay participation is quite general and is highly valued. "Especially helpful in assisting with the evaluation of curriculum content. . . ."; ". . . provide a link between the school and the community. . . ."; "In launching a new curriculum, lay-advisory groups are brought in for advice. . . ."; ". . . excellent device for continuing appraisal of the effectiveness of the college's programs"; ". . . an advisory committee makes suggestions and recommendations. . . ."; ". . . developed the *Community College concept*. . . ."; "The content of the program . . . is determined by a committee. . . ."

From the descriptions of lay participation received and from the examples found in articles, catalogues, and brochures, several important points emerge.

First, the most common use of lay persons is in the development of vocational programs. Very frequently advisory committees are formed, on either a standing-committee basis or long-term appointment, and they help in many ways—defining the need for the program, assessing its desirability and feasibility, outlining the program, evaluating the results, placing the graduates, keeping the offerings up to date.

Second, some cases were reported of the use of lay groups in college-wide program development. One president referred to a "General Advisory Committee made up of the chairman of each of the Curriculum Advisory Committees"; another stated that "Our Advisory Committee, composed of representatives from our major business and industrial organizations, are a great help to us in outlining new areas for instruction." One college, the Los Angeles Junior College of Business, indicated the importance attached to its advisory committee by issuing a printed brochure with pictures and short descriptions of all members.

In Montgomery County, Maryland, informal groups have advised the chief administrator and his staff regarding the total development of the college. The League of Women Voters, American Association of University Women, Montgomery County Junior College Advisory Council, the County Council of the Parent-Teacher Association, and others, performed excellent services by making studies of the junior-college movement and the needs for this kind of education within the county and in interperting the college to the community. The Junior College Advisory Council meets at regular times during the academic year to hear progress reports, to consider recommendations proposed by the dean of the college, and to give judgments on proposals and to suggest others. Fashion Institute of Technology in New York City was founded through the co-operation of the Board of Education and a lay group organized as the Educational Foundation for the Apparel Industries. Three agencies are responsible for program and support of this institution: the state, the city, and the garment industry.

It has been common practice for the technical institutes in New York State to have advisory committees working with them and, as several of these institutes made the transition to community colleges, their advisory committees proved to be powerful agencies for community co-operation.

Third, community junior colleges might well give serious thought to more vigorous utilization of lay groups in planning general-education offerings. The vitality, reality, and vigor which lay committees have introduced into the technical offerings could well be utilized in programs emphasizing such goals as citizenship, community co-operation, and aesthetic values. Several administrators reported serious efforts in this direction, and one tangible result was described as follows:

> Finally, as an evidence of the fact that East Los Angeles Junior College typifies the real community college, it is interesting to note that the Greater East Los Angeles Chamber of Commerce has officially adopted the college as "its community college" and has caused its resolution to be published and widely circulated.

RESEARCH AND EXPERIMENTATION

We can look only briefly at the role of research and experimentation in junior-college curriculum improvement. We shall do this by summarizing the contributions that curriculum studies have made to program improvement and by citing a few junior-college projects that illustrate curriculum experimentation or action research.

Curriculum Studies. At all levels of our educational system a tremendous number of investigations have been carried out in the search for solutions to curriculum problems.[20] Of special significance to junior-college workers are the attempts to evaluate the results of college programs in general education.[21] At the junior-college level, the purposes which the curriculums should serve, the objectives which should be stressed, the content used and needed, the method of organizing content and learning experiences into programs, and

20. Summaries or examples of the more significant studies can be found in such works as B. Othanel Smith, William O. Stanley, and J. Harlan Shores, *Fundamentals of Curriculum Development.* Yonkers-on-Hudson: World Book Co., 1950; J. Paul Leonard and Alvin C. Eurich (editors), *An Evaluation of Modern Education.* New York: D. Appleton-Century Co., Inc., 1942.

21. For particularly stimulating analyses, see Paul L. Dressel and Lewis B. Mayhew, *General Education: Explorations in Evaluation.* (The Final Report of the Co-operative Study of Evaluation in General Education.) Washington: American Council on Education, 1954; and C. Robert Pace and Donald G. Wallace, "Evaluation of Institutional Programs," *Review of Educational Research*, XXIV (October, 1954), 341–50.

the evaluation of curriculum effectiveness have all been studied to greater or lesser degree during the history of the junior-college movement.[22]

A canvass of these investigations yields these conclusions:

1. Many curriculum studies have been carried out, particularly as doctoral studies. Eells in 1950 observed that "a large number of dissertations and other studies have been concerned with the curriculum, but most of these are status studies, based for the most part upon catalogue analysis or questionnaire information. . . ."[23] This observation was probably justified at the time, but there is discernible a trend to encourage graduate students to concentrate on problem-solving attempts rather than simply to engage in fact-finding surveys.

2. Studies of community conditions, student needs, occupational trends, illustrated in an earlier section of this chapter, have vitally affected the junior-college offering.

3. Studies of graduates, their successes and failures in further education and in vocational careers, have furnished curriculum-builders with ideas and evidence regarding program effectiveness.

4. Self-evaluation studies by institutions and realistic evaluation of program results are promising trends. Definitive studies of program results take long periods of time in addition to substantial expenditures of money and faculty energy. Furthermore, the problem of defining what is the result of the instructional program and what are the results of other factors is extremely difficult. Consequently, a great many attempts at evaluation among colleges have been along the line of assaying the attainment of knowledge while students are in school, and the sampling of the opinions of graduates, teachers, em-

22. The reader will find the research summarized and available in such references as Leonard V. Koos, *The Junior College Movement* (Boston: Ginn & Co., 1925); Walter C. Eells, *The Junior College* (Boston: Macmillan Co., 1931); *Bibliography on Junior Colleges* (United States Office of Education, *Bulletin*, 1930, No. 2, coupled with a continuation of this bibliography in the issues of the *Junior College Journal* between 1940 and 1946); Lois Engleman and Walter C. Eells, *The Literature of Junior College Terminal Education, op. cit.;* and W. H. Conley and F. J. Bertalan, *Significant Literature of the Junior College, 1941–48* (Washington: American Association of Junior Colleges, 1948). Later studies have not been summarized adequately nor generally published. Unfortunately, the 1950 edition of the *Encyclopedia of Educational Research, op. cit.,* did not add significantly to the previous edition with respect to junior colleges, nor did the recent issue of the *Review of Educational Research* devoted to post-secondary programs cover community-college research to any great extent.

23. Walter C. Eells, "Junior College," *Encyclopedia of Educational Research,* p. 632. Edited by Walter S. Monroe. New York: Macmillan Co., 1950.

ployers, and students themselves. But there have been a few notable attempts at more basic evaluation.[24]

5. Co-ordination in planning related researches is badly needed in order that studies may build more meaningfully on past efforts. The explorations of the American Junior College Association in this direction should be implemented, or some other means of planning devised by those in the field and those in the universities.

6. A systematic dissemination of research results is needed. This would appear a logical function of the United States Office of Education, and it is to be hoped that greater efforts along this line will be made by that agency.

7. While to date few studies have attacked basic curriculum issues, there is a distinct trend from status studies toward co-operative experimentation and action-research. This is promising and warrants our turning for a look at developments of this type.

Experimentation and Action-Research. The difference between basic research and data collection would seem to be that the former is carried on with the intent to establish, test, or apply theory—"the function of theory being to explain observations in such a way as to make prediction possible."[25] The following analysis of the relationship between theory and practice is highly suggestive of the relationship between curriculum improvement and research:

The development of theories starts often with a re-examination of various researches which have dealt with similar phenomena, in which similar concepts have been employed. Out of such examinations arise more general questions and hypotheses. The development of theories is enhanced if studies are interrelated with one another so that the knowledge gained from one bears on the knowledge gained from another. The planned interrelation of research can be achieved by selecting

24. See Dressel and Mayhew, *op. cit.*; Ward, *op. cit.*, for a detailed report of an effort at evaluation of Wright Junior College; Roy Johnson, *Explorations in General Education, op. cit.*; B. Lamar Johnson, *General Education in Action, op. cit.*; the Orange Coast College survey discussed earlier, as well as Superintendent Peterson's *Annual Report of the Superintendent, 1952–53*; Thomas B. Merson, "A Faculty Study of General Education," *Junior College Journal,* XXIV (January, 1954), 260 ff.; R. J. Hannelly and Wayne Edland, "Phoenix College, Self-portrait," *National Education Association Journal,* XXXVIII (September, 1949), 433; and G. Robert Pace, "How Does an Institution Organize and Conduct an Effective Self-Evaluation?" in *Current Issues in Higher Education, 1954,* pp. 251–59 (Washington: Association for Higher Education, 1954).

25. Marie Jahoda, Morton Deutsch, and Stuart W. Cook, *Research Methods in Social Relations,* Part I, *Basic Processes,* p. 337. New York: Dryden Press, 1951.

a common focus for attention in a series of studies. Whether this focus is "theoretical" in nature—with concepts and hypotheses as foci—or "content-oriented" in nature—with phenomena and settings as foci—each individual study in the series should be designed with both orientations in mind. This is of particular importance because there is in the social sciences at their present state of development a glaring need for theories at an intermediate level of abstraction—i.e., theories in which the concepts can readily be linked to observed phenomena.[26]

Experimentation as educational research has long received significant attention, particularly in the field of learning theory and learning results. Fewer studies in the area of curriculum theory have been carried through, but the recent introduction of the action-research concept has high-lighted the steadily developing belief that "laboratory" experiments and "control-group" experiments were many times ineffectual in arriving at explanations that would stand up in normal situations.[27]

At the junior-college level, three examples of research activity that could be called experimentation or action-research in accordance with the foregoing discussion, and which have influenced or promise to affect curriculum development in significant fashion, warrant brief consideration.

1. *The Terminal Education Study of the American Association of Junior Colleges.* This study has been referred to several times previously in this chapter. In its earlier stages primary efforts seem to have been devoted to bringing together as much information as possible regarding the need for vocational education at the junior-college level and the efforts of institutions to provide that kind of offering. In the later stage, as set forth in the final report, efforts were designed to "determine effective solutions for some of the problems in terminal education, as revealed in the exploratory study, and to serve as a means of disseminating information concerning the findings and the procedures to other junior colleges and similar institutions. As a result, the program of the continuation study involved two major activities—first, a series of nine institutional studies; and, secondly,

26. *Ibid.*, p. 338.

27. The work of the Horace Mann-Lincoln Institute of School Experimentation has been one of the agencies fostering experimentation in typical educational situations that would produce results more applicable to general needs. See, for example, S. M. Corey, *Action Research To Improve School Practices* (New York: Bureau of Publications, Teachers College, Columbia University, 1953); and Gordon N. Mackenzie and Stephen M. Corey, *Instructional Leadership* (New York: Bureau of Publications, Teachers College, Columbia University, 1954).

a series of workshops and conferences for junior-college instructors and administrators throughout the country.[28] Furthermore, in the final reports by Miss Ward, the first part was devoted to "Principles of Terminal Education"—e.g., the attempt to integrate experimentation into theory.

During the post-World War II enrolment bulge and curriculum expansion, the guide lines established by this study were widely studied and implemented.

2. *The California Study of General Education in the Junior College.* This study also has been referred to a number of times in this chapter.[29] Arthur Adams, in the "Foreword," points out the aspects we are particularly interested in at this juncture of our discussion:

"The study presented in this volume has the special value that it is based solidly on what is actually being done. It deals with objectives in terms of tested classroom procedures. Hence, it not only has intrinsic interest as a survey of educational policies and practices of the junior colleges of California, but it also lays the foundation for future progress both in that state and in other areas . . . it seems evident that the conclusions of the study will prove useful to junior college teachers and administrators in other parts of the country and may well have a profound influence on the future course of the general education movement everywhere."[30]

It is too early to appraise whether Adams' enthusiastic observation is borne out, but there are a number of reasons to believe that it will be. The grass-roots nature of the project meant, in general, that the people who were doing the experimenting were in on the ground floor; administrative backing was a part of the picture from the start; and some attempt was made in the report to relate practice to theory, particularly in a chapter titled "Approaches to General Education."

3. *The Co-operative Research Project in Junior and Community College Education for Nursing.* This project grew out of the concern over the shortage of nurses and the possibility of junior colleges developing a new-type of program for the preparation of nurses. Officials of the National League for Nursing Education, the American Association of Junior Colleges, and personnel at Teachers College, Columbia University, particularly in the Nursing Education Division, co-operated in the exploration of what might be done. The latter Division secured the funds and launched the project with the advisory services of a committee representing the two organizations and Teachers College.

The project, now moving into its third year, would seem to be demonstrating the truth of the two major hypotheses underlying the

28. Ward, *op. cit.*, p. x.

29. B. Lamar Johnson, *General Education in Action, op. cit.*

30. *Ibid.*, p. v.

experimentation: that nurses can be educated successfully within two years if the program is designed from an educational rather than a nursing-service point of view, and that a program can be developed within the framework of the typical junior college. Several characteristics make this last project a particularly good example of the effect of experimentation or action-research upon curriculum development: (a) the program is grass-rooted, for the local educational institutions have initiated, planned, financed, and launched the local program with the *advisory* services only of the project staff; (b) the project was designed to test an hypothesis, not just to launch some special kind of a nursing-education program; (c) certain tentative principles were established at the beginning and, to the limit of reasonableness and practicality, have been followed; (d) evaluation of results has been envisioned from the outset; (e) dissemination of findings is a major although future function of the Co-operative Project as well as of the two organizations concerned.

Like all on-going projects dealing with critical curriculum problems, it has been inevitable that some effect on practice would occur from the very outset. The eagerness of the junior-college educators for information and assistance from the project augurs well for the importance that will be attached to the findings.[31]

Readers may well think of other examples of experimentation that are affecting curriculum practices in junior colleges. It is hoped that those cited point up the importance of action-research and experimentation as approaches to the solution of program issues.

Principles and Issues in Program Improvement

The description of activities directed toward the improvement of junior-college programs has of necessity been brief and, consequently, at points, extremely sketchy. The almost inevitable result of brevity is the creation of the impression that programs are all much alike, are all good or all bad. It, therefore, appears desirable to list the curriculum issues and problems facing junior-college educators. These will be classified under four basic curriculum principles.

PROGRAMS MUST BE DEVELOPED TO MEET NEEDS

A good many instances in which junior colleges have surveyed the community and identified the needs of the learners as a basis for cur-

31. While no formal reports of results are available, the interested reader will find many of the concepts alluded to here set forth by Mildred Montag in her study, *Education of Nursing Technicians* (New York: G. P. Putnam's Sons, 1951), and in an article, "A New Program for Nursing in Community Colleges," *Teachers College Record*, LIV (May, 1953), 447–51.

riculum improvement have been presented. Organized studies as well as informal and "personal" approaches were mentioned, and some analysis of purposes, group needs, and group pressures as curriculum determiners was made.

Issues. In connection with needs-approach to curriculum development there are two basic issues which must be consciously faced or unconsciously answered by actions:

1. What concept of need is psychologically and educationally most useful as a basis for curriculum improvement?
2. Is the community junior college responsible for helping individuals meet all kinds of needs or only certain kinds?

Problems. Even granting a consciously established position with respect to the issues, there are many problems which remain to be dealt with in specific program implementation. The following are some examples:

1. How is knowledge regarding needs translated into action leading to curriculum improvement?
2. How can the process of identifying needs be organized so that it can be carried on continuously without burdening the faculty?
3. How can individual instructors utilize knowledge of needs in their instruction?
4. What needs of junior-college students are most pressing and most likely to serve as good motivation for learning?
5. How can adults be stimulated to grow in self-understanding so that expressed needs become a more realistic basis for program-planning?

THOSE WHO ARE CONCERNED MUST BE INVOLVED

Teacher participation in surveys and studies, faculty committees, lay advisory councils, student participation in planning learning experiences—these and other evidences of the involvement of many people in the process of program improvement have been referred to rather frequently in our discussion.

Issues:

1. Who plans the curriculum? This issue might be stated as: What role should different groups play in curriculum improvement—faculty, students, trustees, administration, parents, pressure groups, others?
2. How is curriculum change brought about—through organization or by individual teacher growth?

Problems:

1. How can a college staff be organized for effective curriculum planning?
2. What arrangements regarding teacher load are justifiable and appropriate?
3. How should faculty committees be constituted and how aided in their work?
4. How can students participate in planning the curriculum? in learning experiences?
5. How can lay groups be utilized?
6. What in-service opportunities for teachers are most effective?
7. How is curriculum leadership exercised effectively at the college level?
8. How are individual teachers motivated to improve their own courses? To co-operate in program improvement?
9. How could lay participation contribute appropriately to general-education programs?
10. How can communication among all those concerned in curriculum improvement be improved?

EACH PROGRAM MUST REFLECT MAJOR PURPOSES, COMMUNITY LIFE,
AND FACULTY BELIEFS REGARDING LEARNING

The function of purposes in program definition was discussed early in the chapter, along with such other curriculum determiners as community and student needs, the faculty, and their beliefs. Several issues related to purposes and needs present themselves, and with respect to each the position taken will reflect the belief held regarding learning.

Issues:

1. Who should go to college, particularly to public junior college?
2. Should community colleges serve a great variety of purposes or only selected ones?
3. What does the degree from the junior college stand for?
4. How specific should vocational preparation be?
5. Can college serve both vocational- and general-education purposes effectively, or must the individual student choose between them?
6. What is the curriculum—organized content or guided experience?

Problems:

1. How can purposes be established clearly and made to function as curriculum, instructional, and evaluation guides?

2. How can a multipurpose institution build an effective program for a wide range of students?
3. How broad can the program of a single college be?
4. How should learning experiences be organized: around problems, themes, movements, generalizations, principles, chronology, needs, interests, jobs, activities, or purposes?
5. How can major purposes be stated specifically?
6. How much use should be made of experience in the laboratory, at work, and with community problems?
7. How can general-purpose courses introduce enough specificity to have meaning and reality for students?
8. Should the program for older adults be the same as the one for younger students, even if the purposes are similar?

PROGRAM IMPROVEMENT RESTS UPON EVALUATION

Many evaluation practices and problems were revealed in the examination of what junior colleges are doing, among them the use of surveys, follow-ups of drop-outs and graduates, self-evaluation efforts of institutions, studies of curriculum practices, action-research projects, and experimentation efforts.

Issues:

1. What constitutes evidence of learning: behavior? knowledge? or expressed attitude?
2. Can curriculum principles be experimentally derived and scientifically proven?

Problems:

1. How can regional or national co-operative enterprises be organized for effecting progress?
2. How should a program be evaluated—by its form, by results, by the opinion of experts, by the opinion of its clients?
3. How can accreditation be handled to stimulate improvement of programs?
4. What can a single institution do about setting up an effective evaluation program?
5. How can the research efforts of graduate students be more functionally oriented and interrelated?
6. How can teachers be helped in their evaluation of student-learning?

Summary Statement

In this chapter we have concentrated upon the *how* of program improvement. To secure illustrations of the ways and means that are being tried out in the junior colleges of the country, about forty administrators were asked to describe their plans for program improvement in their colleges. From these, from the accounts of curriculum ventures in the literature, and from the research, an attempt has been made to describe how curriculums are defined, how programs are being improved, and what principles seem to be serving as guides to action.

Several important observations seem to be warranted. Junior-college programs emerge from the purposes of the institution.

Community colleges are striving to fulfil the broad purposes of preparation for further education, vocational education, general education, and community service. Programs reflect the individualities of the communities served; they also reflect the particular ideas of the college staff. Because of this breadth of purpose, and the significant differences among communities and staffs, programs vary greatly.

Junior colleges are utilizing extensively the needs-approach to curriculum development. Surveys of the needs of communities as well as needs of students are frequently reported. Faculty committees for curriculum work are commonly found in junior colleges, and the use of lay advisory committees is almost universal. The intimate participation of lay members of the community in program development is one of the most significant differences between these community-type institutions and the typical four-year college.

Curriculum studies have been numerous, and some real program development has flowed from surveys of needs, follow-up of graduates, and the investigations of practices. Research or experimentation designed to develop and test principles of curriculum improvement, however, has not been extensive, and this would seem to be a serious lack within the junior-college movement.

From the practices and the existing researches, certain principles are apparent and might well serve as guide lines. Programs must emerge from needs and purposes. Those responsible for the program must be involved in the process of defining and improving it. Each program must, to be representative of its community, reflect the individuality of that region. And, perhaps most important, program improvement must rest upon evaluation of results.

CHAPTER X

The Student Personnel Program

A. M. MEYER

AND

ROBERT J. HANNELLY

Student Problems and Needs

The authors of this chapter made a study of the nature of student problems in November, 1954. Replies were received from a questionnaire sent to 41 junior colleges. Respondents included instructors, deans, counselors, and directors of student-personnel. An interesting feature of the results of this inquiry is the appalling evidence of the frustration with which many youth of college age face problems pertaining to their educational opportunities for which they can see no solution. A few examples of the variety and perplexity of such problems are listed here as reported by teachers and counselors who responded to our questionnaire.

PROBLEMS OF STUDENTS VARY

"My ambition is to become an aeronautical engineer. I developed tuberculosis in Korea; had one lung collapsed for a year. Now that I can navigate, do you think I can take it in engineering?" So asks a student in a Michigan junior college.

From a Nebraska junior college comes the question, "I earned only seven out of fifteen credits last semester. Would I do better to change from science to speech and music or quit college?"

"My old man is rich. The police couldn't scare me. Neither will you," said a student in a junior college in the Pacific Northwest.

"I am a girl six feet tall. My brothers tease me. Nobody likes me. Can you help me?" pleads a girl in a junior college in Illinois.

"I worked in the oil fields. I'm rough. Don't leave any money lying around. The only reason I'm here is because of rehabilitation money from the state. Maybe you could make a dean out of me. Ha!" So laughed a junior-college enrollee in Oklahoma.

"Hey, Doc, I've been studying the wrong stuff. Let's see those ratings on the Seashore Music Test again," requested a junior-college co-ed in Louisiana.

"With thirteen brothers and sisters to help support, do you think I should play football?" asked a Latin-American boy in West Texas.

"With only slightly better than average ratings on the Otis and California Mental Maturity, should I study science?" asked a student in Idaho.

"I'm a divorcee. I hate soldiers and lawyers. What course would you advise me to take?" So asked a student in Chicago.

A California junior-college student comments, "Classes are easy for me. I always get high grades, but I can't get along with the other guys. They won't have anything to do with me."

At a Mississippi junior college a boy asks, "How can I get a job so I can earn money and stay in college?"

"I just can't keep my grades up and do a good job on the student council, and yet I don't want to drop off the council. I really need it." This from a youth enrolled in a North Carolina junior college.

These are actual examples of problems brought to workers in student personnel services in public junior colleges. In each instance, whether the student is aware of it or not, the reality of the problem constitutes a genuine need for assistance. Moreover, this assistance will not be secured as a result of routine classroom experiences. The need will be satisfied only through the student's finding someone who will listen to the details of the problem and who, through skilful counseling, may guide the student in his search for a solution.

The junior college which limits its educational program to classroom activities and does not provide a complement of student personnel services can do little for students of the type who presented their personal problems in the manner described above. Persistence of such problems may obstruct students' efforts to attain the full value of their junior-college work. They need the assistance which comes from services such as guidance and counseling, a well-organized program in extraclass activities, and placement and follow-up. The urgent need for these services is further substantiated when it is recalled that the list of student problems is much broader than those mentioned by the students quoted at the beginning of this chapter.

Our questionnaire study of student problems indicated that the problem area having to do with choice of curriculum was by far the most frequently mentioned. The area second highest in frequency was that of dropping a course. Apparently the matter of deciding on a suitable curriculum constitutes one of the most serious of all problems confronting junior-college students. "Dropping a course," as a student problem, may be the result of changes in the curriculum.

All problem areas which were reported with a frequency of 100 or more are shown in Table 1.

TABLE 1

PROBLEMS ON WHICH STUDENTS REQUESTED COUNSELING

Problem	No. of Cases	Problem	No. of Cases
Choice of curriculum	1,568	Armed forces	403
Dropping a course	1,034	Health	379
Absences	963	Complaints about instructor	357
Registration	775	Family matters	263
Getting a job	716	Student-student relations	240
Change of curriculum	601	Student-government problems	233
Use of college facilities	540	Recommendations for students	223
Drop-outs	461	Physical injury	197
Official withdrawal	458	Complaints about marks	165
Vocational testing	441	Marriage	118
Transfer of credit	419	Athletic eligibility	116
Adding a course	416	Minor discipline (man)	106
Aptitude testing	412	Recruitment	100
Emotional matters	407		

PROVIDING FOR INDIVIDUAL DIFFERENCES

So far, attention has been directed to student problems only. Despite their diversity, they constitute only one of the factors which complicate the task of the student personnel worker. The difficulty of providing facilities for helping students meet these problems is increased by the individual differences of the students. Some idea of the extent of these student differences may be obtained from the list of eight educationally significant categories of differences reported by the Educational Policies Commission:[1]

1. *Education for All American Youth: A Further Look*, pp. 26–28. Educational Policies Commission of the National Education Association of the United States and the American Association of School Administrators. Washington: National Education Association, 1954.

1. Differences in intelligence and aptitude
2. Differences in occupational interests and outlooks
3. Differences in availability of educational facilities occasioned by either location of residence or family economic status
4. Differences in the types of communities in which youth reside
5. Differences in opportunity resulting from differences in social and economic status, often aggravated by differences in race
6. Differences in parental attitudes and cultural backgrounds
7. Differences in personal and avocational interests
8. Differences in mental health, emotional stability, and physical well-being

One of the types of student variance studied by the authors in their questionnaire inquiry is that of differences in intelligence. Respondents were asked the question, "How do you identify and develop special kinds of intelligence?" Some of the answers follow:

Only by observations that come to counselor's attention when working with counselees. Study of educational records, interests, hobbies, etc.

We are in process of trying to define mechanical ability with tests. In our course in "Marriage and Family," some students display social intelligence which far exceeds their ability to express themselves in English.

We employ a school social worker.

Through classroom activities and special extraclass functions such as class organization, social functions, student government, dramatic productions, etc.

We use the A.C.E. Co-operative English, Wren Study Habits Inventory, Strong Vocational, and Bell Adjustment. Each student builds a complete file on himself in required orientation. Deans and orientation instructors work together on each student.

Observation followed by testing in particular area of special interests.

Each entering student is given the Seashore Musical Aptitude Test. When we recognize a student who is not participating in school activities, his music test score is consulted.

We use the National College Freshman Testing Program.

Instructors in orientation give personality and interest inventories and make use of entrance test scores.

Identify by examining transcripts, by testing, and by conferences; develop by programming into areas of student's strengths.

We give Acorn Verbal, Differential Aptitude Tests, Acorn Non-verbal, Minnesota Paper Form Board, Aptitude in Engineering (Psychological Corporation), and GATB tests.

Degree of a student's success in certain types of courses provides a clue to certain types of intelligence.

The variety of procedures suggested by these answers is ample evidence of the complexity of the problem of one kind of individual student differences in relation to the student personnel program. While it does not follow that each category of student differences will necessitate an equal amount of work, it does follow that the task of the personnel worker is materially greater than that of simply becoming familiar with the major classifications of student problems. It is the operation of these two factors, differences among student problems and differences among students, which seriously complicate the functions of the student personnel program.

Purposes of Student Personnel Services

The Research and Service Committee on Student Personnel Services of the American Association of Junior Colleges issued, in 1950, a general statement on the philosophy underlying student personnel services. The statement holds that the primary obligation of the junior college is to render assistance to the individual in regard to intellectual training, aesthetic appreciations, emotional problems, physical conditions, social and civic relationships, vocational potentialities and skills, and moral and spiritual values. More specifically, this same report states that the student personnel service has for its objective assisting the individual student in achieving the following goals:

1. To understand himself in all aspects of personality
2. To make the most of all his capacities, qualities and interests
3. To adjust himself to the varied situations in his total environment and . . . to modify some aspects of his environment, whenever possible
4. To make his own decisions and to solve his problems independently
5. To discover his potential contributions to society
6. To decide how he can render these contributions to society to the fullest possible extent[2]

2. Committee on Student Personnel Services, "Philosophy Underlying Student Personnel Service." Washington: American Association of Junior Colleges, 1950 (mimeographed).

An analysis of this statement of philosophy reveals it to be a synthesis of the elements of student problems and student personality. This situation provides the basis for a simplified statement of the purposes of student personnel services: the recognition and provision of means for finding solutions for a great variety of student problems which are encountered by students with widely varying characteristics.

While the program of student personnel services is directly responsible for the functions that have been described, this program can with desirable leadership facilitate progress toward other educational goals. These additional goals include: (*a*) assistance in curriculum-building, (*b*) improvement of the instructional processes, and (*c*) the basis for sound administrative policies.

Satisfactory curriculum-building depends to no small degree on an intimate knowledge of the students to be served by the educational program. Moreover, the success attending the activities of graduates of an educational institution provides a clue for evaluating the effectiveness of the curriculum planning and the basis for needed changes in existing curriculum plans. The information needed for this constructive criticism of the curriculum is a natural by-product of the records which will be a part of any efficiently organized program of student personnel services.

The importance of knowing as much as possible about all the students in a given classroom has long been recognized as essential for effective instruction. The information acquired by the student personnel worker is the information needed by the instructor as a basis for his work. The fact that, in many instances, satisfactory means have not been found to transmit information from the student personnel files to the instructor's files in no way invalidates the importance of this personnel information to the improvement of the instructional program.

The development of sound administrative policies is also dependent on a wealth of knowledge about students and the homes from which they come. Here, again, the student personnel files present a rich reservoir from which the needed information may be drawn.

These three additional goals—improved curriculum-building, improved instructional procedures, and better administrative policies—are not, strictly speaking, within the province of the student personnel service. However, in such a co-operative enterprise as that of making and implementing an educational program, it should be recalled that the comprehensive student personnel program will be planned to facilitate progress toward the additional goals.

The remaining sections of this chapter will be clearly understood against the background of the foregoing description of the purposes of student personnel services. In outline, the ensuing topics of the chapter will be presented in the following order:

1. Identify and report examples of techniques and methods used by student personnel programs in achieving their purposes
2. Report types of organization used by junior colleges for their student personnel services
3. Report plans used by junior colleges for improving their student personnel services
4. Report plans for utilizing student personnel services in curriculum improvement, in the improvement of instruction, and the development of the total educational program of the college
5. Make recommendations regarding the improvement of junior-college student personnel services

Techniques and Methods for Achieving the Purposes of Student Personnel Services

PERSONAL DATA RECORDS

Complete and cumulative personal records are essential to effective personnel services. These records are needed for such diverse functions as (*a*) a basis for student remedial work, (*b*) the means by which the student may obtain a clearer understanding of himself, (*c*) the basis for a student changing his goals, and (*d*) the facilitation of transfer of the student from one level of educational work to the next highest and from educational institutions into business and industry. The cumulative record usually carries academic accomplishment, personal data about the student and his family, interests and hobbies, vocational goals, citizenship, aptitude, and other objective test records.

Much more needs to be done to make cumulative records from high schools available to the junior colleges. Time and money could be saved in this manner by avoiding duplication in testing. In a few of the larger colleges and high schools, the punch-card system seems to give promise of aid in this respect.

An example of continuing practice in testing and record-keeping is reported by a Minnesota college:

A program of testing our college students at the beginning of the Freshman year and at the end of the Sophomore year has been conducted since 1949. In addition to having high-school rank, A.C.E. Psychological Examination for College Students score, Co-operative English Test score for each student, plus his scores from any tests he may have taken in our Counseling Bureau, the Freshman student takes Co-operative General Culture and Co-operative Contemporary Affairs tests during his Freshman orientation. These scores are discussed with each student individually to assist him in getting a picture of his strengths and weaknesses as he begins his Freshman orientation. He receives a copy of his profile of scores for reference. Frequently the students who have not used the services of the Counseling Bureau before entering college become aware of the opportunity for further testing and counseling, and take advantage of it. At the end of the Sophomore year, the student takes the Co-operative English Test, the Co-operative General Culture Test, and the Co-operative Contemporary Affairs Test. These scores are discussed with the student individually and are used in comparison with the Freshman scores. Scores are discussed in reference to selected majors or occupational goals. The student receives a profile of his scores in comparison to those of our junior-college Sophomores and to national Sophomore norms.

It appears that this program is of considerable value to the students in helping them watch their development in various areas of learning. The college faculty analyzes the class scores over the years to determine whether the results are in line with the goals and philosophy of the college.

COUNSELING PROCEDURES

Many acceptable definitions of counseling have been formulated, but all are student-centered. However, the role of the counselor must at all times be recognized in the counseling process. For example, Strang has offered the following definition: "Counseling is a face-to-face relationship in which a person who needs help in developing his most acceptable self or in solving personal problems is given the opportunity to gain insight by thinking through the situation himself in an accepting atmosphere."[3]

Progressive colleges work out techniques for counseling which

3. Ruth Strang, *Counseling Technics in College and Secondary Schools*, p. 11. New York: Harper & Bros., 1949.

seem to serve best their particular situation and needs. There are in practice today many successful counseling procedures. A few of the more common approaches include: (*a*) observation, (*b*) rating scales, (*c*) autobiography and other personal documents, (*d*) the interview, (*e*) projective techniques, (*f*) cumulative personnel records, (*g*) the case study, and (*h*) therapeutic methods.[4]

It is evident that, to meet the needs of a widely varying group of students, the junior college will require a broadly conceived program of counseling service. Although a certain amount of group guidance is effective, the pay-off is in individual counseling. For example, there is definite need for educational and curriculum advisement and for counseling in the fields of such personal problems as vocational choice, religion, social matters, and naturalization. Most progressive public junior colleges are constantly surveying their work to discover whether they are omitting from their counseling service a large block of student problems.

An Illinois college describes procedures of its counseling staff in assisting a veteran of the Korean War as follows:

A married Korean veteran, who had had no high-school work, entered junior college in the spring of 1953. He had a background of delinquency as a juvenile but had become aware of a desire to rise above his past. His counselor, finding him intelligent and receptive but burdened by an extreme inferiority complex concerning his poor background, advised him to take the sociology course in juvenile delinquency—to help him understand his past—and a course in speech to help develop confidence in his ability to express himself. At the same time, he enrolled in high-school courses needed for entrance. A course in English literature awakened in him a real appreciation for poetry. During his second semester he ran into three difficulties: his wife objected to his college work; he was hospitalized for two weeks with a chronic illness; his past caught up with him when he was questioned by the F.B.I. for a robbery and had difficulty proving his alibi because of a long absence from work. By this time, however, he had developed confidence in his instructors and in the dean. He told them frankly of his difficulties and was encouraged to think out for himself what values were most important to him. He solved his home problem and was cleared by the F.B.I.

He had enrolled in the course in rhetoric with misgiving because his grammar background was extremely sketchy; so when his illness and his personal problems caused him to miss classes, he had to decide whether

4. *Ibid.*, chaps. ii–ix.

to drop this required subject. Once again he freely discussed his problem with his counselor, was given the promise of extra help at an hour convenient to him, and is at present doing good work. This man we consider "salvaged goods." His salvation can be attributed to the general atmosphere of our small college, an atmosphere of mutual trust and interest between students and faculty. Such a man probably would not have had the courage to enter a large university in the first place; had he done so, he would, in all probability, have dropped out after a few weeks and perhaps even have returned to his former ways. As it is, he seems well on the way to a useful life.

ORIENTATION AND ADMISSION PROCEDURES

Orientation as a process of making the student ready for accepting change and new responsibility makes use of the psychological law of readiness in learning. If responsibility is to be assumed for the entire person, then the orientation program must cover all phases of college work. To provide such a wide coverage, the entire faculty should be fully informed and willing to pass such information along at every opportunity.

There are numerous methods of applying the principles of orientation in any given situation. Most colleges send out bulletins, newspapers, catalogues, and other printed materials to prospective students. Visits are made to the high schools by student groups and faculty members. High-school Seniors are invited to the college on special occasions for a tour of the campus, for an entertainment program in the assembly, and for brief talks by both students and faculty. Seniors are informed that deans' offices are open at all times to high-school students, and they are invited to make appointments for themselves and their parents to go over admission requirements and other matters. During Freshman week the student personnel workers, faculty-counselors, and older students make definite plans for welcoming the new group of students. Activities of this week include a welcoming assembly, a campus tour, orientation tests, a social mixer of some kind, meetings with small groups to discuss common problems, counseling with temporary advisers, and, finally, registering for courses. Orientation service should not cease with registration but should continue throughout the year.

In addition to such orientation procedures as those listed, some junior colleges provide a formal course as part of the orientation process. The college adjustment course at a West Virginia college, described below, is an illustration.

The college adjustment course is designed to present to the incoming freshmen students the major steps in making the necessary transition from high school to college. The program is developed by employing group guidance to meet the recognized primary needs of most young adults. These basic needs may be grouped into three general classes: (*a*) making a successful emotional and mental break from parental influence and authority; (*b*) developing an interest and obtaining information concerning a vocation; and (*c*) making a satisfactory heterosexual adjustment with a future home in mind. In each area, group guidance is supplemented with individual guidance outside the classroom.

This course helps meet the need of students making a successful emotional and mental break from parental influence and authority, and thus recognizing themselves as individuals, by:

1. Presenting the rules governing students, i.e., absences, grade points, requirements, withdrawals, transfer of credits, etc.
2. Providing opportunities to analyze individual health habits
3. Reviewing correct rules of etiquette
4. Analyzing personality differences

The program develops an interest and presents information concerning vocations by:

1. Guiding the student in analyzing study habits by the use of check lists and by scheduling his time
2. Presenting the basic skills of studying, outlining, and taking notes
3. Giving a basic diagnostic reading test to determine areas of reading difficulties, and suggesting methods to improve vocabulary, speed, and comprehension in reading
4. Presenting information concerning proper use of the library and correct procedure for writing term papers
5. Discussing occupational information, i.e., how to obtain a job, writing letters of application, preparing for an interview, advancement in a vocation, etc.
6. Urging students to take advantage of vocational testing and of counseling and placement services

The course content guides the student in making a satisfactory heterosexual adjustment by:

1. Discussing the etiquette of dating
2. Presenting the mores concerning correct dating and courtship procedures
3. Discussing factors involved in a wise selection of a marriage partner

FACULTY-STUDENT RELATIONSHIPS

The entire student personnel program can actually be said to rest upon the foundation of faculty-student relationships. The tone or atmosphere of faculty-student relationships is set during the first week of the college year—usually during Freshman week or orientation week. After this week it is very important that this impression of general helpfulness be continued as the student goes into routine classwork.

The responsibility for the creation and maintenance of morale rests primarily on the shoulders of the administration of the junior college. Administrators should accept referrals from counselors and encourage and develop any successful rapport that has been created by faculty members. It is they who should provide the climate for successful faculty-student relationships. Procedures which have been found successful in a Texas college are described in the following account.

Perhaps the most important continuing practice in guidance at our college is the early contact with each student. These contacts are particularly valuable in that they set the stage early in a student's college career for easy and often valuable contacts with the personnel workers throughout the entire year, and often throughout two years. These early contacts go beyond the usual practice of faculty advising during registration. By the end of the first month of college, nearly every new student has been contacted by either the dean of men or dean of women at least once, and usually more often. Beginning with the separate assemblies for men and women during orientation week, the dean of each group of students informs them of the services available, gives them a chance to ask questions, and opens the door for immediate interviews if they are needed. By the end of the first week of classes, all veterans have had a meeting with the dean of men. The girls have been asked to small teas with nine or ten other girls by the dean of women. Since on our campus the majority of students (excluding the veterans and nurses) participate in sorority and fraternity rush, individual contacts are again made through the next two weeks with the dean of men and dean of women as these students pick up the invitations and give their preferences in these offices. This offers yet another opportunity to answer questions and establish the habit of friendly and easy rapport on the part of these deans. By the end of this first month, the permanent advisory lists are complete, and each student is contacted for a brief interview by his faculty adviser. These early contacts help break down any hesitancy on the part of the student in coming to the appropriate dean or faculty member with even the most minor question. It also makes it possible for the personnel worker to spot difficulties before they become serious.

STUDENT-LIFE PROGRAM

The curriculum has been variously defined. A widely accepted view is that it is the totality of experiences the student has under the direction of the college. The aim to develop the whole person is consonant with this definition. Also, the values to be derived from a well-balanced program of extraclass activities may be indispensable to the all-round development of students. It may be that such important traits as a sense of responsibility and adeptness in human relations can be taught to certain students only in active situations in which the trappings and restraint of the classroom are not present.

Social growth and social approval rank very high among student goals. To be stimulated and guided in their efforts to grow socially, they need many and varied experiences. One college lists the following activities as extraclass: drama club, choir, band, intramurals for all men, intramurals for all women, press club, book-discussion club, honorary dramatic fraternity, music club, yearbook, newspaper, Panhellenic council, intersorority council, interfraternity council, honor society, student council, student union board, intramural council, denominational clubs, college Y, fraternities, sororities, intercollegiate athletics for men, intercollegiate athletics for women, athletic club; special student committees on orientation, assemblies, social activities, group guidance, and college conferences; dances, monthly open-house meetings, intercollegiate (spectator) sports, and recreation sponsored by the student center. Through such social affairs as coffees, dances, receptions, hobby groups, and intramural sports, social growth definitely may come.

Another value of many of the extraclass activities is the carry-over of learned behavior into adult life. The habits of courtesy, thoughtfulness, poise, demeanor, ease of conversation, musical skills, athletic prowess, and others are often acquired in the college climate. In addition, the experiences students have in extraclass groups often serve to emphasize and clarify many of the classroom teachings. Members of college classes present great heterogeneity. This being true, colleges may expect to find need for a variety of extraclass activities which will afford practically every type of personality an opportunity to develop new knowledge, skills, attitudes, and appreciations. The impact of peer groups on young college students is sometimes revolutionary in its effect on the person. But, in every case, membership in any of the extraclass-activity groups and participation in their programs should be voluntary. This being true, interest is the dominant motive. The sharpening of one's personality results when there is compatibility and mutual interest among members of a group. The social isolate on a modern college campus is a challenge to all staff members and particularly to the student personnel staff. To distribute the total program of extraclass activities in such a way that student leaders are not overworked and every student participates in at least one activity is a genuine challenge to the time, resourcefulness, and energy of the staff for student personnel services.

CAMPUS GOVERNMENT

A knowledge of the wide range of differences among students, which was discussed earlier in this chapter, and the mores and traditions of the junior college impinge upon the program of student participation in the government of the campus. The age-old struggle to maintain freedom within a framework of self-imposed restraint is still extant on college campuses. Full and honest participation by the greater part of the student body is the ideal to be desired. Methods of attaining this goal are, of course, the joint responsibility of the student leaders and the faculty personnel. The latter group, by virtue of their broader understanding and experience in democratic procedures, perforce must serve as guides in spearheading such a program.

PLACEMENT SERVICE

Finding a job in gainful occupations is still a most important goal for most people. The vocational phase of college training, therefore, is of continuing importance to the majority of our students. Vocational guidance has been developed to assist students to choose, prepare for, enter upon, and make satisfactory progress in some vocation. Placement on a job is the culmination of a training course and guidance services during the training. Placement during and after college is a joint responsibility of the student and the placement office of the college. Naturally, placement services are offered former graduates as well as new graduates. Too many college students do very little in planning their training courses so as to meet all the requirements of the jobs for which they apply. Planning the student's course should be initiated in the junior high school or early in the senior high school. Wide study should be given to occupations, general requirements for success in occupations, and finally, after a choice has been made, to the analysis of the job itself and the qualifications of the applicant for it. The vocational counselor and the placement officer have much assistance to offer in this matter if the students will ask for it. The chief burden of guidance, however, falls on the personnel worker in charge of guidance and counseling.

After placement, follow-up service is necessary to insure proper advancement of students and alumni. This calls for an up-to-date file of employees placed on jobs. Publicity which will acquaint prospective employers with the placement services must be generously distributed. This office needs to be sensitive to the study of, and demand for, new employees. Such information helps in placing both the new and inexperienced graduates and the alumni who have had some experience. Full knowledge of these services by many college officials is a guarantee of success; ignorance of them can result in mediocrity.

Organization for Student Personnel Services

VARYING TYPES OF ORGANIZATION

Organization for student personnel service is a necessary but not an exclusive condition for an effective program. Unaccompanied by a tenable philosophy, by excellent preparation of faculty and administrators, by dedication to the welfare of students, by hard work, and by a spirit of co-operation, any organizational plan may be simply lines and rectangles on paper.

There is no uniformity in the titles used to denote faculty members who direct and carry out the various student services. The duties of a dean of students in one college will be markedly different from those of the same official in another college. The degree of authority granted to the registrar varies. Whereas in one college he is considered an administrator, in another he is a clerk. The question of lines of authority is important. Who works under whom? Is it desirable for each college employee to know his niche in the line of authority? Perhaps some confusion is inevitable in a field as vital and complex as human engineering.

In Table 2 the most frequent titles are president, registrar, and some form of title for the financial officer. This latter is variously called bursar, accountant, and business manager.

TABLE 2

MOST FREQUENTLY USED ADMINISTRATIVE TITLES IN 63 PUBLIC JUNIOR COLLEGES IN 14 STATES AND FRACTION OF TIME ALLOCATED TO POSITION, 1955

TITLE OF POSITION	FRACTION OF TIME SPENT ON JOB				NUMBER OF PERSONS
	Full	¾	½	¼ or Less	
Chief Administrator–Director.....	14	0	1	1	16
Chief Administrator–President....	36	0	2	4	42
Chief Administrator–Dean.......	16	0	0	0	16
Vice-President–Dean..	5	0	0	0	5
Dean of Women...............	17	4	9	5	35
Dean of Men.................	15	2	6	1	24
Registrar.....................	34	5	3	3	45
Director of Admissions..........	5	1	0	0	6
Dean of Students..............	10	2	3	1	16
Dean of Activities.............	5	1	2	0	8
Men's Counselor(s).............	21	............83........			104
Women's Counselor(s)..........	13	............46........			59
Testing Officer................	11	0	4	2	17
Nurse.......................	17	1	5	11	34
Vice-President................	13	0	0	0	13
Dean, Adult Evening College.....	6	0	1	0	7
Financial Officer..............	25	0	3	3	31
Dean of Instruction............	11	1	1	0	13

* This table is read as follows: Of the 16 deans of students listed, 10 devote full time to student personnel services; 2 are so engaged three-fourths of their time; 3 of them, one-half time; and 1, not more than one-fourth time.

The two predominant plans of organization include the following officers:

Plan I	Plan II
President	President
Dean of Men	Dean of Instruction
Dean of Women	Dean of Students
Registrar	Counselors
Counselors	Registrar
Financial Officer	Financial Officer

McCreary and Hanson[5] say that in the public junior colleges visited in California, one-third of the junior colleges provide for an

5. William H. McCreary and Joseph T. Hanson, *Student Personnel Programs in California Public Junior Colleges*, p. 3. Sacramento: California State Department of Education, November, 1954.

organized student personnel program under the direction of an administrator whose title clearly indicates the nature of his work. His staff consists of counselors, a registrar, and clerks. His position is on a par with that of a dean of instruction.

A second type of organization, according to McCreary and Hanson, is the traditional dean of men–dean of women–registrar system. This type is frequently found in the older and smaller junior colleges. Other types of organization involve parts of the two main types in various combinations and also other administrators and teachers.

In any plan of organization of the student personnel program there is a need for a specially educated staff member to head up the work. Other staff members with special training are desirable. It will be found, however, that the number of staff members with the special preparation varies directly with the size of the junior college—institutions with large enrolments will normally have a large staff of trained personnel workers, while in the smaller junior colleges, there may be only one person with the requisite training, and frequently this staff member will be working only part time in personnel work.

Improvement of Student Personnel Services

The dynamic nature of the educational program is a product of the ever-changing social environment in which the program is operated. This condition makes mandatory continual attention to improving existing aspects of the program. While there are numerous means for improving the program of student personnel services, two of the more important ones are considered here: in-service training of counselors and co-ordination of all of the elements of the school in providing student personnel services.

IN-SERVICE TRAINING OF COUNSELORS

The status of the training which counselors in junior colleges in one state have received affords a pertinent background against which to consider the topic of in-service training. Hanson[6] says that in 58 California public junior colleges studied, the typical counselor had a few credits beyond the Master's degree, nine undergraduate and

6. Joseph T. Hanson, *Responsibilities, Professional Characteristics, and Training Recommendations of Counselors in Public Junior Colleges of California.* Doctor's Dissertation, University of Minnesota, November, 1953.

twenty-one graduate credits in psychology, sixteen years' experience in schools, twelve years of part-time or full-time counseling experience, and other experience at nonschool jobs.

Apparently the majority of junior colleges keep their counselors so busy that there is little time available for in-service training. However, some junior college counseling staffs hold regular meetings, at which time common problems and better techniques are discussed. In some communities joint meetings with the high-school counselors are held. In still others a psychologist or a psychiatrist leads the discussion at meetings. Faculty members who serve as counselors can best be oriented in faculty meetings in which the burden of leadership is carried by the student personnel staff. It would seem necessary to schedule sessions for important improvement far in advance and very carefully, either for regular counselors or for teacher counselors. Again, the responsibility for an effective program of in-service training rests principally with the chief administrator of the junior college. He should assist with the program and release the counselors for the meetings. Also, he may suggest summer school courses to round out the understanding and techniques of the counselors.

CO-ORDINATION OF ALL ELEMENTS IN STUDENT
PERSONNEL SERVICES

No doubt, a tenable philosophy of education and, as part of it, a tenable philosophy of student personnel services are the chief and most elementary necessities for co-ordination. This philosophy must be shared, communicated, and implemented by the chief administrator. An administrator who does not understand and support such a point of view can only pay lip service to a good program. Prestige and lines of authority must serve the program. Common determination of aims and complete communication will help to formulate a good program. Availability and accessibility of guidance workers are essential.

Cruising the campus to pick up problems and feel the pulse of the student body is a good technique. To an extent, the desk may isolate the counselor from the very problems he means to discover. Incidental counseling is probably the most effective kind. It is not easy to change a subject-minded teacher to one who is student-minded, but neither is it impossible, especially if he notices that his colleagues have a broad point of view. Perhaps the students affected by the program have not been sufficiently consulted for their suggestions. Co-operation and evaluation by students would surely indicate the aspects of the program which are unpalatable. This procedure might indicate new, important, and even inexpensive services to be rendered.

Curriculum Improvement, Instructional Improvement, and Development of the Total Educational Program

The student personnel program can make important contributions toward the improvement of curriculum instruction and the total educational operation. Certain practices used in junior colleges are illustrative of this added value.

SURVEY OF STUDENT CHARACTERISTICS

While the average faculty member has a vague idea of the prevailing characteristics of the student body, his opinion is frequently overinfluenced by the portion of the student body who enrol in his classes, and very frequently the opinion cannot be relied upon as descriptive of the total student body. This deficiency is serious in those cases in which faculty members participate in planning an appropriate curriculum for the students being served.

One device which is effective in providing faculty members an accurate description of student characteristics is that of summarizing and publishing an account based on the records of the student personnel department. Such accounts need to be subdivided into several dominant patterns to prevent obscuring the principal deviations through reduction of all characteristics to medians or means based on the whole student body. Through such a refinement of technique it is possible to present a better picture and a picture which has more usefulness in curriculum-planning.

FOLLOW-UP STUDIES

The logic underlying the follow-up studies in curriculum-planning is that of testing the efficiency of the finished product against criteria imposed by agencies which the product is expected to serve. Junior-college student personnel workers who carry on follow-up studies usually include three fields: (*a*) students who transfer to senior colleges, (*b*) students who go directly into full-time employment, and (*c*) student participation in the various nonvocational roles such as home-life and citizenship.

While the efficacy of follow-up studies as a means for improving the curriculum is generally acknowledged, the number of junior colleges which conduct such studies is comparatively small. The chief reason for this condition is the high cost in time and effort required by an effective follow-up project. Whether or not this disadvantage will ever be overcome generally will depend on the ability of the junior-college administrators to find the financial assistance necessary.

STUDENT PERSONNEL STAFF MEMBERS ON

CURRICULUM COMMITTEES

Probably no member of the staff of any junior college has a better over-all picture of the student body than the student personnel workers. For this reason their membership on curriculum committees provides an excellent system by which this knowledge may be tapped. The advantages are two-way: the work of curriculum committees is facilitated by the contribution of the student personnel worker, and the student personnel worker is placed in an improved situation for understanding the many facets of the educational program.

IMPROVED TEACHING

The necessity for the instructor to have a detailed knowledge of the students he is teaching is an accepted principle basic to good instruction. The records of the student personnel worker provide one of the best sources from which the instructor can secure this needed information.

A less obvious advantage accruing to the instructional program is that which occurs as a result of the instructor's participation in the guidance and counseling activity. Through this means each faculty member gains a better understanding of the values residing in the student personnel operation, and is better equipped to understand the problems of the students whom he teaches. This understanding is indispensable for effective instruction.

Conclusions

The heterogeneity of the student body in junior colleges as well as the wide variety of problems these students have are conditions which make necessary the provision of means for personal adjustment among all students if curriculum plans are to be implemented satisfactorily. Student personnel services provide the best means of affording students the opportunity to make the needed adjustments. This program of services needs to be so organized as to provide its benefit to all kinds of students.

Fortunately, the by-products of the well-developed program of student personnel services are of equal value in the total educational operation of the junior college. The chief concomitant values of the student personnel services are realized in curriculum-building and revision, improvement of instruction, and the adoption of sound policies underlying the over-all development of the educational program.

While it is recognized that much valuable work can be done in the field of student personnel services by regular faculty members who possess only a small amount of specialized preparation for personnel services, it is desirable that the director of the student personnel services have a thorough grounding in principles, common procedures, and theories of successful student personnel work. In junior colleges with smaller enrolments, this director may be the only one with an adequate complement of such preparation. In larger junior colleges, however, many members of the student personnel staff will have the specialized education necessary. For example, the placement officer will be thoroughly trained in regard to variations in the job market and techniques for keeping constantly up to date in regard to job demands.

While no one type of organization for student personnel services exists that is best for all junior colleges, there are principles which are common to all of the organizations. One such principle is the necessity for the administrator to assume the responsibility for the implementation of the student personnel program and to secure sufficient funds to operate it. Another principle which will be common to all types of organization is the clearly indicated route for the flow of referral cases.

It is extremely unlikely that any student personnel service will ever attain the status of complete satisfaction. This situation provides the basis for continual evaluation of all aspects of the program. On the basis of such evaluation, the junior college may be assured of a student personnel program which will approach a satisfactory status and which will be consistent with the needs arising from the current social situation.

CHAPTER XI

Making Teaching More Effective

L. L. JARVIE

Introduction

IMPORTANCE OF INSTRUCTION IN THE JUNIOR COLLEGE

The improvement of instruction is important to any college or university. Particular weight must, however, be attached to high-quality teaching in the junior college. For it is a teaching, not a research, institution, and the achievement of its purposes largely depends upon the effectiveness of instruction.

More than thirty years ago Koos, in an interpretation of pronouncements of leaders in the junior-college movement, identified "offering better instruction in these years" as one of the purposes proposed for the junior college.[1] Similarly, in 1931, Eells reported "superior instruction" and "superior instructors" among reasons cited for having junior colleges.[2] These same claims have been advanced earlier in this volume (chap. iv).

Among the conditions in the junior college which can be expected to encourage effective teaching are the following:

1. Teaching is the major responsibility of junior-college instructors.
2. Instructors are, therefore, selected primarily for their teaching ability.
3. The promotion and establishment of tenure by faculty members is largely dependent upon the quality of their teaching.
4. The relatively small size of most junior colleges encourages individual attention to students.

It will be recognized that these advantages contrast with conditions in many universities, where Freshman and Sophomore courses are frequently taught by teaching assistants (whose major interest

1. Leonard V. Koos, *The Junior College Movement*, pp. 20, 23–24. Boston: Ginn & Co., 1925.
2. Walter Crosby Eells, *The Junior College*, p. 202. Boston: Houghton Mifflin Co., 1931.

is the writing of a thesis) and where professors are appointed and promoted primarily on the basis of research and publication.

The considerations referred to above are largely theoretical in nature. Quite naturally, therefore, the question arises: What evidence is available regarding the quality of junior-college instruction?

THE QUALITY OF JUNIOR-COLLEGE INSTRUCTION

Valid comparative data regarding the results of teaching in different types of institutions are practically nonexistent. The problems of establishing controls and developing valid instruments of measurement have, up to the present, served as insuperable barriers to arriving at conclusions regarding the comparative effectiveness of junior-college instruction. Four types of evidence are, however, regarded as providing support for the claim that high quality teaching is characteristic of the junior college.

Observation of Teaching. During the early history of the junior college, Koos visited 111 junior-college classes and forty-one Freshman and Sophomore classes in four-year colleges and universities. As an aid to appraising the instruction which he observed, Koos used a rating-chart score card. Despite the fact that the college and university classes visited were all in accredited institutions, whereas a number of the junior colleges included were unaccredited, Koos reports that, as a result of his large amount of classroom visitation in higher institutions, he has "a distinct impression of the superiority of the junior colleges" with respect to the quality of instruction offered.[3] To the best knowledge of the author of this chapter, no comparable survey has been made in recent years.

Judgment of Junior-College Experts. The Silver Anniversary issue of the *Junior College Journal* includes eighteen articles by junior-college authorities on the general subject of the most important development within the field during the past twenty-five years. In his editorial comment on these articles, James W. Reynolds notes that "improvement of instruction" is one of the three significant developments on which the authorities appear to be in agreement.[4]

3. Koos, *op. cit.*, pp. 85–86.

4. James W. Reynolds, "The Significance of the Past Twenty-five Years of Junior College Development," *Junior College Journal*, XXV (April, 1955), 425–26.

Success of Transfer Students. Studies of the grades of junior-college students who transfer to senior colleges and universities (chap. v) have long been quoted in support of the claim that junior-college instruction is effective.[5] Recently Brown made this same claim, citing reports to the effect that many of the junior-college graduates who have entered the Junior classes of four-year institutions kept pace with those students who were trained in the first two years of the degree-granting colleges. Thus: "The philosophy that excellent classroom teaching and professional training contributed to the success of freshman and sophomore work became established."[6]

Judgments of Former Students. Educational institutions frequently secure the judgments of students and graduates as an aid to program improvement. Rarely, however, are comparative surveys of opinion made regarding different types of colleges. Of particular interest, therefore, are the findings of Iffert's study of the judgments of 2,661 former students from a random sampling of 170 institutions (universities, technical schools, liberal-arts colleges, teachers colleges, and junior colleges) enrolling undergraduate students. Using a four-point rating scale, Iffert reports the reactions of former students to the faculties and the instruction in the institutions they attended. The ratings were based on such items as teaching ability of instructors, assistance from instructors on how-to-study techniques, opportunity to have private conferences with instructors on class work, and ability of instructors to set forth clear-cut and interesting course objectives. The junior-college faculties rated significantly higher than those of any other type of institution. Interpreting the statistical significance of the results of his study, Iffert explains that the difference between the mean score of 3.28 for junior-college faculties (highest rating) and 3.07 for liberal-arts (next highest) indicates that there is only a "very remote chance that in other samples similarly selected the faculties of liberal-arts colleges will rate higher than those of junior colleges."[7]

The evidence reported above in no sense purports to prove that

5. Koos, *op. cit.*, pp. 92–97; Eells, *op. cit.*, pp. 278–79.

6. Loren H. Brown, "A Contribution of the Junior College," *Junior College Journal*, XXV (April, 1955), 434–35.

7. Robert E. Iffert, "What Ought Colleges and Universities Do about Student Mortality?" in *Current Issues in Higher Education, 1954*, p. 179. Washington: Association for Higher Education, 1954.

junior-college instruction is superior to that found in other types of institutions. Data to support such a claim are simply not available. We have, however, seen that the two-year college is essentially a teaching institution. This characteristic, at least theoretically, should encourage the improvement of instruction.

PROBLEM OF JUNIOR-COLLEGE INSTRUCTION

In developing an effective program of instruction, it must be recognized that the junior college is confronted with a number of problems. Three of these are sufficiently widespread and important to warrant identification here.

Heterogeneity of Students. Students in two-year community colleges are notably heterogeneous as to age, socioeconomic background, range and type of abilities, educational and vocational goals (chap. iii, iv, and x). The needs of widely dissimilar students can, in part, be provided for by varied course offerings and programs (chap. ix) and by effective student-personnel services (chap. x). Typically, however, the heterogeneity of students places heavy responsibility upon the teacher who has in his classes some students preparing for professional careers, others who will be skilled workers or tradesmen, some who are in their late teens, others in their forties or fifties, some with really superior verbal ability and achievement, and others decidedly deficient in these areas. To an unusual degree, junior-college faculty members must be proficient in recognizing and dealing with individual differences not only in curriculum-building and in guidance but also in teaching.

Preservice Preparation of Faculty Members. Programs of preparation are rarely established for junior-college teachers. The problem posed by this situation is illustrated by the comment of a California junior-college administrator to a visiting educator: "We don't have any junior-college teachers in California. We have simply borrowed them from high schools and universities."

The junior college has some of the characteristics of the four-year college or university and some of the high school, but it has other characteristics which are uniquely its own. Nevertheless, faculty members for junior colleges must ordinarily be recruited from those who are prepared to teach in high school or from those trained in and interested in research of the type needed for university positions.

Teacher Shortage and Overloading. Mounting college enrolment, predicted for the forthcoming decade, points to a likely shortage of teachers and to an overcrowding of facilities. These situations are faced by junior colleges in common with all other institutions of post-high-school education. But it is clear that the anticipated rate of enrolment increases in two-year colleges plus the difficulty of securing qualified instructors for these institutions at any time are likely to accentuate the crisis faced by the junior college.

PURPOSE OF CHAPTER

With this background regarding (*a*) the special importance of high-quality instruction to the junior college and (*b*) some of the obstacles to effective teaching in the two-year community college, these questions arise: What is being done to improve instruction in the junior college? What more should be done? In the following pages of this chapter, these questions will be considered from two viewpoints: (*a*) the preservice preparation of teachers and (*b*) junior-college programs of instructional improvement and in-service training.

Preservice Preparation

As recently as 1950 Wood reported that not a single college or university offered a program of preparation for junior-college teachers.[8] With this knowledge, it is not surprising to learn that the major direct source of public junior-college instructors is the high school —not the four-year college or university. In a study of some fifty public junior colleges in the Midwest, the South, and California, Koos found that almost three-fourths of their faculty members were recruited from public and private high schools and only one-eighth had been teaching in colleges and universities.[9] Moreover, courses in education taken by junior-college teachers are usually the same as those taken by high-school teachers. Less than one in ten has taken a course in "The Junior College."[10]

Merson found that, of the courses in professional education which

8. William R. Wood, "Professional Personnel for Community Colleges," *Junior College Journal*, XX (May, 1950), 513–22.

9. Leonard V. Koos, "Preparation for Community-College Teaching," *Journal of Higher Education*, XXI (June, 1950), 309–17.

10. *Ibid.*, p. 313.

California colleges and universities offer in preparation for junior-college teaching, only 8 per cent give primary attention to the junior college and only 2 per cent are exclusively devoted to the two-year college.[11] It is, of course, possible that the courses in education to which reference has been made are adequate for the needs of prospective junior-college instructors—though not planned specifically for them. This possibility will be explored later in the chapter.

Several inquiries have been made regarding the academic preparation of junior-college teachers. On the basis of information assembled in 1950, Koos reported that about three-fourths of the academic teachers in the public junior colleges held Master's degrees. A smaller proportion but probably more than half of the special teachers at the junior-college level at that time held Master's degrees. Also the Koos report showed that many teachers in public junior colleges had taken graduate courses beyond the requirements for the Master's degree. On the average, the training which followed the Master's degree amounted to almost an additional year of graduate study.[12]

In a study of 463 public and private junior-college faculties, Punke found that approximately two-thirds (64.4 per cent) of the instructors held the Master's degree.[13]

Typically, then, the preservice preparation of public junior-college instructors is similar to that of high-school teachers, with one significant difference: Most junior-college instructors in academic fields have Master's degrees plus additional graduate work.

RECOMMENDED PROGRAMS OF PRESERVICE PREPARATION

The problem of just what should constitute the preparation of junior-college instructors has frequently been discussed. One of the more thoughtful statements on this subject emerged from the Conference on the Preparation of Junior College Instructors, sponsored by the American Council on Education. At this conference twenty-seven representatives of junior colleges, technical institutes, colleges, universities, and national agencies discussed the findings of a survey

11. Thomas B. Merson, "Certification Standards for Junior College Teachers in California," p. 315. Unpublished Doctor of Education thesis, University of California, Berkeley, 1952.

12. Koos, *Preparation for Community-College Teaching, op. cit.,* pp. 314–15.

13. Harold H. Punke, "Academic Qualifications of Junior College Faculties," *Junior College Journal,* XXIII (March, 1953), 366–79.

of sixty junior colleges and technical institutes. The group then adopted the following recommendations regarding the selection of faculty for the junior colleges and the other institutions represented at the Conference:

We recommend that the institutions designated above select and advance faculty members who have the following qualifications:

1. A clear conception of the philosophy and background of these institutions, their relationship to the whole educational structure, and especially their place in the community.
2. An understanding of human growth and development and of the special problems of age groups enrolled in these institutions.
3. Adequate skill in curriculum construction, evaluation, and other areas related to the art and science of instruction in these institutions.
4. Adequate supervised teaching experience—at least a quarter or a semester—in the type of teaching in which they are planning to engage. . . .
5. A clearly balanced appreciation of both the occupational and general educational services of these institutions.
6. For occupational instructors, occupational competence—which includes practical experience—with due recognition of this practical occupational experience.
7. For instructors in fields of general or academic education, competence in their special fields, and also in broad functional fields (for example in *social factors in the life of the community* as well as in history and social sciences; or in *communication in the community* as well as in English and the humanities; or in *health in the community or conservation of human resources in the community* as well as in the biological sciences, etc.)—with practical experience also in community service agencies, on newspapers, in camps, or the like.[14]

Dolan reports a study of the preparation needed for junior-college teachers based on information provided by some five hundred instructors in Illinois junior colleges. These teachers were asked for three sets of opinions: (*a*) an evaluation of their own professional education in terms of the relative value of the different courses taken; (*b*) a statement regarding professional education courses they had not taken but later felt they should have taken in order to prepare themselves properly for junior-college teaching; and (*c*) a listing of the professional education courses all students preparing to become junior-college teachers should take.

14. *Wanted: 30,000 Instructors for Community Colleges*, pp. 11–13. Washington: American Council on Education, 1949.

On the basis of his finding, Dolan recommends that junior-college teachers take the same education courses required of high-school teachers plus a general course in the junior college and a course in the junior-college curriculum, along with courses in the psychology of adolescence and in guidance and counseling. He further recommends two years of graduate work, including the Master's degree.[15]

Punke, whose study is limited to the academic qualification of junior-college faculties, suggests that the requirements for junior-college teaching should include a Master's degree based on two years' work beyond the Bachelor's degree.[16]

In an investigation of credential standards for California junior colleges, Merson secured the judgments of 263 junior-college instructors regarding elements of teaching competence which should be required of all junior-college teachers and regarding the value of courses in education which they had taken. He also secured the opinions of 90 junior-college teachers regarding teaching problems and the need for including consideration of these problems in programs of preservice preparation for junior-college teaching. In addition to the opinions of faculty members, he requested the recommendations of a jury of fifty-four junior-college leaders regarding desirable practices for the certification of junior-college instructors.

On the basis of the findings of his several investigations Merson recommended the following basic requirements for teachers in junior colleges:

1. Six years of college education beyond high school.
2. A Master's degree in a subject field.
3. One-sixth of the total program (28 units) of professional education in a program designed for preparation for junior-college teaching including:
   3.1. Work organized to include thorough preparation in the basic factors of teaching competence.
   3.2. A thorough knowledge of the characteristics of junior college students.
   3.3. Work organized to develop attitudes, skills, and knowledges necessary to fulfill the functions of the junior college.
   3.4. Work emphasizing means of adapting methods of instruction and

15. F. H. Dolan, "The Preparation of Junior College Teachers," *Junior College Journal*, XXII (February, 1952), 329–36.

16. Punke, *op. cit.*, p. 377.

subject matter presentation to meet the needs of junior college students.

3.5. Field work in typical junior college organized as an integral part of each of the courses used in fulfilling the requirements in professional education, and illustrating the practical applications of the theory contained in the courses.

3.6. An interneship of directed teaching and related activities of at least one semester in an approved program in a typical junior college teaching situation.

4. Work experience in a field related to the major subject. This related work experience shall be longer than three months for teachers of transfer students and a year or longer for teachers of terminal students.[17]

Merson and the Conference on the Preparation of Junior College Instructors have given particular emphasis to the need for employment experience on the part of teachers of vocational courses. Koos, too, supports this view:

Without actual vocational experience, the teacher's instruction, in such subjects as agriculture, commerce, secretarial subjects, home economics, and the engineering and industrial arts, is likely to be unrealistic and to fail to equip the community-college student to meet the conditions and responsibilities of employment. . . .[18]

The results of the studies referred to above lead to the following recommendations regarding the preparation of junior-college instructors:

1. Thorough preparation in the field of teaching must be provided. In academic fields a master's degree is suggested as essential, with an additional year of graduate work recommended. In vocational fields, actual employment experience is urged as essential.

2. Courses in education should include materials directly related to the junior college, its philosophy, its program, its students, and its problems.

3. Practice-teaching should be done in a junior college, not in a high school or in a university.

The writer of the present chapter questions the proposals of Dolan and Merson regarding the *number* of credits in education courses which junior-college instructors should be expected to take. With the amount of graduate academic work and/or vocational experience

17. Merson, *op. cit.*, pp. 530–31.
18. Koos, "Preparation for Community College Teaching," *op. cit.*, p. 312.

expected of junior-college teachers, it is unrealistic (and also, in the opinion of this author, unnecessary) to require up to twenty-five or thirty units of work in education. From twelve to fifteen units in education (including work in the field of the junior college) should comprise an adequate and defensible minimum.

CURRENT DEVELOPMENTS

Despite the general agreement on recommendations of the type suggested above, little is actually being done to strengthen programs of preparation for junior-college instructors—much less to develop new and experimental programs. There are, however, at least three developments which deserve attention.

Interdivisional Curriculums. Reference has been made to a recommendation regarding the need of junior-college instructors for competence in broad fields of learning.[19] A number of universities are currently providing interdivisional curriculums designed to prepare for such competence. Teachers College, Columbia University, for example, offers a comprehensive and basic graduate program in the communication arts in the modern community. Through the cooperation of several departments, a core offering is developed and related to a series of specialized courses in the social, psychological, and technical aspects of communication.

There are also indications that technical divisions of universities are willing to experiment in developing programs planned for junior-college personnel. New York University and Cornell University are among the institutions which have recently introduced programs combining advanced technical study with appropriate offerings in the field of professional education.

Courses in Junior-College Education. The need for teachers who have an understanding of the junior college, its philosophy, and its program has been reported in preceding paragraphs. This discussion was concluded with a recommendation that courses in the junior college (including practice teaching) be introduced into programs of preservice preparation for junior-college teachers.

A number of colleges and universities now provide offerings designed to meet these needs as well as to provide training for teachers now in service. Colvert and Baker identify twenty-three institutions

19. *Wanted: 30,000 Instructors for Community Colleges, op. cit.,* p. 13.

as having such courses—in addition to several others which hold summer workshops in the field of the junior college.[20] The credit value of these offerings ranges from two units at the University of Colorado to twenty-four at the University of Texas.

Of the institutions surveyed by Colvert and Baker, only one (the University of California at Los Angeles) reports a program of practice-teaching in the junior college. Requirements for the junior-college teaching credential at this university include a Master's degree in a teaching field, a course in the junior college, and junior-college practice-teaching.

A Two-Year Graduate Program. Thorough preparation in his teaching fields is, of course, essential for the junior-college instructor. Many, in this connection, would agree with Koos that the Doctor's degree should ultimately become the prevailing standard.[21] Such a proposal would, however, be unrealistic for the foreseeable future. Nevertheless, there is a widespread belief that a Master's degree is presently inadequate for the academic preparation of junior-college teachers. This has led Punke, Dolan, and others to recommend a two-year program of graduate study for junior-college instructors. Such a program is currently being developed at the University of Texas.

A SERIOUS SITUATION

The inadequacies reported in the current preservice preparation of junior-college instructors do not, however, represent new findings or observations; they have repeatedly been pointed out and discussed throughout a major part of the history of the junior college. Likewise, the recommendations for improvement presented in this chapter are not new—they, too, have been urged by individuals, committees, and commissions throughout much of the past quarter-century.

And yet, little is being done today to improve the preservice preparation of junior-college instructors. It also seems likely that the current situation will deteriorate before it improves. With the forthcoming expansion of enrolment, a shortage of teachers can be anticipated. Under these conditions, the quality of teacher preparation

20. C. C. Colvert and M. L. Baker, *The Status of College and University Offerings and Services in the Area of Junior College Education and Professional Up-Grading of Junior College Faculty Members.* Austin, Texas: Research Office, American Association of Junior Colleges, University of Texas, 1955.

21. Koos, "Preparation for Community College Teaching," *op. cit.,* p. 316.

is all too likely to decline rather than to improve. The situation is serious. It demands local, state, and national attention.

Programs of Instructional Improvement and In-Service Training

Plans for the improvement of teaching are important to any educational institution. Such plans are particularly needed, however, in the junior college—not only because it is primarily a teaching institution but also because, as has already been noted, the preservice preparation of junior-college instructors is notably deficient.

JUNIOR-COLLEGE PRACTICES

In earlier chapters we have noted faculty participation in program development (chap. ix) and in guidance (chap. x). These activities have high potential value for increasing the insights and understandings of teachers and for improving instruction. A wide range of additional activities are, however, used in junior colleges as aids to raising the quality of teaching. The most extensive survey in this area has been reported by Reynolds, Gray, and Davis,[22] who summarize practices in 228 junior colleges. In the paragraphs which follow, reference will be limited to activities in the 126 public institutions included in the survey.

Reynolds reports the use of a number of co-operative staff projects. Most often listed are curriculum construction and revision (by 80 per cent of the colleges) and surveys of student interests and needs (49 per cent). Community surveys by faculty members are carried on in more than one-fourth of the colleges. Although securing the aid of consultants is widely recommended, only 13 per cent use such assistance. It will be observed that these practices are planned for use in program development and improvement. Staff participation in these activities can contribute significantly to the improvement of instruction—hence their inclusion in Reynolds' report.[23]

22. James W. Reynolds, "Administrative and Supervisory Practices for Improving Instruction, I," *Junior College Journal*, XVIII (December, 1947), 181–90; John E. Gray, "Administrative and Supervisory Practices for Improving Instruction, II," *Junior College Journal*, XVIII (January, 1948), 238–46; Joseph B. Davis, "Administrative and Supervisory Practices for Improving Instruction, III," *Junior College Journal*, XVIII (March, 1948), 365–73.

23. Reynolds, *op. cit.*, p. 183.

Selected practices identified in the survey are found in Table 1. Audio-visual aids (including motion pictures, film strips, foreign-language recordings, dictaphone, and typewriting and shorthand recordings) are used by more than nine-tenths of the colleges. Undoubtedly, if the survey were repeated today, television would also be described as an aid to teaching by a number of colleges.

Intervisitation of classes is reported by nine out of ten institutions. Under this plan instructors visit classes in their own college, in other colleges and universities, or in high schools. In this connection, Mac-

TABLE 1

SELECTED PRACTICES USED IN 126 JUNIOR COLLEGES AS
AIDS TO THE IMPROVEMENT OF INSTRUCTION*

Practices	Per Cent of Colleges Using
Use of audio-visual aids	90
Intervisitation of classes	90
Conferences with administrative head of college	81
Classroom visits by administrative head of college	72
Encouragement of classroom experimentation and research	64
Presession faculty conferences	63
Use of teacher rating plan	25
Use of demonstration teaching	6

* Adapted from Reynolds, *op. cit.*, pp. 188, 189; Gray, *op. cit.*, pp. 239–41, 245; and Davis, *op. cit.*, pp. 366, 367, 369.

Lean has recently pointed out one of the major values of visiting classes in other colleges:

It may be possible for instructors who are puzzling over how to use best the lecture-demonstration method in science, role playing, phonograph discs and earphones in language teaching or the physical setup of a writing laboratory, to visit other colleges where these kinds of materials and processes have long been established. An administrator will often find, as I have, that standing the costs of even extended trips for his teachers pays large dividends.[24]

In almost three-fourths of the colleges, the administrative head of the college visits classes. Deans and division and department chairmen also observe teaching in a sizable number of colleges. The value of routine, inspectorial visits to classes is open to question. Such visits may actually do more harm than good. Morse holds, however, that such need not be the case:

24. Malcolm S. MacLean, "The Role of the Administrator," in *Accent on Teaching*, p. 289. Edited by Sidney J. French. New York: Harper & Bros., 1954.

If the observer is a dean or department head with responsibility for selection and advancement of faculty in the college or department, there may be legitimate fear that he appears in the role of judge, jury, and executioner rather than as a guest at the feast of reason. If, however, it is understood that the purpose of visitation is to gain information about the course, about instructional methods, about the instructor's thinking, to the end that the entire program of the college may be articulated more effectively, then the instructor need not feel he is on trial for his professional life every time a visitor appears.[25]

Approximately two-thirds of the colleges claim to encourage classroom experimentation and research, and a like number hold presession faculty conferences. Teacher-rating plans are used by one out of four colleges, and demonstration teaching by 6 per cent. Other aids mentioned in the survey, but not in Table 1, include faculty meetings, encouragement of advanced study, and the provision of professional libraries.

The use of a practice in a large percentage of colleges in no sense indicates that it is employed effectively or that it is a desirable practice. It may simply be the easy or the traditional thing to do, and it may be carried on in a highly perfunctory fashion. Likewise, the infrequent use of a practice in no way suggests that it lacks value. Demonstration teaching, for example, is used in few colleges—and yet is reported to have a high degree of value. The class in general biology taught by Dean H. Ferris of Graceland College before a general session of the 1954 national convention of the American Association of Junior Colleges was one of the highlights of the conference program—demonstrating as it did to an audience of four hundred the development of a unit through the extensive participation of students (individual study, group study, and committee work), the use of varied audio-visual aids (lantern slides, microprojector, charts, motion picture, and opaque projector), and the relationship of the facts and principles of biology to the life and experience of students.[26]

25. H. T. Morse, "Improving Instruction in the College Classroom," *Junior College Journal*, XXV (May, 1955), 520-21.

26. "An Exploration in College Teaching." Demonstration presented under the auspices of the Teacher Preparation Committee at the 1954 Convention of the American Association of Junior Colleges.

A PROGRAM IN ACTION

The foregoing practices are used in various combinations and to
varying degrees by different colleges. The survey presents, however, a composite of practices rather than descriptions of the total
programs of particular colleges. As a matter of fact, the literature of
education includes few reports of such college-wide plans. McCammon has, however, published a comprehensive description of one
junior college's program of in-service training.[27] Reference is here
made to parts of this report from a private junior college because of
the implications they have for public institutions. Among the practices which McCammon describes are these:

1. *Participation in research.* In this connection, research is defined
as the "systematic investigation of possibilities for improving administration and instruction. With the guidance and assistance of the
college research service, approximately half of the faculty annually
participate in one or more voluntary studies—as, for example, an
evaluation of experimental classes in group piano; a study of the time
students spend in extraclass activities; appraising the value of a science field trip; or an inquiry into the educational and employment
history, the community activities, and the marital status of 13,000
graduates" (pp. 4–7).

2. *Fall faculty conferences.* These meetings are held for from one
to two weeks each year preceding the opening of college. The success
of these conferences, during which faculty members draw their regular salaries, is in no small measure due to the fact that the conference is of sufficient length to permit real work and achievement.
Given over to the consideration of institutional emphases and problems (individualized instruction, the meaning of a functional curriculum, and the role of extraclass activities at the college—for example)
as well as to individual and group work, conferences include general
all-faculty sessions, division, department, and committee meetings—
not to mention social and recreational activities (pp. 7–16).

3. *Work with expert consultants.* Members of the staff, individually and collectively, are encouraged to invite a consultant to the
campus to provide guidance and direction in meeting a problem or

27. Hugh McCammon, "Continuing Growth: A Statement concerning the
In-Service Training of College Faculties." Columbia, Missouri: Stephens College, n.d. (mimeographed). 97 pp.

in projecting a new development. Off-campus experts have been called upon in such fields of instruction as foreign languages, art, business education, and occupational planning; in college-wide programs in the improvement of reading skills and student counseling and guidance; and in evaluating the results of teaching (pp. 17–21).

4. *Work with national advisory boards.* In the fields of radio, health education, and the use of audio-visual materials in teaching, men and women of national reputation have been appointed to advisory boards which meet on campus to study the college program in their particular fields—and to recommend plans for improvement (pp. 21–31).

5. *Summer workshops.* College faculty members are, from time to time, employed for work during the summer on individual, group, or all-college problems and plans for improvement. Under such arrangements, instructors of a particular course (communication skills, or problems of contemporary society, for example) meet together for a period from one to three weeks to project plans for their course for the succeeding year (pp. 32–38).

6. *Training as an adviser.* Each member of the faculty serves as a faculty adviser. Training for this responsibility is carefully planned and carried out—not only through faculty meetings but particularly through advising groups of from fifteen to eighteen staff members representing a cross section of fields and areas of work (pp. 45–50). McCammon particularly emphasizes the relationship of advising to teaching and the contributions which serving as an adviser can make to an instructor's teaching. He further points out the existence of important common elements in good teaching and good counseling (pp. 66–67).

7. *Learning in the case conference.* An example of this activity would be a called meeting of faculty members who are working most closely, in and out of the classroom, with a student known to be encountering some difficult problems. The author explained that, as a result of participation in such conferences, a teacher often gains information about students which had not become apparent in their normal teacher-student contacts. Out of this understanding may come new insights regarding students in general—and improved classroom teaching (p. 55).

8. *Working with librarians.* Librarians are recognized as members

of the instructional staff and are assigned to work with the faculty of various departments. McCammon describes the favorable outcomes of this co-operative procedure in the following statement:

Their constant practice is to call to the attention of the teachers with whom they work the availability of materials they can use. To make this possible, their teaching colleagues must take pains to help the librarian get and maintain close acquaintance with the aims and methods of the instruction. Librarians in common practice attend classes frequently, take active part in departmental and divisional meetings, work as members of committees, have a voice in course changes and in starting new courses. Thus the individual teacher or the staff that wants information or advice from the library service need not consider an "embassy" or "negotiations." The librarian is there beside him, on the job, every day [p. 71].

McCammon reports such other practices as these: faculty meetings, professional reading, writing professional books and articles, committee work, conferences with administrators, and annually prepared course outlines which include recommendations for improving each course the next time it is to be offered.

Perhaps the most noteworthy feature of the program which McCammon describes is the wide variety of activities used by a single college. It should also be observed that considerable emphasis is placed upon experimentation and evaluation. Even in his report on in-service training McCammon appraises the practices which he has reported by holding evaluative interviews with forty members of the faculty. On the basis of the results of these conferences and of his own observations, McCammon arrives at such conclusions as the following:

The individual teacher learns most, and changes most, from getting a new point of view about experience he considers part of his necessary and legitimate job. He is far less helped by any sort of "training program" set up apart from that basic task [p. 92].

. . . *an experience is most valuable to a faculty member if the initiative lies with him from beginning to end . . ."* [p. 94].

. . . *a teacher can learn things in an experience with a heterogeneous professional group which he will never come to see or do if his contacts are limited to others in his own field.* . . . The teacher who reports to a case conference a student's work in algebra is heard by representatives of almost every division and service of the college organization. He finds around him the same sort of mixed groups as he studies his job of advising, or serves on an all-college committee, or takes part in a fall conference for his own job which makes him a better counselor and a better teacher [p. 95].

. . . the faculty member learns most from the experience in which he does something, in which he acts rather than being acted upon (p. 95).

. . . the teacher grows most in an institution which does not dread and oppose change, but expects it and welcomes it [p. 96].

. . . in-service training costs, and is worth, money. . . . But the dividends from this investment can be found in the increased strength of a really healthy institution [p. 96].

RESPONSIBILITIES OF THE ADMINISTRATION

A variety of practices which junior colleges use to improve instruction have been reported and the pattern of activities used by one college has been noted. These are followed by suggested conclusions regarding desirable characteristics of a program of in-service training. There is here no disposition to propose that all of the activities reported or any pattern of them can or should be used in a particular institution. Rather, it is hoped that the activities described may suggest possible lines of planning and development for many junior-college faculties interested in the improvement of teaching.

Particular emphasis has been given to the importance of faculty participation in improvement programs. Mention must also be made of the responsibility of the administration for providing leadership, through such means as the following:

1. Creating a working atmosphere conducive to high group and individual morale.
   a) Faculty participation in program planning and development.
   b) Desirable working conditions with respect to salary, tenure, teaching load, and leaves of absence.
2. Stimulating and aiding faculty members to identify problems and developments on which to work.
3. Helping faculty members develop and carry out plans and procedures for working on problems and projects, including, when necessary, the assistance of expert consultants.
4. Providing facilities (classroom, laboratory, library, and audio-visual materials) which encourage high quality teaching.

Conclusion

The improvement of instruction is basically important to the junior college. This necessarily involves the preservice preparation of staff members and also institutional programs of instructional improvement and in-service training. Junior-college teachers need a high degree of competence in their teaching fields and an acquaintance with and understanding of the junior college, its role, its program and its students. Universities must, therefore, be expected to give more attention, in their programs of graduate work, to the particular needs and demands of the junior college and its faculty members.

At the same time junior colleges must develop programs of instructional improvement in which faculty members assume major responsibility and have opportunities for personal and professional growth—and for work on programs and developments.

CHAPTER XII

Legal and Extralegal Influences for Improving Junior Colleges

JESSE P. BOGUE

AND

NORMAN BURNS

Introduction

Controls over institutions of public education come from many sources. One form is the action of state legislatures. Other forms include administrative regulations of boards, federal legislation in such areas as vocational education and veterans' subsidies, the action of the people voting on bond issues or tax rates, the action of tax assessors and tax boards, and the decisions of courts. This list, while not exhaustive, gives some indication of the nature of the sources of controls which may legally be exercised over the administration of a public junior college.

It must also be recognized that there are many extralegal sources of control. Among these are regional accrediting agencies; other accrediting agencies which confine their work to a single field such as music, medicine, or teaching (as the state departments of education); universities, either through formal accreditation procedures or through informal admission of transfer students on the basis of the registrar's evaluation of transcripts; and foundations which grant subsidies for specified purposes.

A third general source of control is public opinion, particularly in the geographical community within which the junior college is located.

The university as a source of control is discussed in chapter v, and the force of public opinion has received some attention in chapter ix. Accordingly, the present chapter will be limited to the consideration of legislation and accreditation.

Legislation

Public education in the United States from the beginning of the nation has been regarded as a responsibility of the states. In discharging part of this responsibility, the states have delegated a large portion of control to local districts. This has been true particularly of public elementary and high schools. As public junior colleges increased in number and spread among the states, the prevailing practice has been to classify these institutions with the public schools of elementary and secondary grade, over which local governmental units exercise a marked degree of control.

The status of public junior-college legislation in the United States may be characterized as highly satisfactory in some states and of relatively little value in others. For instance, we might begin with Texas at a high point on the curve of legislative support of junior-college purposes, dip down for Louisiana, rise with Mississippi, go to zero for Alabama, rise again for Georgia and Florida, and descend for South Carolina. We could begin with a very high point for California, go down the chart for Oregon, and ascend again for the state of Washington. Various combinations of states in different sections of the nation could be charted similarly. We could scale New England at almost zero, the Middle Atlantic States much higher (particularly New York), the Southern States higher yet, advance upward for the North Central region, and reach the peak of present status in the Northwest and in California. It is significant indeed to observe the extent to which, in these states and regions, public junior-college development has paralleled the progress of liberal legislation.

While state legislation is necessary as a basis for the establishment and operation of public junior colleges, it is well to recognize that two general classifications of legislation are found on the statute books. One class, referred to as basic legislation, defines the conditions that must be satisfied in establishing and operating junior colleges in general. A second type, special junior-college legislation,[1] covers such situations as establishing state-controlled junior colleges, authorizing junior colleges to be established as a part of or to become a part of the state university or the state system of higher edu-

1. S. V. Martorana, "The Legal Status of American Public Junior Colleges," in *American Junior Colleges*, p. 25. Washington: American Council on Education, 1952.

cation, and authorizing establishment of local public junior colleges. Consideration in this chapter is restricted to basic legislation.

PROVISIONS OF BASIC JUNIOR-COLLEGE LEGISLATION

In the main, state legislation providing for the establishment and operation of junior colleges in general should define procedures and authority with respect to the following items: purposes of public junior colleges, permission to establish public junior colleges, conditions under which public junior colleges may be established, provisions for support of public junior colleges, provision for control of public junior colleges, and the relationship of public junior colleges to state departments of education.

Purposes of Public Junior Colleges. Customarily, state legislation providing for public junior colleges gives some consideration to a definition of purpose. This statement of purpose should avoid the imposition of crippling restrictions which might result from an over-emphasis on detail. An example of an appropriate statement of purpose is found in the section, "Junior College Defined," of the Colorado Junior College Organization Act:

A junior college established pursuant to the provisions of this act within the state of Colorado is hereby defined to be an educational institution which shall provide not to exceed two (2) years of training in the arts, sciences, and humanities beyond the twelfth (12th) grade of the public high school curriculum and/or vocational education.[2]

Permission To Establish Public Junior Colleges. Most legislation eventuates from well-known and recognized needs and from the concerted demands of the people. This is especially applicable with respect to education, which involves acceptance by political subdivisions. Any legislature would be more than reluctant to devise and promulgate a system of public education without the approval of the people. This statement may be judged by the fact that no state, regardless of the forward steps it may have taken in junior-college legislation, has enacted directives that public junior colleges shall be established. That is, present legislation providing for the establishment of junior colleges is permissive in character.

Conditions under Which Public Junior Colleges May Be Estab-

2. *School Laws of the State of Colorado, 1941,* p. 201. Denver, Colorado: State Department of Education, 1941.

lished. Most permissive authorizations are surrounded with restrictions of one kind or another. These restrictions may be classified under two general headings: (*a*) minimum requirements for the establishment of public junior colleges and (*b*) legal procedure for establishing public junior colleges.

The designation of minimum requirements should provide satisfactory answers to the following questions: (*a*) Do the citizens in the geographic area involved want a junior college? (*b*) Is there a large enough potential of students to assure an enrolment needed for a desirable educational program? (*c*) Is the potential in financial resources large enough to support the junior college adequately? While it is true that other items are included occasionally in the minimum requirements, the usual list provides for answers to the three questions listed.

Basic junior-college legislation should define the procedures for establishing public junior colleges. In considering these procedures, it will be seen that the first question in the preceding paragraph has pertinence for the matter of procedures for establishment. In addition to providing the voters of the proposed junior-college district an opportunity to express their opinion through the ballot, legislation should provide for (*a*) ascertaining by public agency whether the minimum requirements have been met, (*b*) describing the form of the petition to be used in calling for an election, (*c*) naming the agencies (state board of education, local board or boards) whose approval is necessary before holding the election, and (*d*) describing the election procedure.

Provisions for Support of Public Junior Colleges. Support for public junior colleges generally falls into two classifications: (*a*) maintenance and operation and (*b*) capital outlay. Legislation in the several states varies widely in designating stipulations regarding each of these classifications. Moreover, there is no uniformity among the states in regard to prorating financial costs among the students, the local unit, and the state. Some states follow a tuition-free policy for students, the state and the local units sharing the cost; other states place all the financial burden on the students and the local unit; while still others undertake to find some formula for apportioning the cost to the students, the local unit, and the state.

Generally speaking, the best development of junior colleges will be found in those states in which the following conditions prevail: (*a*) the students' share in the financial responsibility, if any, is small; (*b*) the local unit takes care of its share of the financial responsibility through tax levies for current expenses and bond issues for capital outlay; and (*c*) the state's financial responsibility is met through legislative appropriations.

Provision for Control of Public Junior Colleges. Provision for the establishment of junior colleges and for local control, as well as authority for a considerable measure of local support, should be defined in the laws of the states. In practice, permission for local action of this type is almost always limited by the specified procedures and requirements of such action. Junior colleges are found which are organized, controlled, and largely supported by high-school districts. All junior colleges in Iowa, Kansas, and some other states are of this type, although counties, as in Michigan, may contribute to the support of the junior colleges if they wish to do so. In other states junior colleges may be organized on a county basis. Eastern Arizona College at Thatcher, Montgomery Junior College in Maryland, San Benito County Junior College in California, and Mesa County Junior College in Colorado are good examples. Still others are organized as districts, embracing two or more high-school districts, or independent school districts, or various combinations of sponsoring political subdivisions on a flexible pattern. Chaffey Junior College and several others in California are good examples of district organized-and-controlled institutions. Tyler Junior College District in Texas is composed of the city of Tyler and sixteen independent school districts. The law in New York State permits community colleges to be organized on a flexible basis by a city, a county, two or more counties, or by combinations of school districts. There are also state junior colleges as in Utah, for example.

Relationship of Public Junior Colleges to State Department of Education. The relationship of junior colleges to state departments of education rests legally on four functions generally assigned to state departments: (*a*) supervision of the expenditure of funds appropriated by the legislature for public education, (*b*) enforcing standards of teacher preparation included in teacher certification laws or state department regulations, (*c*) certifying teachers for public schools, and (*d*) administering educational programs in agencies of education. Martorana makes the following comment on administrative and academic standards for junior colleges:

That state legislatures consider the state board of education, state department of education, or similar agency best able to supervise the general administration of junior-college programs is evident from an analysis of the state laws. The statutes in ten states provide that the state board of education shall act, at least in part, as the standardizing agency for the junior colleges. . . . In five other states . . . the state department of education or the state department of public instruction is authorized by statute to perform this function. In [three other states] the state superintendent of public instruction sets the standards for the junior colleges.[3]

STATE LEGISLATION CONSISTENT WITH ACCEPTABLE JUNIOR-COLLEGE PRACTICE

Legislation of real and lasting value to the organization and operation of junior colleges must be consistent with the basic concepts and functions of these institutions. What are they? In what respects may legislation be consistent with them?

Near to the People. The public junior colleges must be as near to the people as possible. Emphasis should be placed upon the fact that these institutions are essentially local public colleges established to serve all the people who live within a reasonable commuting area. Some legislation has been enacted to take care of situations of this kind. In Mississippi, for example, public junior colleges have been organized by zones, varying in size from one county to seven. Jones County Junior College at Ellisville serves an area embracing seven counties. This college and all others in the state (with the single exception of Meridian Municipal Junior College) have dormitories. These facilities make it possible for students to attend without the necessity of traveling great distances. In California practically all public junior colleges are so located that students may commute daily and live at home. Provisions are frequently made for free transportation. In Texas some colleges have dormitories, and others do not. Even in those schools with boarding facilities, transportation is provided either free or at a small cost for nonboarding students.

Flexibility. In every state, communities should be authorized to establish public junior colleges on a flexible basis consistent with

3. Martorana, *op. cit.*, p. 23.

their particular needs. Some needs are common to all communities. These may be met by general-education programs. On the other hand, even communities in the same geographical area may differ sharply. In view of such variations, state legislatures should consider the importance of flexibility in legal provisions for the operation of public junior colleges.

DATA NEEDED AS BASIS FOR STATE LEGISLATION

In any undertaking in which legislation plays a significant role, there is a need for factual information to serve as a basis for action by the legislature. Surveys within the state have proved to be a satisfactory means of gathering this information. Such surveys should be conducted in advance of the initial action by the legislature, and periodic resurveys may be needed as a basis for revision of junior-college laws.

State-wide Survey as a Basis for Initial Legislation. The justification for this step is obvious. While it is true that proposed legislative action in any given state will benefit from reference to similar action in other states, it is generally agreed that the recognized differences among states constitute a strong argument for the individual state survey as a basis for initial legislation establishing public junior colleges.

Simms stresses this point in his discussion of the legal status of public junior colleges. Following a report based on an exhaustive study of state laws, he presents an evaluation of existing legislation in the form of a series of recommendations. The following is his first recommendation: "Before any general legislation is passed, in those states not having such legislation, a survey of the state should be made to ascertain if there is a need for public junior colleges."[4]

Periodic Resurvey for Revision of Junior-College Laws. No state legislature is wise enough to pass laws which are good for all time. There should, therefore, be periodic studies to keep legislators and administrators well informed regarding desirable modifications.

For example, in 1955, California completed a state resurvey of

4. Charles Wesley Simms, *The Present Legal Status of the Public Junior College*, p. 97. Contribution to Education No. 403. Nashville, Tennessee: Bureau of Publications, George Peabody College for Teachers, 1949.

higher education. Recommendations are made to expand all public junior colleges and to establish several new ones.[5]

The Minimum Foundation Program studies in Florida brought forth legislation for the establishment of public junior-college districts by county or joint-county action and provided for state aid.[6]

Mississippi has had junior-college legislation since 1928. In 1950 House Bill No. 541 codified all previous enactments and laid the groundwork for increased state aid. One factor which brought this legislation into effect was background information from which emerged a state program for a balanced economy of agriculture and industry. The comprehensive character of this legislation may be seen in the statement of purposes:

An *Act* to establish junior colleges in the State of Mississippi, and to declare their purpose and function; and to provide for the personnel of the junior college commission, and to define their powers and duties; and to authorize the levy of taxes for the support and enlargement of junior colleges, and to provide for the distribution of revenue thereby derived; and to validate existing junior college districts; and to provide for the operation, management, maintenance, enlargement and improvement of junior colleges; and for other purposes.[7]

Moreover, up-to-date information tends to prevent the establishment of junior colleges in areas and under conditions which do not warrant their establishment. At one time, for example, Iowa had twenty-seven public junior colleges. Today there are sixteen. Practically all of those which have been discontinued were too small to operate with reasonable economy and efficiency. Now, Starrak and Hughes[8] have shown how a state system of public junior colleges could be financed on a district basis with free tuition. They could

5. Liaison Committee of the Regents of the University of California and the State Board of Education, "Draft of a Restudy of the Needs of California in Higher Education." Sacramento, California: State Board of Education, 1955 (mimeographed).

6. *Financing Florida's Elementary and Secondary Education: A Survey of the Minimum Foundation Program of State Aid to County School Systems.* Reported to the Select Committee on Education for Consideration of the Legislative Council. Tallahassee: Florida Legislative Reference Bureau, 1950.

7. Knox Broom, *History of Mississippi Public Junior Colleges: A State System of Public Junior Colleges, 1928–53.* Jackson, Mississippi: State Department of Education, 1954.

8. James A. Starrak and Raymond M. Hughes, *The Community College in the United States.* Ames, Iowa: Iowa State College Press, 1954.

be located within commuting distance of every potential student in the state and be large enough to provide for the variety of programs which Iowa needs now because of changing agricultural, industrial, and business conditions. If data of this sort had been fully considered initially in Iowa legislation, many pitfalls could have been avoided in establishing the early junior colleges. At the same time, this kind of information can help legislators realize what their obligations are to all the youth of the state rather than being limited to those who live in the more populous and wealthy sections.

Georgia is now engaged in a study to determine its responsibility for junior colleges. There are five state-supported junior colleges under the Georgia University System. In addition, there are two which are operated on a local community basis and one which is supported by a county. These latter three public junior colleges receive no aid from the state, an obvious inconsistency. There appears to be a growing conviction that the best interests of all youth of the state cannot be met short of the establishment of a state system of public junior colleges.

Recent events in Utah illustrate the need for continuing studies and up-to-date information. Late in 1953 the Utah legislature voted to discontinue support of junior colleges and to turn some of them back to the Church of Jesus Christ of the Latter Day Saints. Armed with the legal provision for a referendum, aroused citizens hastily secured more than twice the number of signatures to place the issue of public junior colleges before the people in the November elections of 1954. The citizens of Utah voted overwhelmingly to reverse the action of the legislature. During the election campaign, a great deal of publicity was given to the accomplishments of public junior colleges. In all probability legislators in Utah, and other states, will take less drastic actions in the future without having at hand sufficient evidence to support their actions.

Accrediting Agencies

There are two kinds of accrediting agencies: (a) the professional agencies which limit their concerns to particular professional-education programs in medicine, law, social work, and the like; and (b) the general accrediting associations which evaluate institutions as a whole. Professional associations operate at the national level, and the general accrediting associations at the regional level.

Junior colleges have not been strongly influenced by professional accrediting associations. Some junior colleges have music programs approved by the National Association of Schools of Music. At least one institution has a program in Medical Record Administration which has been approved by the American Medical Association. Other examples of programs approved by professional associations could doubtless be found. The major influence on junior colleges, so far as accrediting is concerned, has, however, been that of the regional accrediting agency.

THE BEGINNINGS OF ACCREDITING

The extralegal accrediting agency is a distinctly American phenomenon. It first appeared on the scene at about the end of the last century as a result of the recognition by educators of the serious shortcomings in institutions of higher education. The great need at that time was for the introduction of some measure of order into higher education. There was so little uniformity among the institutions presumably concerned with the higher learning that the Carnegie Foundation for the Advancement of Teaching, established in the early years of the twentieth century to provide pensions for retired members of college faculties, found that it had first to define a college before it could identify the persons eligible for college-faculty pensions. Accordingly, the early efforts of the accrediting associations were in the direction of encouraging uniformity among institutions through insisting on conformity to a set of definitions or standards.

At the time of the beginning of general institutional accrediting, the liberal-arts point of view was dominant in the higher educational scene since the great majority of institutions were of that type. Even the German-type university which was coming to occupy a place of great importance in America was itself built around a program in the liberal arts. Furthermore, universities were very much concerned with the quality of liberal-arts education—were, in fact, instrumental in starting the accrediting movement in an effort to insure adequate preparation for the students who entered their specialized and graduate programs as transfer students from the liberal-arts colleges. It is small wonder, then, that the standards used during the early years of the accrediting movement were based on the practices and characteristics of the liberal-arts college.

The first public junior college came into existence at just about the time the earliest regional accrediting associations were initiating their programs. As the junior-college movement gained momentum, it became amply clear that here was an institution which, if it were to meet the expectations which lay behind the creation of it, would bear little resemblance to the liberal-arts college. Nevertheless, the liberal-arts-college point of view was dominant in the accrediting process until fairly recent times. So long as this was true, it is fair to say that the influence of the accrediting agency on the developing junior college was more likely to be negative and restrictive than positive and constructive.

RECOGNITION OF INSTITUTIONAL UNIQUENESS

Regional accrediting associations have now come to recognize that the complex educational needs of American society can only be adequately met through the maintenance of a wide variety of institutions, and that institutional evaluation is valid only if made in terms of an institution's objectives and the situational characteristics that are peculiar to it. Adoption of this concept as a basis for accrediting activities has permitted the accrediting association to give attention to the particular characteristics of junior colleges as educational institutions of post-high-school grade and thus to make a positive contribution to the development of the public junior college in a number of ways. For one thing, the criteria used in evaluating institutions are sometimes useful guides to junior colleges concerned with strengthening their programs. Further, the institutional examinations made by persons skilled in techniques of evaluation and possessing a broad understanding of junior-college education are of value to institutions in identifying points of weakness and suggesting means for bringing about improvement.

It is probable, however, that so long as the accrediting association limits its efforts mainly to institutional evaluation by groups external to the institution it will fail to make its maximal contribution to educational progress, even though it approaches the problem of evaluation with due regard for the nature of the institution under consideration. Recently there has come an awareness of certain weaknesses, or perhaps incompleteness in this approach, not only as applied to junior colleges but to other kinds of institutions as well. In the first place, traditional accrediting lays primary emphasis on the separation of those institutions which have reached a minimum level of performance from those which have not. The concern is with status rather than growth. Once the level of accomplishment needed to gain accredited status has been reached, the major objective of the accrediting association has been attained. This objective—that is, the attainment of minimum status—though important, is too limited. The accrediting association should be concerned not only with minimum status but with institutional improvement regardless of the level of performance already reached by an institution.

It is also true that modern psychology has made us aware of the importance of widespread participation in the decision-making process on the part of those to be engaged in putting the decisions into practice. In educational institutions this means that improvements in the educational process are most likely to be real and enduring if they grow out of a study in which the staff of the institution has participated in response to a need which it feels. This kind of thinking has resulted in less reliance being placed on the use of the "expert"—one who has ready a stock of answers which are presumed to be widely applicable in a variety of situations. In place of the "expert," we now make use of the services of the "consultant"—one who does not pretend to know all the answers but who helps those operating in the situation to ask the right questions and who suggests techniques by which solutions appropriate to the particular situation might be found.

These observations suggest the means by which the accrediting association may best contribute to the sound development of the public junior college. First, it should approach the institution seeking accreditation with full regard for the fact that it should not be expected to be like other educational institutions. The junior college must be evaluated in terms of its success in discharging its particular responsibilities as it sees them. It is not enough, however, merely to develop standards specifically for junior colleges as distinguished from other kinds of institutions. Recognition must also be given to the fact that, in certain respects, every institution is unique. This is particularly true of the community-centered public junior college.

The accrediting agency should, then, in its evaluation procedures, encourage the institutions to play an active role in the process. The institution seeking accreditation should be expected to make a good case for itself rather than, as has been the typical procedure in the past, passively wait for the inspecting team—the "experts"—to tell the institution whether or not it is acceptable. Essential to the playing of this more active role is a carefully and imaginatively conducted institutional self-study as a part of the accrediting procedure.[9] Where this has been done, the results have not only been found useful in reaching a decision as to the accredited status of the college but also have been an extremely valuable experience for the members of the staff who carried on the study.

STIMULATING AND ASSISTING IN SELF-IMPROVEMENT

In its dealings with institutions which are accredited and whose status is not in doubt, as well as with those seeking accreditation, the accrediting agency should devise procedures designed to encourage improvement. As was mentioned earlier, its maximal contribution can only be made if it concerns itself with institutional improvement regardless of the level of educational excellence that has been attained; it should not confine its attention to those institutions that have not yet reached a minimum level of acceptability. This calls for an extension of the activities of the accrediting agency beyond that of approving institutions. It might, for example, encourage the initiation of research studies and assist in the investigation of the different aspects of the educational process, either by individual institutions or by groups of institutions desirous of attacking a common problem. In the rapidly expanding junior-college field a program of studies of this kind would do much to strengthen junior-college education through adding to the store of knowledge about education in this kind of institution, through the discovery of new techniques to be employed by individual institutions in seeking answers appropriate to the particular conditions under which they operate, and

9. Harry E. Jenkins and Jesse P. Bogue, "A Guide for the Self-evaluation of Junior Colleges." Washington: American Association of Junior Colleges, March, 1954.

through the stimulation which junior-college faculties would get from participation in this kind of activity.

In a program of this kind, the accrediting agency would serve as a catalyst—encouraging and stimulating through providing consultant service to junior colleges and other institutions seeking assistance, arranging conferences and workshops, serving as a clearinghouse of information, and providing the channels through which the junior colleges and other institutions could communicate. The transition from accrediting associations conceived of as agencies primarily concerned with policing to mutually helpful educational communities is still in the early stages, but that the movement is in the direction indicated here is clear. The accrediting association which draws together the wide variety of institutions comprising the American educational system with this objective of mutual benefit will play a role of great significance in the strengthening of American education in days ahead. In the councils of such an organization, the junior colleges must, of course, occupy the position which their importance in the educational system justifies.

Conclusion

The concept of legal and extralegal controls is, in its negative implication, inimical to a developing institution. The evolving policy of regional accrediting associations presents an illustration of the operation of this assertion. The early efforts to standardize and to suppress innovational developments have given way to an emphasis on institutional growth and improvement. Thus, the concept of control in its repressive interpretation has been replaced by a concept of judicious encouragement of institutional efforts to meet more effectively the educational needs which are peculiar to their respective constituencies.

Legal control, however, may be viewed in a different sense from absolute repression. It may be the means by which uninformed but enthusiastic promoters will be prevented from taking steps consistent with their current ardor but destined in the long run to prove unsuccessful. In this sense, it is not the junior college which is repressed but the activity of junior-college promoters who are insufficiently informed to plan well for future success.

Moreover, legal control in still another sense serves to eliminate the uncertainties which plague the life of a public institution which has no legal base. In this instance, the control applies to the opponents of the institution whose major ambition is to destroy it.

It should be realized, however, that with both legal and extralegal influences, stagnation results from excessive prescription. A desire to avoid this extreme has led both legal and extralegal agencies to adopt procedures allowing for greater flexibility. In the field of legal influences this has been accomplished through the assignment to lay educational boards of greater responsibility for exercising regulatory activity. Among the extralegal agencies, the desired end has been attained through greater emphasis on co-operative ventures in institutional improvement.

The junior college must be kept dynamic if it is to serve satisfactorily its role as a community educational agency. Policies of legal and extralegal control can and must evolve in a manner consistent with the needed adaptability.

CHAPTER XIII

Financing Public Junior College Operation

LELAND L. MEDSKER

Introduction

How much does it cost? How can we pay for it? These are the questions asked daily by literally thousands of American families about the goods or services they desire or must have. They are asked by the average high-school graduate as he contemplates his further education. They are asked by the older worker or housewife who sees the need for returning to school for one of many possible reasons. They are asked by the public about the services considered desirable for the welfare of all.

The preceding chapters have presented the case for the public junior college—its role in the American system of free schools, the types and numbers of students it serves, and its program. Implicit in all the chapters is the usefulness of the junior college as an institution in today's social and economic order and its apparent potentiality for greater usefulness in the decades ahead.

Now we must consider the question of the cost of public junior colleges, for education, like all public services, has an invoice figure which must be billed to someone. How great that cost figure may be and who is to pay the bill is the subject of this chapter. Patience and serious study are needed in the consideration of the subject. There are so many problems involved in the financing of public junior colleges that there is danger either of oversimplification of proposals or of becoming discouraged about the prospects for a logical solution. Because school plant facilities of public junior colleges are so frequently provided in conjunction with local public high schools, the ensuing discussion of financial problems deals with operational costs only.

Problems in Financing Junior Colleges

Although many problems grow naturally out of the fact that there never seems to be enough money to carry on adequately all the functions of government, the problems involved in the financing of junior colleges seem to be unusually complicated. The first step, then, will be to consider some situations with respect to the junior college which result in a lack of clarity and definiteness in planning its financial program. Three such situations are considered here.

THE PLACE OF THE JUNIOR COLLEGE IN AMERICAN EDUCATION

As has been indicated in earlier chapters, the public junior college is not only relatively new in American education but it has also developed in different ways in different parts of the country. In some states it is regarded as a phase of higher education under the general supervision of some type of board for higher education. In other states all or part of the existing junior colleges are organized as state institutions, with most or all of their support coming directly from the state government.

Such circumstances are not only confusing to legislative bodies but they also result in differences of practice in the support of junior colleges in the various states. The high schools and four-year colleges have been in existence for many decades, and organizational patterns for them are well established. Universally the high school comes under a local school district and is supported either by local tax levies or by a combination of local funds and state aid. The public senior college generally receives its major support from state legislative appropriations. There is little wonder that the financing of public junior colleges is in a state of confusion, since, as institutions, these colleges do not conform to the established patterns of either the institutions above them or those below them. The lawmakers in many instances are prone to regard the junior college as a stepchild, with a result that there is not the same sharing of financial responsibility for them that there is for other divisions of public education.

There is also much variation and confusion regarding the junior college at the local level. In Oklahoma, the several state junior colleges are completely supported by the state, while the junior colleges maintained by local high-school districts are operated without state aid. In some states junior colleges may be maintained by unified districts, separate high-school districts, or separate junior-college districts. This tends to cause bewilderment on the part of the public regarding the junior college, thus militating against proposals of more appropriate measures for financial support.

This is by way of saying that the newness of the junior college, its lack of tradition, its in-between characteristics—all combine to prevent it from being fully understood by the lay public. In this situation it is inevitable that financial patterns will not be uniform.

RAPID GROWTH OF THE JUNIOR COLLEGE

When it is remembered that the public junior college has developed within a period of slightly more than fifty years and that its growth, both in number of institutions and in individuals served, is as variable as has been indicated by reports presented in previous chapters, it can be understood that those communities and states which have embarked on junior-college programs have not only been hampered by lack of tradition but also have had to find ways of providing for an institution that was growing very rapidly. When the number of students to be served by 1960 and beyond is considered, it is certain that new and unprecedented financial problems will arise.

MULTIPLE RESPONSIBILITIES OF THE JUNIOR COLLEGE

Previous chapters have outlined the various and extensive educational services to different groups of people provided by the junior college. It has been noted that the colleges must serve those who are expecting to transfer to higher institutions and also offer a vocational program for those who do not expect to transfer to higher institutions. Moreover, for both groups, it must provide rich experiences and activities contributing to general education. It is obvious that the service load entailed by these responsibilities is increased by the fact that counseling and guidance in the junior college are considered highly important and that community services of all kinds, including adult-education programs, seem properly to be junior-college functions. All these give the junior college an apparent diversity of function which not only tends to make its operational procedures expensive but raises doubts in people's minds as to how far any public institution can go in "being all things to all people."

The last item alone, namely, the responsibility of the junior college for extending services to older youth and adults, is one which is much discussed and debated. There are few people in any community who would not recognize the importance of junior-college services, and generally they would concede that any available public junior college, no matter how organized, is an appropriate agency to render such service. The issue arises when the community needs to decide how the service should be financed. If the institution happens to be tuition free and is entirely supported out of either local or state taxes or by some combination of these, there will be those who will conclude that the operating expenses of the institution should be entirely financed out of receipts from tuition. There will be others who will contend that it is permissible for such services to be financed out of local funds, but that state funds should not be used for such purposes.

The Problem of Financing All Public Education

It is, of course, impossible to consider the matter of financing public junior colleges outside the context of the nation's promise of financial support for *all* public education. In these United States we have, since early days, assumed that education is primarily a function of the state. And while private means of education have contributed significantly to our culture and to progress in the methods of education, as a nation we have continued to increase markedly the amount spent out of public funds for the education of the populace from kindergarten through college.

Now we must look to the future. The story of projected college enrolment as presented in chapter ii points to increased expenditures for public education even if we do nothing more than maintain present standards. If we desire to improve the educational program, greater financial support must be provided.

Beardsley Ruml[1] has suggested that we bring up the expenditure for each child in the lower half of our public school budgets to the level of the average for the nation. He has estimated the cost of meeting this standard for the number of children that will be of school age by 1960 at $3,000,000,000 more than we are spending today.

1. Beardsley Ruml, "Financing the Public Schools," an address at the Fifth Annual Dinner of the National Citizens Commission for the Public Schools, San Francisco, California, March 19, 1954.

This, he believes, will be possible in light of increased national production.

The National Citizens Commission for the Public Schools explains that the amount of money to be spent on educational opportunities of appropriate quality for children of school age in the next decade will depend upon three principal factors:

1. The increase in the number of school-age children.
2. The increase in productivity of the United States economy.
3. The amount of educational expenditures that will be considered appropriate for each child of school age.[2]

On the basis of estimates of increases in school population and in national income and production, the Commission expresses the view that there will be ample opportunity for the American people to provide for continuing improvement in the nation's educational services. The following explanation is given:

The rise in public education expenditures of $5 to $10 billion by 1965 will occur when the level of national productivity is rising [from $365 billion in 1953] to $525 billion a year. The increased costs of education will not be impracticably large, then, when projected against the increased level of gross national productivity. A substantial increase in expenditures for education will be possible without being a burden to the economy, as follows:

1. On the basis of our projections stated above, the increase in the gross national product between 1953 and 1965 will be $160 billion.
2. The increase in public expenditures for education can be estimated at $5 to $10 billion.
3. The increase for public education will then be 3 to 6 per cent of the increase in productivity.

As public education expenditures rise and the number of children increase, the percentage of gross national product used for public education purposes will increase slightly—from 2.4 per cent in 1954 to between 2.6 per cent and 3.6 per cent by 1965. This increase will not interfere with other types of expenditures for goods and services required by our expanded population, nor will it affect significantly public expenditures for other services such as hospitals and highways.[3]

2. *Financing Public Education in the Decade Ahead*, p. 1. New York: National Citizens Commission for the Public Schools (2 West Forty-fifth St.), 1954.
3. *Ibid*, pp. 5–6.

A committee of the National Conference of Professors of Educational Administration recently pointed out that thorough study of the means of meeting the problem of financing the public school system of our nation involves some conclusions or assumptions with respect to the rights of citizens to liberal educational opportunities and the obligations of the government to provide such opportunities. This committee's reckoning of the outcome of an attempt to match the nationwide demand for educational advantages with the requisite tax exactions upon the material resources of the country and its people was summarized in the following statement:

If the problem of public school financing were merely a matter of ascertaining the total money needed and determining the financial ability of the nation to provide for school needs, the treatment of the subject could be relatively brief. At the midpoint of the twentieth century the people of the United States are providing approximately $5,000,000,000 annually for the support of the public schools—a sum which is less than 3 per cent of their income. It is generally recognized that the people could double their expenditures for the public schools without unfavorably affecting the economy of the country. However, as implied above, the problem is not that simple. There are numerous complications and many related issues which must be considered.[4]

There is little need to belabor the point that the American public must think seriously about its obligation to its public schools in the next decade. Junior colleges that are a part of American public education must accept a share of the responsibility that all education will have to meet in getting the bill paid. The fact that many junior colleges are local institutions and may share in local tax revenues makes them more likely to be singled out by critics as competitors for the money that would otherwise be used for elementary- and high-school instruction. On the other hand, they may be just as vulnerable for being regarded as competitors of state-supported colleges and universities. Those who wish to provide adequate financing of junior colleges will have to be unceasing in their efforts to inspire public confidence in the services of such colleges to the community.

In general, there are two primary sources of revenue for the support of public education: (*a*) the levy made by a local district, and (*b*) the aid given by the state to local districts or to institutions main-

4. National Conference of Professors of Educational Administration, *Problems and Issues in Public School Finance*, p. 1. New York: Bureau of Publications, Teachers College, Columbia University, 1952.

tained by the state. Other revenues include tuition receipts, subsidies for specialized programs often coming from the federal government through the state, and, in the case of local districts, payments made by one school district to another for the cost of instruction of non-resident students. But for the most part, the local school district or the state institution must depend upon the revenues from local taxes on real and personal property or upon these resources and state funds arising out of revenues and taxes at the state level.

The local school district, which may maintain an elementary school, a high school, and a junior college, raises its local money by a given tax rate on the assessed valuation of the district. This rate may be restricted by law to a "legal maximum rate," above which the governing board of the district may not go without a majority vote of the people of the district.

In many states the local revenues may be supplemented by state aid given either on a "flat-grant" basis in an equal amount for every student (usually on some basis of equivalent full-time or average-daily-attendance formula) and/or on an equalization basis whereby the state guarantees a stated amount of revenue per student enrolled in any district in the state. This basis of distributing state aid to local school districts is employed in recognition of the fact that the wealth behind each student varies greatly from district to district and that each child within the state is entitled to at least a minimum program. Formulas for such programs may be complicated, although in general they first set a minimum amount per student that should be spent and then require each district to impose at least a minimum tax rate on its assessed valuation which, if not sufficient to obtain the considered minimum, is supplemented by the state in order to bring revenues up to the desired goal.

Colvert has presented an analysis of the allocations of state aid to public junior colleges of the fourteen states which were providing such aid in 1951–52. The situation at that time was summarized in a brief introduction to the report on the pertinent legislation in those states.

The laws covering the administration of state aid to junior colleges are quite varied in the fourteen states in which such aid is provided. California and Florida have minimum foundation programs, complicated in the case of Florida by an elaborate formula for arriving at state aid based on an economic index. California, Colorado, and Florida have equalization features and Mississippi provides a sort of equalization in giving each college a fixed amount ($10,000) before distributing per capita aid.

With few exceptions state aid is based on some sort of per capita formula. Arizona pays operating cost on another basis. New York State has a novel feature in supplying one-half of the capital cost and one-third of the operating cost if these amounts are matched by the local sponsor. Idaho has an unusual sort of state aid in the form of county appropriations from the Liquor Control Act Fund.[5]

Other studies have dealt with the income patterns of junior colleges operating under the authority of a state agency in comparison with those under the management of municipalities, including school districts. One report shows that state junior colleges have depended almost entirely on state funds and student fees for their income. In 1934, the first year in which comparable records could be assembled, the state junior colleges received 67.8 per cent of their income from state governments. In 1950 state funds provided 64.7 per cent of the total income of such institutions. There was no disturbing deviation from this pattern in the intervening years.[6]

The income pattern of local public junior colleges during the same period of years is indicated by the following excerpt from the report of the same investigation.

Local public junior colleges depend for their support primarily on local funds, state funds, and student fees. In 1934, the first year for which relatively complete data are available, localities supplied 84.3 per cent of the income of this category of institutions. By 1948 the importance of local funds had dropped to 41.4 per cent; in 1950 it increased to 48.8 per cent. State funds supplied 22.4 per cent of income in 1938, 27.9 per cent in 1942, 15.3 per cent in 1946, then increased to 21.6 in 1948 and 25.5 per cent in 1950.

Student fees supplied 13.2 per cent in 1934, rose to a high of 14.2 per cent in 1938 and dropped to a low of 8.9 per cent in 1950. Federal payments for veterans' fees supplied 7 per cent of the income in 1946, 23 per cent in 1948, and 13.5 in 1950.[7]

5. C. C. Colvert, *Legally Prescribed Methods for Allocation of State Aid to Public Junior Colleges*. Research Bulletin of the American Association of Junior Colleges, III (June, 1952), 1.

6. *Higher Education in the Forty-eight States*, pp. 107–8. Chicago: Council of State Governments (1313 East Sixtieth St.), 1952.

7. *Ibid*, p. 110.

Present Practice in Financing Junior Colleges

Believing that those concerned about the public junior college would be interested in knowing how such institutions are currently financed in the different states, the author undertook a survey of present practices. At the same time he sought the opinions of the chief state school officers on matters pertaining to the financing of such institutions. Two instruments were sent to the chief state school officer in each state—one form (a simple one-page opinionnaire) to be filled out by that officer and the other (a two-page questionnaire) to be completed by a person in the state department of public instruction who would be able to supply basic facts about junior colleges in the state. There are sixteen states in which there are no public junior colleges. All but two of the remaining states responded, and all but three of those responding completed both of the instruments submitted. Information regarding tuition charges, tax rates, and state aid to local school districts is here summarized as reported for the school year of 1954–55.

1. To what extent do public junior colleges charge tuition?

It has been noted that sixteen states do not have any public junior colleges. Of the twenty-nine states responding to this question, twenty reported a tuition charge in all public junior colleges in the state, four reported a tuition charge in some but not in all of them, and five reported a tuition-free situation throughout the state.

2. What is the tuition rate for resident students in public junior colleges?

While information received on this question was somewhat less complete than on others, fifteen states reported tuition among junior colleges as shown in the accompanying tabulation.

According to the data presented in Table 1, the reports from five of the fifteen states indicate that the tuition charges are uniform in all institutions of junior-college grade operated under public jurisdiction within the state. Among these five states, the annual charge for tuition varies from $50 to $180. Ten states reported variable rates among the institutions of the state, the amount of the tuition varying from $30 to $105 in the state in which the lowest rates were reported and from $200 to $300 in the state where the highest rates prevail.

3. What is the maximum local tax rate for public junior colleges?

One question in the inquiry form sought to determine the legal maximum levy for the support of those junior colleges for which part of the cost is borne by the local district. As would be expected, the range reported was so great that no common pattern could be observed. For example, Illinois has established a maximum tax rate of 17.5 cents for operation expenses, while the California rate is twice as much. Five states reported no legal maximum, the supposition being that a local governing board may establish whatever tax rate is

TABLE 1

COMPARATIVE RATES OF TUITION IN
PUBLIC JUNIOR COLLEGES
OF FIFTEEN STATES

State	Annual Resident Tuition
1	$114
2	$100 to $150
3	$50
4	$90 to $180
5	$9 per semester hour
6	None to $90
7	$30 to $105
8	$45
9	Less than $100
10	$45 to $60
11	$200 to $300
12	Up to $200
13	$180
14	$50 to $150
15	$110 to $140

needed and feasible. The lowest rate reported was two mills. Several reported five or six mills.

Obviously, a reported maximum rate is not in itself indicative of sufficiency or a lack thereof, since there are other factors to be considered. In the first place, there is the possibility of the local community voting to exceed the maximum rate, although the states reporting indicated this to be the exception rather than the rule. More important factors are the amount of state aid, the richness of the junior-college program, the enrolment, and the taxable wealth of the district.

While it cannot be expected that any status survey of legal rates would set an example or pattern, the range does indicate the necessity for thorough consideration of the rate that can or should be levied.

4. *To what extent and on what basis is state aid given junior colleges?*

Nineteen states reported that state aid is given public junior colleges. In three of these states—Utah, Georgia, and Louisiana—all the junior colleges are supported entirely by the state. The junior colleges in Georgia and Louisiana are integral parts of the university system. In Oklahoma, state aid is limited to the fully state-supported junior colleges and is not extended to the six municipal junior colleges maintained by local communities. In the remaining fourteen states the aid granted by the state supplements the local support. The states thus financed are: Arizona, California, Colorado, Florida, Iowa, Michigan, Mississippi, Missouri, New Jersey, Montana, Indiana, Texas, Maryland, and Washington.

There is great variation among the states in both the amount of state aid given the public junior colleges and the method used in determining the amount a given institution would receive. Likewise, there is little consistency among the states relative to the conditions of eligibility for state aid placed upon junior colleges with reference to the type of program to be offered or the qualifications of the students to be enrolled. The following table is designed to show the general pattern of aid provided by the various states. The information as reported by the respondents to our inquiry is shown in condensed form with details of operation omitted.

While a report of dollars spent by states on junior-college aid is not in itself significant since the amount spent depends in part on the magnitude of the state program, it is interesting to note the amount reported by certain states as having been apportioned for junior-college purposes in a recent year. In 1954–55, California leads the list with an apportionment for junior colleges of $12,381,777. New York State followed with a reported expenditure of $6,500,000. Texas reported $2,610,000, Michigan $1,485,000, Utah $939,400, Georgia $512,640, Colorado $231,912, and the other states lesser amounts.

An interesting question is raised concerning the percentage that a given state's support of its public junior-college program is to the total support of all higher education in the state. In attempting to accumulate such information, insufficient data were received to indicate a general pattern. However, the information from some of the states gives a general idea of the relative amount of state money going for junior-college purposes. California, New York, and Utah each

TABLE 2

BASES OF STATE AID ALLOCATIONS TO PUBLIC JUNIOR COLLEGES, BY STATES

State	Basis for Aid	Limitations Imposed	Equalization Factor if Any
Arizona	Flat appropriation for each college.	None.	None.
California	Flat grant of $120 per unit of A.D.A.	None, except students must be high-school graduates or 18 years of age.	When needed to supplement required district taxes so that there is insured $380 per student. (Students in "classes for adults" not counted for equalization purposes.)
Colorado	Flat grant of $900 for each seven equivalent full-time students.	None.	None.
Florida	One unit of aid for each 12 students in A.D.A.	None.	A formula to adjust differences in tax-paying abilities among counties.
Georgia	Special appropriation (part of University system).	None.	None.
Illinois	Flat grant of $100 for each equivalent full-time student in attendance.	None.	None.
Indiana	Special appropriation (one college only).	None.	None.
Iowa	25 cents per day for each student.	Must be college work. Student to be counted must carry 12 or more hours of college work.	None.
Louisiana	Appropriation (one junior college only, and it a part of university system).	None.	None.
Maryland	$150 per student.	Must be matriculated for A.A. degree.	None.
Michigan	Annual appropriation for junior-college aid distributed on basis of full-time equated students in all junior colleges (officially called community colleges).	Limit of $130 for each full-time student.	None.

TABLE 2—*Continued*

State	Basis for Aid	Limitations Imposed	Equalization Factor if Any
Missis-sippi	Lump sum appropriation for all junior colleges with State Board disbursing funds to each college on basis of number of full-time students in attendance on last day of sixth week in fall semester.	Student must be "full-time academic day students." Only Mississippi students counted.	Each junior college receives $10,000. Remainder is distributed as indicated.
Missouri	Flat grant of 1.3 cents per day per student in A.D.A. plus $100 per year per teacher, supervisor, and administrator devoting more than one-half time.	20-year-age-limit courses approved by State Board of Education.	None.
Montana	By foundation program only. If 10-mill county limit not enough for high-school and junior-college foundation program, state contributes difference.	None.	See first column.
New York	One-half the amount of capital costs and one-third of the amount of operating costs.	Such maximum limitations as may be prescribed by state university trustees.	None.
Oklahoma	Seven state junior colleges supported entirely by state through special appropriation. No financial aid to six municipal junior colleges.	None.	None.
Texas	Over-all state appropriation with distribution on per capita basis as follows: $230 for first 250 equivalent full-time students enrolled (15 semester hours) and $189 for all over first 250.	Aid only on first 64 semester hours. Students must be enrolled in courses comparable to those in 4-year state-supported institutions.	None.
Utah	Special appropriation.	None.	None.
Washing-ton	Approximately 88 cents per day per full-time student from general fund with deficiencies from Equalization Fund. In addition, all districts maintaining junior colleges receive same teacher-unit support for instructors as do districts for elementary and high schools. Amount of A.D.A. 1953–54 = $283.70 per unit.	None.	If required 14-mill limit does not equal 40 cents per A.D.A., remainder comes from Equalization Fund.

report that for a given year 14 per cent of the money spent for higher education was for junior-college purposes. From this percentage comes a graduation downward to 9 per cent for Mississippi, 4.4 per cent for Texas, 3.9 per cent for Georgia, 3.8 per cent for Michigan, to less than .2 of 1 per cent for Missouri.

Another significant question is the extent to which the state aid to public junior colleges in the various states covers the cost of operation of those colleges. Some information on this point was revealed in the survey by asking for an approximation of the percentage that the state aid was of the cost of operation for the last school year. While data were readily available in only a few of the states, the following states did report these percentages: Colorado, 10 to 15 per cent; Iowa, 20 per cent; Michigan, 29 per cent; Mississippi, 25 per cent; Texas, 23 per cent; and Washington, 52 per cent. New York provides state support in an amount not to exceed one-third of the operating costs of the college. From this limited sample, it may be observed that regardless of state aid, a high percentage of the cost of operating a junior-college program is presently borne at the community level either by local taxes or tuition.

Twenty states reported that their junior colleges carried on extended-day and/or adult-education programs. In response to the question, "In what respect, if at all, does the financing of such a program differ from that for the regular program?" only five states reported little or no difference. Those states are California, Colorado, Florida, Illinois, and Utah. Two states, Michigan and New York, declare options for their junior colleges so that the extended-day program may come either under regular financing or special financing of adult-education programs. The other states reported differences in the financing of such programs, such differences being usually a lack of state aid and/or a heavier tuition charge—in some cases tuition bearing the total cost of operating the program.

What Lies Ahead in the Financing of Junior Colleges?

The survey of present practices reviewed in the preceding pages is at least a springboard for further consideration of what may or should be the basis of financing public junior colleges in the future. Also in projecting probable junior-college financial situations, it has been considered desirable to secure the opinion of the chief state school officer in each state concerning the future of the junior college and how it should be financed. Accordingly, one of the inquiry forms referred to previously asked certain questions of the chief administrators. One question sought to determine the administrator's opinion concerning the probable place of the junior college in caring for the increase in college students in the years ahead. A second question specifically asked for an opinion of how the public junior college should be financed. It was felt that while the second question was patently germane to the topic, the first was also extremely important since, if junior colleges are to hold either the same relative position or if they are to serve an even greater portion of the college group, there are definite implications for finance.

Sixteen chief administrators reported that, in their belief, the junior college will serve an *increasing* percentage of college-age youth. Eleven said that the percentage served would, in their opinion, remain the same.

Seventeen of the administrators said that in order either to serve the same percentage or a greater percentage of college youth, new junior colleges would need to be established. Seven said no new ones would be needed. When asked whether or not new state legislation would be necessary for the establishment of new public junior colleges, eleven administrators said such legislation would be essential, five said it would be desirable, and nine said it would be unnecessary.

As to how public junior colleges *should* be financed, regardless of the current practice or whether or not there are now public junior colleges in the state, the officers reporting revealed some common opinions. Twenty-seven of them said that such institutions should be financed by a combination of state and local effort. No one answering this part of the query said that the support should be entirely by local district taxes or entirely by state funds. Four respondents did, however, indicate that while in their belief there should be joint effort of the state and local community, there still should be a tuition charge for part of the support. On the other hand, nine of the officers indicated their belief that a public junior college should be tuition-free. Some did not express themselves on the matter of tuition.

Some General Conclusions

While conclusions are always hazardous, there are circumstances under which they seem warranted—not so much as undeniable truths but as assumptions based on evidence that can serve as guideposts to those concerned. The following such conclusions result in part from the studies mentioned in preceding paragraphs and in part from some firsthand information on the part of the author arising out of experience with junior-college programs in different sections of the country.

1. *There is a strong probability that no single pattern of financing junior colleges will emerge.*

If the survey of present practices revealed any one definite conclusion, it is to the effect that to date no two states follow the same pattern in the financing of their public junior colleges. Even at the local level there exist tremendous differences, and in those states where state aid is given, an even greater variety in practices is observed. This, of course, is not surprising since public education itself has long been recognized as a function of the state, and each of our forty-eight states tends to shape its own pattern in providing support for its common schools and its colleges. By the same token there is great variety in not only the amount spent on public education among the various states but also on the degree of *effort* in terms of ability in the support of education.

What is perhaps even greater reason for this variation is that public junior colleges in most states are associated closely with the common schools of the states. True, there is often the debate as to whether or not junior colleges are "secondary" or "higher" institutions. This argument incidentally is perhaps more fictitious than real, due to the fact that while such institutions often are units of local public school systems and are closely associated with the community, they still perform many of the functions of "higher" education. The situation then tends to be somewhat of an anomaly, and, for purposes of considering how best to finance junior-college programs, the argument may well be abated. Nevertheless, so long as junior colleges are units of local school systems, it can be expected that even in the matter of local support, there will exist rather sharp differences among them.

The question of predicting how the national pattern of supporting junior colleges may unfold would perhaps be easier if we were to consider only the states in which junior colleges *now* exist. However, if it can be anticipated that other states, in an attempt to provide greater opportunities for the increasing number of youth, may consider and establish junior colleges as one method of providing such opportunities, new and different possibilities of financing patterns may appear in those states.

The conclusion that no single pattern likely will emerge is perhaps most important for individuals, communities, or states that look forward to establishing new junior-college programs or improving those now in existence, and its greatest implication perhaps is that, since no entirely ideal arrangement has yet been effected, there exists the opportunity for experiment and initiative to work out the most effective plans.

2. State participation in financing junior colleges is to be desired.

As reported in the preceding section, the chief state school officers are fairly unanimous in their opinion that the ideal method of financing is by combinations of state and local effort. It is interesting to note the extent to which development of junior-college programs in the various states has tended to be greatest in those states which provide for rather generous state aid. This development is reflected in the numbers of both the institutions and the students served and is true in such states as California, Texas, Washington, and more recently Mississippi and New York. While Illinois ranks third in the number of junior-college students enrolled, the enrolment there is due to the fact that the city of Chicago has been willing to carry the program of the City Junior College until 1955 without state aid. However, in the remainder of the state there has not developed the large effective junior-college programs in communities that would seem to require them.

Aside from the consideration of opinion and apparent correlation of state aid and junior-college development, there is the plain theoretical consideration that unless the state's help is somewhat material, the growth and development of the junior-college movement cannot expect to make any rapid progress. Despite the fact that local control and partial local support for a junior-college program may be desirable, its dual nature and its responsibility for serving in the realm of higher education makes state support important for two reasons: (*a*) Many local communities cannot afford the entire burden on top of the strain in caring for elementary- and high-school students, and (*b*) it seems just as fair for the state to assist in the support of a segment of higher education carried on by junior colleges as for it to support the same kind of education in four-year colleges or state universities.

In considering state support, there arises the question as to what form it should take. As was noted in the survey of present practices, there are those states which organize junior colleges on a "state basis," such colleges tending to serve a region with full support by the state. These institutions may or may not be a part of the over-all university or higher education system of the state. The state of Mississippi, as was noted, has another plan where its colleges are in part local and in part regional and where there is fairly generous state support for each institution. The majority of the states, however, give state aid on the basis of some kind of flat grant, and some of them supplement such a grant when necessary by an equalization plan so that communities will, in general, be guaranteed minimum programs.

It is not for the author to render an opinion as to which method of state support is desirable, for to do so would take careful study over a period of time concerning many factors to be found in the different states. Furthermore, it has been conceded that it is best for each state to work out its own solution. Since, however, so many of the states follow the plan of authorizing both local and state support, it may be concluded that the majority favor this method even though in many of the states, the amount of money appropriated by the state government appears to be inadequate.

3. *Studies are needed to guide the future course of action.*

A sampling of practices and problems in those states that have junior colleges and the tendency toward complacency in some of the states that do not have them lead to the conclusion that more information is needed in most of the states on such areas as that of junior-college costs, comparative costs with other types of institutions, potential enrolment, and related problems. Adequate data on over-all unit costs in junior colleges are difficult to obtain. Even more rare is information about the cost of component parts of junior-college education. Reliable information on the costs of educating junior-college students as compared with lower-division students in four-year colleges is seldom available. Not all states have estimated enrolment in their post-high-school institutions for the next decade, nor have they studied carefully the facilities that will be needed to care for the load of students. Likewise, there should be studies that would continue those made by Koos a few years ago on the social effects of a tuition charge.[8]

There are states that have made considerable progress in some such studies. To cite California once more, there can be reported the action taken by the legislature in 1953 authorizing a complete re-study of the needs for higher education in the state. This study has been completed and provides invaluable data on many of the points referred to in the preceding paragraphs and undoubtedly will be used as a basis of legislation having to do with the financing of all institutions engaged in higher education in the state.

It is not inconceivable that the problem of how best to provide opportunities for at least the first two years of education beyond high school will become so acute that federal agencies may be encouraged to study the problem and its financial aspects from a national point of view, out of which may come specific recommendations for the several states.

4. Society has a stake in the junior college.

One look ahead to the wave of college enrolment leads at once to the question as to how collegiate educational opportunities are to be provided for the numbers seeking them. Again, the answer may not be the same in all the states, but in many, particularly in the thickly populated ones, a strong case may be made for the public junior college whereby students may live at home, thus eliminating the cost to society of providing housing and the cost of students' living therein while attending college away from home, and where the more simple facilities needed for lower-division work may be separated from the more elaborate ones required for upper-division and graduate work.

8. Leonard V. Koos, "How To Democratize the Junior College Level," *School Review*, LII (May, 1944), 271–84.

Assuming that this hypothesis is shown to be correct by those who continue to study it, the planning within most states should define the place of the junior college in the over-all state program and provide the necessary encouragement to local communities to initiate or to further develop their own community colleges. And though the cost may seem high, it is to be remembered that another choice may mean the denial of opportunities to worthy youth.

In the final analysis there is a possibility that as a nation we could be penny-wise and pound-foolish concerning our educational program beyond high school. For years we have realized that the more education our people possess, the higher the standard of living and the level of productivity and consumption. Twice the United States Chamber of Commerce has confirmed this fact, not just for the United States but for other nations as well. To ignore it in the years ahead when thousands more than ever before will be graduated from the high schools of the country is not the step America should take. To recognize it may well have implications for the public junior-college movement and for adequate means of financing a sound junior-college program.

SECTION IV

MOVING AHEAD

CHAPTER XIV

Establishing a Junior College

ELBERT K. FRETWELL, JR.

How Junior Colleges Have Been Established

ORANGE COUNTY, NEW YORK, COMMUNITY COLLEGE

Middletown, New York, needed a college. The secretary of the chamber of commerce, officials of the city school system, and a local photographer-artist recently returned from military service knew this and were concerned. Their county was located only sixty-five miles from one of the world's great metropolitan centers, yet in proportion to population fewer young men and women there continued their formal education past high school than in any other county of the state. Institutions of higher education were located in many parts of this relatively wealthy state, yet were failing to serve the great majority of youth of the Middletown area. What to do?

This situation, furthermore, had existed for some time, but the return of World War II veterans accentuated the need for expanded services to the young people of the community. Ex-G.I.'s who considered going away to college found it difficult to gain entrance because of crowded conditions. Those seeking employment at home frequently found they needed more training to qualify for the jobs they were seeking.

Sparked by one man's first-hand knowledge of the problems and another's ability at organizing, an informal group came into existence calling itself the Committee on Higher Education. Developing out of a meeting of the Middletown board of education, the committee collected information from the city superintendent of schools on capable high-school graduates not able to go away to college. In a matter of weeks, a report on the needs of young people of the area was on the desk of the governor at the state capital. Attached documentation from a recent polling of thirteen high schools in the county indicated that 183 high-school Seniors—slightly over 13 per cent of the upper half of each graduating class—wished to attend a local college in Middletown, should one be organized.

"Knowing your stand for educational improvement and our need for facilities," wrote the chamber of commerce secretary to the governor in his covering letter, "we make this appeal to you at this time." A few months later Freshman-level courses were offered in Middletown on an interim basis. A collegiate center under a somewhat unusual four-way arrangement made this possible. Space was provided by the city high school during late afternoon and evening hours. Legal authority and general supervision were handled by the state. Instruction was offered on a contract basis by staff provided by an existing private university in the near-by metropolitan area. Costs were covered largely by tuition collected from students—almost entirely ex-servicemen financed through Federal veterans' benefits.

Middletown's citizens were pleased with these interim arrangements but realized the necessity of banding together to organize a *permanent* junior college with its own regular staff, plant, local control, and courses of study suited both to students who would complete a Bachelor's degree elsewhere after two years in the local college and to those who would enter the county employment market immediately. As an editorial in the local paper pointed out, "Only when a definite plan is mapped out showing that Middletown not only needs but is able to provide for a junior college will the powers-that-be at the state capital consider the city as a site." So, in brief, the continuing Committee on Higher Education found itself faced with such problems as these:

1. How could enough funds be raised locally to provide half the capital outlay which the state would then match, as provided in state law, for the establishment of a community college?
2. Where should such a college be located, and to what extent should proposed gifts of real estate influence the decision?
3. How could the use of local initiative and citizen groups be co-ordinated with the need for expert educational and legal advice from state authorities?
4. Would the county board of supervisors, a permanent and legally constituted group, agree to sponsor the college, even though it would involve expenditure of tax funds for one-third of the college's oper-

ating expenses? (State law provided another third from state sources, with the final third coming as tuition from students or their families.)

5. Assuming all of the above were worked out, would it be possible to secure an administrative and teaching staff, develop a curriculum, and build or renovate appropriate buildings in order to take over when the temporary collegiate center closed?

Almost immediately the Committee on Higher Education expanded its membership to include interested citizens from various occupations in all parts of the county. Liaison was established with the specialist for two-year colleges at the state university. Offers for various sites were considered. Finally the ideal location appeared to be an eighteen-acre estate in Middletown which included a forty-room, four-story residence of substantial and attractive stone construction, with various outbuildings, among them a large concrete barn-garage. The owner was willing to give the estate to the college, but there was the complication that, upon her death, the property was to go to a local hospital, as per the terms of her late husband's will.

After considerable discussion officials of the hospital agreed to relinquish claim to the property if the friends of the proposed community college would sponsor a fund-raising drive to enable the hospital to pay off its indebtedness, a sum approximating $60,000. This arrangement proved to be a real bargain for the county, inasmuch as state officials later applied the figure of $242,000 as appraised "educational value" of the property. The fact that the state would match this amount with an identical sum, to be used for plant renovation, was good news to the backers of the college.

The next step was to secure the official support of the thirty-seven-member board of county supervisors. The idea of sponsoring a college was new to most members of this group, but as a result of effective promotion by members of the Committee on Higher Education, officers of the local Grange, and parents of potential students, the college idea gained favor. A cloud of pessimism settled briefly in the Middletown area as a daily paper in the county's other major city predicted that an "economy-minded bloc" of the supervisors would vote down the proposal. At this point the indefatigable secretary of Middletown's chamber of commerce secured radio time and announced that if economy were really the goal, the supervisors should "provide that which is most beneficial to our people for the least sum of money—education." The vote was carried, thirty-two for, five against.

With official local backing gained, the new community college was included in the so-called Master Plan of the State University, trustees were appointed by the governor and by the county board of supervisors, as provided by law, and the college came into legal existence. Quite appropriately, the first offices of the college were in the headquarters of the chamber of commerce, since it took several weeks to have the buildings on the future campus vacated and renovated. The chamber of commerce secretary became acting president until a professional educator could be selected to head the college. In the meantime a teaching staff was assembled, and a catalogue was prepared with the assistance of staff members of two-year institutes in other parts of the state.

In the four years since the community college at Middletown opened its doors in the renovated mansion with approximately two hundred students, it has grown in enrolment to over twelve hundred, including part-time students. Its day enrolment has increased yearly, but perhaps of greatest significance is the rapid expansion of courses attracting the adults who now comprise two-thirds of the number of persons attending. For a county which once had no higher institution at all, and even entertained doubts as to whether tax money should be spent for a local college, the Middletown region has come a long way. This new institution, in keeping with the community-college concept described in earlier chapters of this yearbook, is becoming a true center and resource to which county citizens are turning to meet their educational needs—whatever they may be.

————

All over the United States junior colleges have come into existence during the past half-century because people believed in them and were willing to work hard to establish them. The example of Middletown, New York, in developing Orange County Community College is certainly not a blueprint, for no two junior colleges have developed in exactly the same manner. But the light that this case throws on the problems of founding *future* junior colleges should be of considerable value to educators and lay citizens alike. If the various needs of youth and society described in earlier chapters are to be met, it is apparent (as explained in chap. iv) that new public junior colleges are going to be needed in large numbers.

Two major questions arise at this point regarding the establishment of these community-centered institutions. What person or agency first brings to the attention of the community the need for a public junior college in a particular locality? Once the need is recognized, what steps are necessary to bring the new college into operation?

Rather than attempt to answer in general terms at this point each of these two closely related questions, this chapter will describe, first, the birth process of five other public junior colleges in different parts of the United States and then draw from these selected examples common problems and basic guiding principles. In conclusion there will be described practices and recommendations to assist in the establishment of new junior colleges.

The junior college, like a hardy plant, has been able to grow and to adapt its functional operations to prevailing local conditions. It will be the purpose of this part of the chapter to delineate the variety of social climates in which the junior-college idea has taken root and flourished. As in real gardening, however, all the know-how of planting, cultivating, pruning, and protecting against unfavorable conditions cannot be described in any one standard manual to be distributed to all would-be practitioners.

Here, rather, the reader will become acquainted with the germination process described in a wide range of localities: Chicago, Illinois, a huge midwestern center of commerce and industry; Phoenix, Arizona, an expanding trading and resort center in the Southwest; Jones County, Mississippi, a rural area in a Southern agricultural state; Everett, Washington, a community on the shores of Puget Sound; and Contra Costa County, a heavily industrialized sector of the San Francisco bay area.

As the discerning reader will note, however, it is not only the soil and the seasons which affect growth but also community attitudes and available resources such as the "prime movers" pressing the college idea, general acceptance by local citizens, extent and nature of assistance provided by state authorities and by other educational institutions, the degree of financial help available, and the ability of administration and staff to create a dynamic organization dedicated to serving community needs.

In the foregoing report on the initial interests and the developmental procedures resulting in the establishment of Orange County Community College, most of the particularly significant factors and influences contributing to the success of the enterprise were mentioned. These circumstances were explained in great detail because the Orange County institution is the newest of the six junior colleges selected for presentation in this chapter. The following reports will necessarily be presented in briefer form but with due regard for the purposes and practices which mark these five institutions as additional examples of the readiness with which the recognized objectives of the public junior college tend to adapt the instructional program to community needs.

CHICAGO, ILLINOIS, CITY JUNIOR COLLEGE

In the years preceding the first World War, junior-college programs developed gradually in Chicago as informal "upper divisions" of three city high schools. In 1911 initial organization problems were held to a minimum as regular high-school instructors in Crane Technical High School, and shortly thereafter in Lane Technical High School and Senn High School, taught classes for secondary-school graduates who returned for a postgraduate year. In this manner students were able to gain credits which often enabled them to enter four-year colleges with advanced standing. This practice had been developed as early as the turn of the century in another Illinois city, where such postgraduate courses at Joliet Township High School comprised the program of the earliest public junior college in the United States which is still in existence.

In Chicago the principal of Crane Technical High School apparently had no orders to start a junior-college program, nor had there been committee action, polling of citizen groups, or taking of community surveys. Certain members of the Crane staff were merely called together at the start of the 1911–12 school year and told that there were thirteen postgraduate students who should receive college-level work. From this modest beginning developed the now-flourishing Chicago City Junior College with its three separate campuses. By 1953–54, the total enrolment of the three branches had passed the twenty-thousand mark, with over half of those enrolled classified as adult or special students.

Those interested in the establishment of new institutions should observe from the Chicago example that *merely starting a junior-college program does not guarantee its permanent status.* The Chicago program suffered three major body blows, one of which caused its closing for a year, but public demand gave it rebirth. The first of these blows was loss of accreditation. The second was questionable legal status. The third, which proved most formidable, was inadequate financing.

Accredited in 1917, the Chicago junior college (then known as Crane Junior College) was dropped from the North Central Association approved list in 1930 because of such practices as failure to require appropriate credentials at admission time, insufficient personnel records and services, a notable lack of instructional, library, and office space, and excessive teaching loads placed on staff. As a member of the staff noted, Crane had grown too fast for its clothes and suffered from malnutrition. The faculty was not unaware of the inadequate conditions but hardly hoped for relief from a superintendent and board under great pressure to economize.[1]

Various reforms resulted in reaccreditation within a year, but at that ponit a survey of the school system revealed that the college had no official legal status. This matter was overcome by a special act of the Illinois legislature. By 1932, however, the city of Chicago was in such dire financial straits, as a result of depression-caused tax delinquency, that the tuition-free junior college had to fight for its life against repeated slashes in the school budget. Despite recommendations by students, citizens, and educators that the college be retained, 1933 saw the arbitrary termination of Crane Junior College in the name of economy, along with radical cuts in staff and services in the elementary and secondary schools.

Public indignation was great. Mass meetings resulted, as well as petitions, a "battle of pamphlets," and formation of city-wide committees including organized labor, religious and cultural leaders, and citizens generally. Major newspapers and such leading educational figures as Robert M. Hutchins and Charles H. Judd urged the reinstatement of the junior-college program. A year later, in 1934, they were successful. The present three-unit system was organized, in-

1. J. Leonard Hancock, "Letter to the Editor," *Junior College Journal*, I (January, 1931), 205–6.

creasing emphasis was placed on terminal-vocational programs, and students again flocked to the three newly organized campuses.[2] It was thus, twenty-three years after the first class had been held, that the Chicago City Junior College took on signs of permanence. This fact, together with the notation that the city school system received no state aid for its junior-college program until 1955, would be of interest to other communities where a public junior college is needed.

PHOENIX, ARIZONA, JUNIOR COLLEGE

While Phoenix Junior College, despite its name, did not have to be reborn from its own ashes, this Arizona institution faced two of the same problems evident in the Chicago development: organization prior to official enabling legislation and lack of sufficient space. The college in Phoenix, however, was able to surmount its comparatively minor difficulties more easily than did that in Chicago.

A member of the school board for the union high-school district at Phoenix had first proposed a public junior college for that city as early as 1910. Action was delayed for ten years, however, until adverse economic conditions following World War I made it impossible for many parents to send their sons and daughters away to college, even to the comparatively low-cost University of Arizona at Tucson. Backed by favorable newspaper publicity and the organizing ability of at least one member of the high-school board of education, the high-school principal, and the instructor who became Phoenix Junior College's first dean, the new unit was set up in the high-school plant. An arrangement was worked out with the state university whereby two years of satisfactory work at the junior college would be accepted at the state university for transfer to Junior standing there. Comparable arrangements, as noted, were utilized by the Chicago junior college and no doubt others at that time.

In Phoenix, as elsewhere, junior-college teachers were usually regular staff members of the high school who devoted part time to their college duties. Since there was no major cost increase, official authorization to begin junior-college instruction was not required from taxpayers. Expenses were met as part of the high-school outlay, and no tuition was charged. State approval was reached earlier in Phoe-

2. See, for example, Butler Laughlin and Given C. Aikman, "The Chicago Junior Colleges: A New Deal in Education," *Chicago Schools Journal*, XVI (September, 1934–February, 1935), 4.

nix than in Chicago, with the Arizona State Board of Education granting the high-school board special authority in 1921 "to create an additional two-years' course" beyond the high school.[3] This was actually a year after the first classes were held.

The road to permanent status was not always a smooth one, however, for the emerging new junior college. A survey report of Phoenix Union High School indicated in 1924 that while no fault was found with the college administration or with the salary level of instructors, the shared plant facilities were not satisfactory. "There is little opportunity to build up the community spirit in the present inadequate, inconvenient, and unsatisfactory housing conditions," stated the survey report as published in the *Arizona Gazette*, a leading Phoenix newspaper, on September 17, 1924. "The inability of the students to have an adequate building in which they may develop the college atmosphere is a serious handicap," the survey committee's report continued. In conclusion, it was recommended that the needs of the elementary schools and the high schools should be met first and that the junior college might be maintained out of whatever funds were available after these other programs had been adequately provided for. The growth and development of the city as well as a "real community demand" for the junior college were to be determining factors in the ultimate decision to continue the college.

After discussion, appointment of a new superintendent of the high-school district, and consideration of statements, both from parents as to why their children were attending the junior college and from other citizens favoring its continuation, the board took action. Acquisition of the college's new home—a large former residence located across the street from the high school—was a positive step forward indicative of the board's desire not only to continue Phoenix Junior College but to provide the necessary space as recommended.

Outlays for expenses were voted by the high-school board of education which has always operated Phoenix Junior College. State aid was hoped for but was not forthcoming in sufficient measure until 1935, at which time $15,000 per year was made available by the state for each junior college of one hundred students or more. Despite the dependence on local tax funds, by 1926–27 the core of liberal-arts

3. "Minutes" of the Phoenix Union High School Board of Education, April 21, 1921.

courses offered had been broadened to include more terminal and vocational work. In 1928 residents of the high-school district authorized a $625,000 bond issue, a portion of which was used to erect a larger junior-college building. North Central Association accreditation was granted in the same year.

While subsequent years were to see the name shortened to Phoenix College, educational opportunities broadened by acquisition of a more spacious campus, and an even wider array of course offerings, the new unit was firmly established by 1928, eight years after its first classes were held. In retrospect, it becomes apparent that both the controlling board and the general public found the college to be a good thing from its inception. As a result, unhappy crises of the Chicago type did not come to pass.

JONES COUNTY, MISSISSIPPI, JUNIOR COLLEGE

Jones County Junior College, like the two institutions described in Chicago and Phoenix, developed under the wing of a "parent" high school, but in a strikingly different manner. The two earlier examples were those of pioneering institutions, Chicago representing one of the first metropolitan junior colleges and Phoenix being the first of its kind in the Southwest outside of California. Impetus for establishment of both of these colleges came entirely from local initiative with little encouragement or assistance from the state during the first few years.

In Mississippi, on the other hand, the 1920's saw the establishment of at least eleven public junior colleges, all of which grew out of older county agricultural high schools. Here local initiative was coupled with over-all planning on a state-wide basis. In this predominantly rural and agricultural state where there were few urban centers and few good roads or effective means of transportation early in the century, boarding high schools were authorized by the county agricultural high school law enacted in 1908. With improved roads, the coming of the automobile, and state equalization funds, the mid-1920's saw the growth of consolidated high schools which enabled pupils to live at home. Consequently, the county agricultural high schools found themselves losing most of their students.[4]

4. See, for example, Jesse P. Bogue, *The Community College*, p. 263. New York: McGraw-Hill Book Co., 1950.

At that point legislators as well as county school people became increasingly aware of the emerging junior-college movement in other parts of the country. They also realized the important role the physical facilities of the agricultural boarding high schools could play in expanding educational opportunities *beyond* the high-school level. As a result, an act was passed in 1924 authorizing the county agricultural high schools to add college-level offerings to help prepare teachers. Four years later the Public Junior College Law of 1928 was passed, enabling agricultural high schools or municipalities of ten thousand population or more to extend their educational offerings upward for two years.

During the preceding year, 1927, post-high-school courses were added to the offerings of the agricultural high school at Ellisville, one of the two county seats of Jones County, in the southeastern part of the state. The lower division continued as an agricultural high school serving the immediate area, but the region served by the junior college was extended beyond Jones County to include seven adjacent counties. Starting with a handful of students, the college program proved increasingly popular. By 1953–54, for example, the enrolment was over one thousand, of which about one-third were adults or special students.

How did Jones County happen to be sponsoring one of the eleven junior colleges operating in Mississippi by the end of 1927? Local pride was certainly a factor. In addition, J. B. Young, president of the college, points out that the county operated one of the stronger high schools and had a good tax base.[5] These, together with such advantages as a good staff, suitable library, and sufficient laboratory equipment, enabled the budding college to meet state standards. A state-wide regulatory plan had been deemed necessary to encourage appropriately located, well-supported junior colleges, rather than an excessive number of small and struggling units in each of the state's eighty-two counties. "It was obvious," Knox Broom declared, "that definite methods for the birth control of this new member of the educational family in Mississippi had to be found if the movement was not to die aborning."[6] Broom, who has been termed the father

5. J. B. Young, statement in interview, January 13, 1955.

6. See *History of Mississippi Public Junior Colleges: A State System of Public Junior Colleges, 1928–1953*, p. 8. Compiled by Knox M. Broom. Jackson: Mississippi Junior College Association, 1954.

of the Mississippi junior-college movement, was the first state supervisor for these institutions.

The expansion of the service area of Jones County Junior College, like that of the ten other junior colleges, was permitted by state law and encouraged by the Mississippi Junior College Commission provided for in the 1928 act. Under the auspices of this commission, informal agreements were worked out whereby the state was zoned, so that junior colleges did not overlap each other's territory or engage in unfortunate competition. All of the junior colleges shared in the initial state appropriation of $80,000 for 1928–30. Later appropriations gradually became larger.

Like its sister junior colleges, the new institution at Ellisville not only prepared students to transfer to four-year colleges but also placed considerable stress on terminal-vocational programs geared to near-by employment requirements. In recent years work has been offered in such fields as aircraft and auto mechanics, machinist and metal work, horology, radio-television repair and maintenance, textiles, and wood manufacturing. A joint product of local and state endeavor, Jones County Junior College is typical of those serving broad community needs over a multi-county region.

EVERETT, WASHINGTON, JUNIOR COLLEGE

In each of the junior colleges described thus far, gradual public acceptance was gained for the new institution even though organization and earliest promotion came largely as a result of initiative by school people rather than by public demand. In the Pacific Northwest, Everett Junior College was also started as a result of action by local school authorities. But in this instance the college founders moved far ahead of public opinion in the beginning, an action which caused exceedingly difficult public relations during the initial weeks of the new college's existence.

Today the junior college in Everett is the second largest in the state of Washington. With an enrolment of almost three thousand (1953–54), it is a thriving institution. At the time of its establishment in 1941, however, it operated under a most unusual handicap: local citizens were seeking an injunction to prevent its board of control from maintaining the college in an elementary-school building which it had taken over on short notice for that purpose. With the

denial of the request for an injunction, the building used by the college suffered a number of broken windows. On the heels of this confusion came United States entry into World War II. Certainly Everett Junior College was off to a difficult start.[7]

As in other communities, the new junior college in Everett came
into existence as a result of a conviction on the part of local school
authorities that establishment of such an institution would be desirable. The superintendent of schools, for example, had previously
served at Mount Vernon, Washington, where he had helped establish the second oldest junior college in the state. Unlike the earlier
colleges in some other states, however, establishment at Everett took
place under specific provisions of state authority, despite the seeming
lack of broad local support.

Laws of the state of Washington provided that a local board of
education might petition state education officials to sanction the
founding of a local junior college. The five members of the board of
education for the Everett school system took this step, apparently
on their own initiative. Their request was granted, and the five were
appointed by the governor to a separate board of trustees for the
new college—a distinct unit set off from the city school system. The
trustees, taking advantage of their "double identity" as the board for
both the college and the city school system, arranged for the college
to enjoy free use of the Lincoln Elementary School. This action necessitated the removal of a number of children from the building,
which was the newest school building in the city, having been
erected in 1938. Public response to this development was noticeably
unfavorable.

The college started with a dean, four full-time instructors, and
three part-time instructors shared with the local high school.[8] The
college charged a tuition fee of $125 per year and also received state
aid of $75 per year per academic student, and $100 per year per vocational student. With this income and no capital outlay for plant,
the new institution was able to function without requiring direct
local tax money. While the early offerings concentrated largely on

7. Information from interview with J. F. Marvin Buechel, January 10, 1955.
Buechel was on the staff of Everett Junior College from 1941 to 1953, having
served as chief administrative officer from 1943 to 1953.

8. Revised Budget of Everett Junior College, submitted to the trustees of
the college on November 12, 1941, by George N. Porter, then dean.

lower-division liberal-arts courses and a terminal business curriculum, technical instruction was provided for workers in the near-by pulp mills. The initial enrolment of about 125 dropped below one hundred the second year, as the armed forces and other war-related activities drew manpower.

The value of the college became evident to the community, however, with the introduction of short-term instruction in such fields as welding, riveting, blueprint reading, and clothing manufacturing —all directly concerned with defense work in the region. At the end of the war Everett Junior College petitioned the state board of education to permit it to merge, under terms of a new state law, with the Everett school district. The petition was granted and the college was then able to draw upon local tax funds. Facilities were expanded to serve returning veterans and others, and eventually charges were dropped to a fee of three dollars per credit hour per quarter for state residents. An increase in state aid helped make this possible.

It is apparent that despite a difficult start, Everett Junior College was able to win an important place in the community it serves. State financial assistance and tuition income weathered the new institution through its first storms until it gained popular acceptance and eventually became a community college in the broad sense of the term.

<h2 style="text-align:center">CONTRA COSTA COUNTY, CALIFORNIA, JUNIOR COLLEGE</h2>

In California where public junior colleges have long been tuition-free, clearly demonstrated local demand and a commitment to provide financial backing are required before a new two-year institution can be established. This is true even though the state meets about one-quarter of operating expenses. Prior to the founding of San Bernardino Valley Union Junior College in 1926, for example, citizens of that area of Southern California voted by a ratio of as much as 25 to 1 to establish a junior-college district and to finance it. In Contra Costa County in the San Francisco bay area, however, it took three attempts to establish a junior college. Effective action by citizen groups, together with startling population growth and inability of existing institutions to meet expanding needs, finally helped bring about approval of a county-wide junior-college district in 1948.

A junior college had first been proposed by the superintendent of schools of Contra Costa County in 1938, but the idea was dropped because of lack of support. Six or seven years later, after the county had become even more heavily industrialized, a postwar planning committee of the county development association considered a two-year college with emphasis on technical education as a memorial to county war veterans. This proposed post-high-school unit was to be organized through creation of a junior-college district eligible for state aid, if the voters approved in a special election in January, 1946.

Several months in advance of the election, proponents of the junior college had held discussions with a representative of the state education department. Based on the observation that the regular day enrolment in California junior colleges averaged between one-fifth and one-fourth of the average daily attendance at high schools in the same region, it was estimated that between five hundred and seven hundred students would enrol at the proposed institution. Opposition appeared, however, in the form of the county taxpayers' association, a property owners' protective committee, and the county farm bureau. Raising serious objections to the presumed costs of the institution in question, these elements hired a publicity manager and settled down to fight this second plan to found a junior college.

Those favoring the proposed district included organized labor, service clubs in various county communities, women's organizations, and an American Legion unit. As an oil company official pointed out, the county ranked second in eleven western states in the value of its manufactured products but was one of the poorest in providing post-high-school education for its youth. Despite strong statements from various quarters urging its approval, the plan to establish a junior-college district in Contra Costa County was turned down by a 500-vote margin. Local observers credited the defeat to an opposition that was well organized and vocal, lack of enthusiasm for an institution with only vocational objectives, and unfortunate competition between eastern and western portions of the county as to location of the proposed campus.

Even after these two apparent failures, the junior-college idea persisted in Contra Costa County. Two years later, in March, 1948, citizen committees studying school-district organization in various parts of California were urged to make proposals for educational improvement. Out of one such group came a recommendation that

Contra Costa County again consider forming a junior-college district. At that time attention was drawn to a recent survey of publicly supported higher education in California which cited Contra Costa County as being in the "most notable" area lacking junior colleges.[9]

This time, those favoring the college lost no time in organizing. While the tax-conscious opposition remained formidable, a Junior College Citizens' Committee developed to obtain support from various other existing groups for the junior-college plan. The publicity manager who had helped fight the preceding proposal was hired this time to work for the college. Again organized labor played an important role, as did parent-teacher groups and school administrators. Among the indorsements given were those by a unit of the American Association of University Women, the Democratic party's county central committee, and the Richmond *Independent*, a major newspaper, and other journals in smaller communities. A pamphlet entitled "They Got It" explained that Contra Costa students were attending junior colleges in neighboring districts, thus forcing the county to pay substantial amounts of tuition to those other colleges as provided by California law.

Although the opposition raised its familiar cry against excessive costs, the junior-college proposal was victorious at a special December election in 1948. Approval was gained by a margin of less than eight hundred votes, but the way was now paved for the actual organization of the district, acquisition of facilities and staff, and course planning.

As authorized by state regulations, the county superintendent of schools appointed an interim board of trustees. A superintendent and an assistant superintendent for the junior-college district were selected by the trustees, and a former residence was acquired and altered to serve as a central office. An initial tax levy at the rate of 27.5 cents per $100 valuation assured income, so the major problem became one of securing facilities. Instructional space was secured in buildings at a wartime shipyard in the western part of the county and in an unused elementary-school building at the county seat.

Curriculum offerings were classed under four major headings:

9. Monroe E. Deutsch, Aubrey A. Douglass, George D. Strayer, *et al.*, *A Report of a Survey of the Needs of California in Higher Education*, submitted to the Liaison Committee of the Regents of the University of California and the State Department of Education, March 1, 1948, p. 78.

general education, occupational training, university parallel, and refresher or remedial work. Citizen committees, including representatives of labor and management, helped plan the vocational offerings
to meet employment needs in the region, while close co-operation
with the University of California assisted with the development of
programs for students who wished to transfer to upper-division
courses. A broad community-service program included offerings for
adults ranging from home furnishing to literature and anthropology.
This program used a downtown center in Richmond, the county's
largest city, and such additional off-campus space as chamber of
commerce rooms, community centers, city halls, banks, markets,
business offices, clubrooms, restaurants, youth centers, industrial
plants, schoolrooms, and auditoriums.[10]

With a staff of 144 instructors, and an enrolment of 1,300 students
on its two campuses and 3,000 in its adult programs by the end of
1950, the district was serving wide interests of county residents.
Two permanent buildings have now been erected on a new East
Campus, with a similar number on a new West Campus. Despite
early opposition to this junior college, it has gained a wide degree of
acceptance in the broad, diversified community it is serving.

Common Problems and Guiding Principles

While the reader will have noted considerable variation in the
conditions surrounding the establishment of the six junior colleges
just described, certain problems have been identified that were common to each situation. Organized around four major areas of concern, guiding principles have been identified that should be of considerable value to those interested in the establishment of new junior
colleges.

THE PRINCIPLE OF NEED AND DEMAND

In each of the six communities described here, student response
was evident once the new junior college was in operation, thus indicating that the institution was meeting at least some individual needs.
It has been shown that, in some instances, enrolments were very
small during early years and that in four of the six instances organ-

10. For additional information see J. Graham Sullivan and Phebe Ward,
"A New Community College," *Educational Leadership*, VIII (February, 1951),
299–302.

ized opposition was present in the locality where the junior college was proposed and even after it had been in operation for a time. Despite such deterrent factors as a fear of additional taxation, alleged weakening of support for an existing school system, or failure to recognize the value of the junior college, each institution sooner or later gained permanent status in its community. Each new college met one or more of the following four needs.

No Other Near-by Colleges. In Jones County, Everett, and Orange County, institutions of higher education were almost entirely lacking in the immediate area. While those willing to travel from twenty to sixty miles to attend college could have done so, the distance in each case was sufficient to discourage at least some of the potential students.

Existing Institutions Crowded. Too many students, or fear of crowded conditions, in existing collegiate institutions helped accentuate the need for a local college in Orange County and in Contra Costa County. In these two cases general enrolment bulges following World War II were of major importance. In another situation, reports of overflowing classrooms at the University of Arizona were circulated in Phoenix following the first World War.

High Cost of Tuition. In a community such as Chicago where a number of other colleges and universities were in existence, the major need for a city junior college system grew out of inability of many students to pay tuition required by the established private institutions in that city. During the depression of the 1930's many students dropped college work entirely when tuition-free Crane Junior College was closed.

Appropriate Programs Not Offered Elsewhere. There was a need for types of instruction not offered by existing institutions. While the two oldest junior colleges described here (Chicago and Phoenix) placed early emphasis on transfer curriculums, establishment of the other colleges was aided in each case by terminal programs not otherwise available. Preparation for occupational proficiency in major fields of local employment loomed large as a reason for the other four and now receives major attention from all six. Adult-education offerings, seldom receiving major emphasis at the time of establishment, have become significantly more important. Woven into the warp and woof of all the college programs has been attention to the aims of general education.

THE PRINCIPLE OF ACTION BY "PRIME MOVERS"

It should be clearly recognized that identification of some or all of these needs does *not* automatically lead to establishment of a junior college. Effectively organized *demand*, as outlined below, is necessary to develop action.

Who actually started demand for junior colleges in these six communities? Who were the "prime movers" who effected initial action? The move to start a college is like football in that co-ordinated team action is necessary, but, as on the gridiron, there are kick-off plays and quarterbacks calling signals. It is desirable, therefore, to identify individuals or groups responsible for the first play in each case. These prime movers fall into two categories.

Action by School People. In the four oldest colleges described, people already involved in school work were the initiators of action. In Chicago, principals of three high schools developed their own postgraduate programs beyond the twelfth grade. In Phoenix, high-school administrators, including a school board member, were among those urging founding of a college. In Jones County and in Everett, the high-school administration working with approval or aid of state education officials developed the new colleges.

Demand by Local Citizens. Citizens not officially connected with any existing educational organization were the effective prime movers in both Contra Costa and Orange Counties. It is recalled in the former case that the county superintendent had suggested a junior college but that the idea did not come to fruition until some years later when organized lay committee work and the substantial backing of labor, service clubs, and other existing groups culminated in the formation of a junior-college district. In Orange County the chamber of commerce secretary was a central figure in organizing local demand and setting up a county-wide committee for higher education. In Chicago, while school people had started the junior-college program, it was aroused citizen action that brought about the reinstatement of the program closed by city officials in the name of economy.

THE PRINCIPLE OF CITIZEN SUPPORT

It is obvious that a local junior college cannot operate on a permanent basis without citizen support, whether it is officially expressed or tacit in nature. Official approval of the voters was recorded in Contra Costa County by a county-wide election and in Orange County by vote of the county supervisors representing the people. Both of these actions took place *prior* to college organization. In Phoenix, approval of a bond issue including funds for a new junior-college building took place *after* the college had been in operation for eight years. In the other cases, however, general public approval was sensed from the beginning, or developed, as in Everett, after a period of some antagonism.

Real citizen support, however, involves more than mere approval of the junior-college idea. As has been indicated in description of the first principle, public response is mirrored also in the extent to which people (*a*) utilize the services which the college offers and (*b*) urge additional courses or services. The college in Orange County, to cite only one example, started out with major attention to needs of veterans and recent high-school graduates who wished to attend on a full-time day basis. Within a short time, however, local banks were among those requesting short-term programs for their current personnel; a near-by air base asked if college instructors could offer instruction in general education; and local hospitals called on the college to offer certain courses in their nursing schools and then arranged to send student nurses to the college for instruction in specific areas.

Hand in hand with an expansion of junior-college services to the community comes the growing recognition by more and more local residents of the many values of this versatile type of institution. And with this recognition comes less and less resistance to necessary requests by the college for continued financial support. Even the taxpayer groups in Contra Costa County eventually submitted a favorable review of the budget of the junior-college district there.

THE PRINCIPLE OF OVERCOMING BASIC ADMINISTRATIVE PROBLEMS

Although the three principles just described are of great importance, a new college cannot really operate in the face of unsolved problems involving official legal status; methods of securing funds;

organization of administration; and development of buildings, instructional staff, and an acceptable program.

Existence of Enabling or Permissive Legislation. None of the six junior colleges was established illegally. Instead, each was either encouraged or permitted by legislation already in existence or passed by the state legislature after the college had come into existence. A special act had to be passed by the Illinois legislature legalizing Crane Junior College twenty years *after* its birth. In Arizona, informal approval of Phoenix Junior College was obtained from the state education department at the time of founding, but state-wide law was not developed until 1927. Jones County Junior College was being established concurrently with the Mississippi junior college law of 1928. The three more recent examples, however, took place under the specific terms of laws in effect in the respective states at the time of community action.[11]

Adequate Financial Support. At least four general patterns of financial support are exemplified by the six colleges considered here.

First, since the junior-college program in Chicago developed as an upward extension of local secondary education, it operated without tuition and has continued to operate since its inception entirely from taxes collected by the city for school purposes until 1955, when the legislature provided aid for junior colleges.

Second, while the colleges in Phoenix and Jones County also originated as parts of high-school districts and received their first support from common school funds, they depended upon state aid to supplement local taxation after state laws were passed to that effect. Contra Costa County may be considered in this broad category, inasmuch as California law requires a new junior college to operate for its first year on local tax income before becoming eligible for the state assistance which now pays roughly one-quarter of its operating expenses.

Third, Everett Junior College charged tuition as well as receiving state aid in its early years. When union with the local school system

11. In at least one case the founders of a particular public junior college initiated state legislation to provide a legal basis for their proposed college and others which might follow. This took place in Massachusetts in 1946 as a result of action by those interested in establishing Newton Junior College, Newtonville.

was effected, local tax funds became available and the former tuition was dropped.

Fourth, Orange County Community College operated under the State University of New York's "Master Plan" whereby costs are split three ways. The state, the sponsoring body (in this case, the county supervisors), and the students each contribute approximately one-third.[12]

Administrative Procedures. Legal authority and financial backing alone do not make a college, even though each of these is obviously indispensable under present conditions. Once these two advantages are gained, a board of control must be selected to be the legal operators of the institution. In three cases (Chicago, Phoenix, and Jones County), the boards serving the "parent" high school served this function. In Everett, the governor of Washington appointed board members. An interim board for the separately organized junior-college district in Contra Costa County was appointed by the county superintendent of schools until voters could choose regular members at an election. Under New York State law, a board of trustees for Orange County Community College was selected jointly by the governor of the state and the board of supervisors. In all cases, boards of control have responsibility for designating a president, dean, or superintendent to act as executive officer.

Plant Facilities and Teaching Staff. Buildings and instructors are considered together here inasmuch as, in three of the cases presented, both plant and instructors were shared with the supporting high school. In the cases of new junior colleges in Chicago, Phoenix, Jones County, and Everett, the first space used was in previously-erected school plants. Additional buildings were required later in all of these situations, but acquisition of such space was not a major problem at the time of establishment. In Orange County and Contra Costa County, on the other hand, the junior college organization was completely separate from the local public school systems. The almost providential acquisition, in the former case, of a large residence and a barn-garage, all of which could be converted to classroom, library, and office space, solved the college's housing problem for the first few years. Temporary offices, prior to the first classes, were set up

12. For details, consult State University of New York, *The Master Plan*, pp. 35–37. Albany: State University of New York, 1950.

in the chamber of commerce rooms. Contra Costa County acquired a much wider array of plant facilities, ranging from wartime ship-yard buildings to an unused elementary school. From the beginning, administrators of these two colleges, along with those of Everett, assembled their own instructional staffs. The institutions with shared facilities utilized part of the time of high-school instructors already on the faculties of the "parent" high schools. Additional instructors were hired sooner or later as the need arose.

Development of Courses. Lower-division courses were developed in all cases with at least some attention to comparable offerings at existing four-year institutions, most notably the appropriate state universities. With regard to vocational programs, personnel of the agricultural high school in Jones County were already familiar with regional needs and were able to organize junior-college courses in appropriate areas on this basis. Committees including membership from labor and management in Contra Costa County aided in the development of technical offerings there. Orange County Commu-nity College secured the services of experts from older two-year institutions in New York State.

It is observed that development of appropriate curriculums cannot be entirely completed prior to the opening of instruction. Each of the six junior colleges has expanded, reduced, or otherwise modified its offerings according to expressed needs and demand. Constant re-evaluation and improvement are required if a community-centered junior college is to develop and play a truly dynamic role in the improvement of educational opportunities for the community it serves.

Practices and Recommendations for Establishing New Junior Colleges

In the preceding section principles were described which were derived from observing growth of individual junior colleges in dif-ferent parts of the United States. Already the discerning reader will have begun to select from among these guiding principles those factors of seemingly greatest importance to him. In this final portion of the chapter there will be described certain practices and recom-mendations with direct practical implications. Junior colleges, of course, cannot be exported from one area to another and then put together like so many parts of a prefabricated house. On the other hand, effective practices in establishing junior colleges can and should be studied, and then modified to suit unique local conditions.

Five recommended steps follow. They are listed essentially in chronological order, although once the first step is taken, the next three may be taken more or less simultaneously.

ASSAY COMMUNITY NEEDS AND PROBABLE STUDENT RESPONSE

The initial step is one of assaying the nature and extent of post-high-school needs in the community in question. This can be done by referring to data already compiled and by gathering new and additional information. Impetus was given to studying "the needs for more and better educational facilities at the thirteenth- and fourteenth-grade level" by the report of the President's Commission on Higher Education in 1947.[13] Since World War II at least ten state or national surveys have been made pertaining to the need for public junior colleges.[14]

Of more specific local value would be information obtained through principals of near-by high schools. Knowledge should be obtained of how many members of each graduating class plan to go away to college and how many would attend a local junior college if there were one. Information about types of skills desired by local employers might already be on record with the board of trade, chamber of commerce, or similar organization, or be available in census reports. If not, a regional occupational survey might be in order.

How many students are needed in order to justify a junior college? John S. Allen[15] lists authorities who believe at least 150 are necessary to keep per capita costs at a reasonable figure. This may be a satisfactory minimum for a narrowly defined academic program, but 300 might be a more desirable minimum if the relatively

13. President's Commission on Higher Education, *Higher Education for American Democracy*, Vol. III, *Organizing Higher Education*, p. 9. New York: Harper & Bros., 1948.

14. See Hugh G. Price, "Planning for Public Junior College Development through State and National Surveys," *Junior College Journal*, XX (September, 1949), 16–22.

15. John S. Allen, *Criteria for the Establishment of Public Junior Colleges*, p. 77. Unpublished Doctor's Dissertation, New York University, 1936.

expensive equipment associated with some vocational programs were to be used. The desirability of much larger student enrolments is reported by August W. Eberle.[16] He states that in order to provide sufficient administrative and student personnel services and to operate at an annual cost of not over $350 per student, a community college requires an enrolment of from 700 to 1,500 full- and equivalent full-time students. The lower number pertains to a college organized as part of a local school system; the higher number, to that of one organized as an administrative unit in its own right.

CONSIDER PROVISIONS OF APPROPRIATE STATE LAWS AND
AVAILABILITY OF EXPERT HELP

It has been demonstrated that some older junior colleges were born first and legalized afterward. This procedure is not to be recommended, and, in fact, is probably impossible in most states at the present time. It is generally observed that enabling legislation is not for the purpose of making it arbitrarily difficult to start a new junior college but, rather, to require the potential supporting locality to demonstrate need and ability to support. In some cases these state laws spell out arrangements whereby costs may be shared by the state and the locality. In others, they are merely permissive, authorizing establishment of junior colleges where there is need and a sufficiently broad *local* tax base to assure operation without state aid.

In addition, potential college founders should learn whether provision is made for organization through an existing school system or high-school district, through an established political subdivision such as a county, or whether a new junior-college district with its own boundaries should be developed. They should seek assistance of junior-college experts of the state education department, state college or university, or staff members of other junior colleges. The University of California at Los Angeles, Michigan State College, the State University of New York, and the University of Texas are among those larger institutions having staff members particularly

16. August William Eberle, "Size of Satisfactory Community Colleges," in *Summaries of Doctoral Dissertations, University of Wisconsin*, Vol. XIV, pp. 362–64. Madison, Wisconsin: University of Wisconsin Press, 1954.

assigned the responsibility of working with junior-college people throughout their state.[17]

In addition, new prime movers should become familiar with earlier proposals for junior-college plans. Mississippi, as has been shown, has had a state-wide plan for years. Ohio is in the process of developing one,[18] which is significant since it is a state with only a single public junior college as of 1953–54. An informal master plan for Iowa has been prepared by Starrak and Hughes,[19] based on a minimum of three hundred full-time students and sufficient taxable wealth for each college. Their plan includes also a proposed bill which might be submitted to the Iowa General Assembly.

IDENTIFY PROMISING PRIME MOVERS AND PROBABILITY
OF GENERAL CITIZEN SUPPORT

Persons considering establishment of a new junior college are by definition prime movers themselves. These individuals or groups may follow through from inception of the idea to actual operation of the new institution. On the other hand, these individuals may succeed in enlisting the aid of other citizens who can make a valuable contribution to the movement. There is no one best way. In a given community, the initial idea might come from a parent-teacher association, from a labor union, a high-school principal, a businessmen's organization, or from a variety of other sources.

Whether the idea originates with an individual or a group, it is essential that the idea gain wide support from many elements of the proposed area to be served if it is to meet with early success. This is important if a desirable attention to broad community needs is to be given. It is important also in this day of strenuous competition for the tax dollar to secure necessary financial support. If extensive citizen support is not forthcoming or cannot be brought about by

17. Michigan State College, to cite one instance, has an office of Junior College Co-operation "to expand our services to the state's two-year institutions, personalize those services, and co-operate in every way possible with junior college interests." From Thomas R. Ford, "Office of Junior College Co-operation," *Basic College Newsletter* (May, 1954), p. 3 (Michigan State College publication).

18. See D. H. Eikenberry, *The Need for the Upward Extension of Secondary Education in Ohio.* Columbus: College of Education, Ohio State University, 1954 (preliminary draft).

19. James A. Starrak and Raymond M. Hughes, *The Community College in the United States,* pp. 93–109. Ames, Iowa: Iowa State College Press, 1954.

effective public relations, then perhaps there is no real need for a junior college at the moment. Correct timing is certainly of the essence. In a situation such as existed in Contra Costa County, California, where general favorable response does not appear to be forthcoming after a reasonable amount of discussion, it may be wise to wait a few years for increasing population, greater need, or better understanding.

In any event, it seems undesirable that the movement to establish a junior college be a one-man show. Leadership from informed, skilled, dedicated individuals is a necessity, of course, but citizen interest and active involvement is highly desirable if plans are to meet with initial success. Principles of effective group action should be brought into play. Hugh G. Price was credited by a local newspaper as being the individual with the persistence and foresight which led to the founding of Montgomery Junior College, now at Takoma Park, Maryland, yet he involved existing and newly-formed community groups in the continuing development of the college for years after its first classes met.

In brief, "Let us all work together in an effort to see if a junior college could improve our area" is a better slogan than "Give me your support to make possible the college I have decided you need."

DETERMINE PROBABLE AVAILABILITY OF FACILITIES AND FUNDS

In locating state laws and measuring citizen support, the prime movers will have learned already of the nature and extent of state aid, if any, and of possible local plant facilities. Even where state sources match local resources in providing funds for buildings and equipment, it may be desirable to keep capital outlay at a minimum during the early years of the college. In many cases this has meant utilization of existing housing which could be altered satisfactorily with comparatively small expense. Use of high-school buildings on a late-afternoon and evening basis has been employed in some instances, but this has been a deterrent to rapid development. However attractive a building may be, sharing it with high-school pupils may make difficult the development of a mature college spirit or atmosphere. In one instance, young women responded only in small numbers when many classes met during the evening. Both of these observations have distinct recruitment implications.

With regard to tax income from local sources, sometimes an increase in tax outlay may develop so gradually that there is little realization by the public that the new junior college is costing much money. Where there is immediate necessity for collecting and spending large sums, however, special measures may be required to assure citizen support. Basil H. Peterson,[20] president of Orange Coast College, Costa Mesa, California, reports thirteen methods successfully used in bringing about a two-to-one victory at the polls for an increase beyond the usual maximum in the tax rate for the new college. Although Orange Coast College had obtained for its campus a former air base with existing buildings, capital was needed for considerable reconversion, as well as for new construction, in order to meet exacting state standards. It was proposed that funds be secured through seven years of higher taxes rather than through a bond issue. This action would actually save taxpayers the additional expense of interest on bonds. Methods used ranged from radio publicity to invitations to visit the college in its temporary buildings. The psychology of encouraging people to give greater support to an organization already on the road to success is worth noting. "Complete Coast College—Vote YES," was the motto used in Costa Mesa.

SELECT THE BEST-QUALIFIED ADMINISTRATORS
AND INSTRUCTIONAL STAFF

Provision for election or appointment of members of a board of trustees is usually contained in enabling legislation. The official or voters responsible for selection of this important group should consider placing on the board representation from the various groups that helped bring the college into existence. Even broader support may be gained by inclusion of one or more leading citizens not as yet identified with the junior-college movement who can offer wise counsel.

One of the most important, and frequently most difficult, decisions facing the new board is selection of the executive officer who will operate the junior college. Successful presidents and directors of junior colleges have served previously as faculty members of similar institutions in some cases and, in others, have come from the ranks

20. Basil H. Peterson, "Converting an Army Air Base into a College Campus," *School Executive*, LXIX (May, 1950), 48–51.

of school superintendents and high-school principals. There appears to be no one most desirable type of past experience. Irrespective of age, sex, or experience, the new executive and his professional staff should be in sympathy with the aims of the community-college movement and be able to contribute specifically to its success. This would involve competence in the position for which hired, a desire to create new ways of doing things, involvement in community activities, demonstrated ability to get along with people, and in many cases experience in fields other than education. Use of part-time specialists from vocational fields who teach one or more classes has frequently worked out well.

A novel and worth-while idea would be to appoint the administrative officers, and possibly a number of key instructors, well in advance of the first day of classes. The salary expenditures involved in making possible organized preplanning of course offerings and other services to students would be a good investment in terms of encouraging a truly first-class program. Such planning should not, however, structure a rigid curriculum.

As the five above steps are being taken, the question might arise as to whether there are any sure-fire criteria for measuring the probable success of a junior college in a particular location. In 1936 Allen[21] proposed eight criteria not unlike some of those included here. He tried out his measuring instrument on ten cities in New York State then having a population of twenty thousand or more but no colleges. On the basis of this study he identified seven of the ten cities which he considered likely places for junior-college establishments. Two-year colleges now exist in three of these seven cities as well as in one which Allen did not select as a probable location. It is worth noting, however, that of the four junior colleges established in these cities since Allen's study, three were set up by the State University of New York and financed entirely by it over a five-year period. The solitary example of a college developing largely from local demand is Orange County Community College, in Middletown, a community which apparently measured up to all of Allen's eight standards.

When the five steps are completed, some people will think that a

21. Allen, *op. cit.*, pp. 174 ff.

junior college has been created. It hasn't, quite. True, these are certain of the steps necessary in order to measure need and probable response, meet legal requirements, identify prime movers and citizen supporters, and work out arrangements for facilities, funds, administrators, and staff. The new junior college is really in operation, however, only when it is offering a program in keeping with the principles outlined in the chapters of this yearbook—a program that really means something to the people it is set up to serve. If the new institution does these things well and continues to merit community confidence and support, it has reached full stature. By then its prime movers will have rendered a lasting service to the community.[22]

22. For accounts of the establishment of three additional junior colleges (Joliet, Illinois; San Bernardino, California; and Montgomery County, Maryland) as well as a checklist of questions to be applied to a community considering establishment of a local junior college, see Elbert K. Fretwell, Jr., *Founding Public Junior Colleges.* New York: Bureau of Publications, Teachers College, Columbia University, 1954.

CHAPTER XV

A Look to the Future

B. LAMAR JOHNSON

In the preceding chapters we have noted certain social and technological trends which, along with an emerging public concern regarding the educational problems and needs of individuals, are uniting in a demand for sharply expanding provisions for post-high-school education; we have identified and interpreted the role and purposes of the public junior college; we have reported the growth and development of the two-year college; and we have noted some of the important problems of these institutions. In the light of these findings we have reported program practices and have suggested needed directions for improvement and development of public education at the junior-college level.

Against this background we now address ourselves to the questions: What are our basic recommendations for the public junior college? What is its probable future?

Recommendations

It is not our purpose here to discuss the wide variety of proposals presented in preceding chapters. There are, however, three basic recommendations which warrant restatement. We have made each of these suggestions in earlier chapters—perhaps somewhat repetitiously—in varying contexts and in differing terms. But at this point it is important that we restate these proposals, clearly and succinctly —for by so doing we actually epitomize the focus and direction of our thinking concerning necessary junior-college development.

The proposals outlined in the following pages of this chapter represent a three-point program under which the public junior college can make the contributions which it, as an institution, is uniquely qualified to make to our nation and to its citizenry:

1. Expand the public junior college
2. Build the educational program of the public junior college to achieve these purposes:
    a) Preparation for advanced study
    b) Vocational education
    c) General education
    d) Community services
3. Develop the public junior college as a community college

1. *Expand the public junior college.* Enlarge existing junior colleges. Build new ones. In brief, multiply junior-college facilities.

We have noted the sharply increasing college-age population. We have seen the apparently irreversible trend toward a consistently larger percentage of our youth continuing their schooling beyond high school. We have identified social and technological developments and considered others (automation and atomic power, for example) in the offing which create a demand for vastly larger numbers of highly trained workers and citizens. And we have observed needs, problems, and other characteristics of youth and adults which make it essential for more and more to continue their schooling beyond high school, if our national health, productivity, and leadership are to improve.

The increased demand for higher education will clearly tax to the utmost all possible facilities, public and private, day and night, rural and urban, including extension centers and junior colleges, universities and four-year colleges. New institutions of learning must be established, and present colleges of all types must be expanded. We have found, however, a particular need for two-year programs and for colleges located in the home communities of eligible students.

Similar conclusions have been reached by two different survey commissions, both of which have been conducting state-wide studies of needs in higher education while the chapters of this yearbook were being written. *Time* magazine cites the tentative recommendation of Florida's special council of educators that the state set up from 12 to 16 two-year community colleges. In the same news report, *Time* refers to California as a state in which the pattern of the educational future is already indicated by the fact that 66 publicly supported junior colleges are now in operation.[1] Even here, however, further development is proposed. The report of the Restudy

1. *Time*, LXV (February 21, 1955), 59–60.

of the Needs of California in Higher Education[2] recommends the expansion of public junior colleges sufficient to take care of at least half of the college population of the state in 1965. This undertaking would require the enlargement of present institutions and the establishment of new junior colleges in areas of the state which are not now adequately served.

The evidence we have examined and the developments we have reported clearly support a recommendation to expand greatly the public junior college.

2. *Build the educational program of the public junior college to achieve these purposes: (a) preparation for advanced study, (b) vocational education, (c) general education, and (d) community services.*

These four purposes have been identified as important and as appropriate to the public junior college. Most two-year colleges will address themselves to each of these objectives—with, however, varying degrees of emphasis based upon the particular characteristics of the community which the college serves. Some individual colleges may validly limit their attention to one or two purposes which are particularly useful to their clientele.

We do not, therefore, hold that it is essential that each of these purposes be emphasized by every junior college. What is important, however, for our nation and for its citizens, is that these purposes be achieved, and at the level of post-high-school education. This places a heavy responsibility upon the public junior college—collectively, to make certain that none of the objectives is neglected and, individually, to identify the particular purposes to which each college can most appropriately address itself.

3. *Develop the public junior college as a community college.* The demand for the community college merges from a number of trends and findings which we have examined: bringing colleges close to the homes of prospective students removes one of the major obstacles to college attendance; communities have complex problems and opportunities—economic, social, educational, religious, political; these problems and opportunities vary widely from community to community.

2. Liaison Committee of the Regents of the University of California and the State Board of Education, "Draft of a Restudy of the Needs of California in Higher Education," chap. ii, pp. 44–45. Sacramento, California: State Board of Education, 1955 (mimeographed).

The complexity and variety of community life and needs point up the value of colleges in which the educational program is planned and developed on the basis of the characteristics of the particular town, city, or region which it serves. Such institutions must clearly depart from traditions, for they must build curriculums and provide services adapted to the changing requirements of their particular settings in an age in which change is taking place at a faster rate than at any period in history.

As we have noted in chapter iv, a four-year college or a university can become a community-centered institution of learning. The public two-year college is, however, particularly adapted to this role. As a recently developed unit of American education, it is much less hampered by the restrictions of tradition. It can develop its offerings and services on the basis of changing community needs with a minimum of interference from the restrictive confines of standard and unyielding course, credit, and degree requirements. Since the public junior college is ordinarily controlled locally, it can also be readily responsive to local needs.

The two-year community college is, however, as has been indicated in previous chapters, more than a dream and an idea. It is an actuality in a considerable number of cities, suburbs, and agricultural areas in all sections of our country. Mayville College, Tech Institute, Moulton College, Suburban Junior College, and Seaside City College —introduced in the opening paragraphs of chapter i—are all, in varying degrees, community colleges planned to meet the requirements of the particular areas which they serve.

Examples of community-centered developments are described throughout the pages of this volume. Vocational programs related to the needs of the community are provided in agriculture or electronics, horticulture or instrumentation, apparel design or nursing— or, indeed, in all of these and a number of others (chap. vi). Courses for adults, forums, consultation service, conferences and workshops are planned for local citizens (chap. viii). Courses such as "The Citizen and His Community" are offered as parts of general-education programs (chap. vii). No longer are all students required to go to their instructors; in some community colleges, teachers come to the students—at neighborhood churches or assembly halls, at industrial plants, or wherever the armed services have their bases (chaps. i, viii, ix).

Paralleling in importance these offerings and services is the process by means of which interested and experienced lay citizens participate in community-college program planning and development. Community surveys are used as a basis for establishing a new junior college (chap. xiv), for making decisions regarding what vocational programs to offer (chap. vi), and for developing community service activities (chap. viii). Lay advisory boards participate in decisions affecting curriculums and in securing necessary equipment and institutional facilities, particularly in vocational fields (chaps. vi and ix). Citizen groups similarly take responsibility for suggesting college-wide program organization and activities (chaps. viii and ix). The values of drawing upon community resources—business, industry, labor, and government, as well as individual citizens—as aids to vitalizing instruction (chaps. vii and viii) are assessed, as is also the utilization of a community counseling and registration committee in enrolling and advising adult students in the evening division (chap. ix).

Throughout our nation, progress has indeed been made in clarifying the concept of the community college and of translating this concept into the program and activities of two-year colleges and thence by feedback into the enrichment of community life. Despite already great achievements, only a few of which have been outlined in these chapters, the concept of the community college constitutes a greater dream for the future—so vast are the possibilities, as the enthusiasm and support, the talents and ingenuity of lay citizens are enlisted along with those of educators in the projection, development, and operation of programs specifically designed to meet the needs of youth and adults of their community and of the nation.

These are our conclusions. These are our recommendations. But what are our expectations?

Expectations

As these chapters are being written, the *Junior College Journal* has published in its Silver Anniversary issue a symposium in which eighteen junior-college leaders answer the question, "What has been the most significant junior-college development during the past twenty-five years?"[3] Consideration of this query suggests another question: What is likely to be the most significant junior-college development of the forthcoming twenty-five years? It seems appropriate to project an answer in the concluding chapter of this yearbook. It is important not only to yearbook authors and readers but also to the total citizenry of our nation. Accordingly, the author addressed this query to seventy-nine educators and certain other leaders of American thought.

Forty-nine replies from seventeen states and the District of Columbia were received early enough to be summarized in this chapter. Professional respondents included college and university presidents and deans, city school superintendents, junior-college deans, university professors, and state superintendents of public instruction. Lay leaders in labor, industry, government, and the professions also answered.

In presenting a summary of these letters, there is no implication that the exact future of the junior college can be predicted and charted by a statistical poll of any group, however wise. Considerable weight must, however, be given to speculations of experienced and informed educators and lay leaders of thought who have expressed their judgments regarding the long-term outlook for the junior college. It will be observed that a considerable number of the respondents did not limit themselves to predicting a single junior-college development but rather suggested several changes which they see as probable, inevitable, or desirable.

EXPANSION

The junior-college development most frequently anticipated (stated in 43 of the 49 letters) during the next twenty-five years is *increase*. "An unprecedented growth in the number of junior colleges" is foreseen by President O. C. Carmichael of the University of Alabama; "a tremendous growth" by President John A. Hanna of Michigan State College; "vigorous growth" by Frank W. Abrams,

3. In commenting on the symposium, James W. Reynolds, editor, points out the three developments particularly singled out for recognition in the symposium: (*a*) emergence of the community-college concept, (*b*) the improvement of instruction, and (*c*) public recognition and acceptance of the junior college. James W. Reynolds, "The Significance of the Past Twenty-five Years of Junior College Development," *Junior College Journal*, XXV (April, 1955), 425–26.

Chairman of the Board (retired) of the Standard Oil Company of New Jersey; "consistent expansion" by Benjamin C. Willis, General Superintendent of Chicago Public Schools; expansion "at a much faster rate than has been thought possible" by Professor Francis L. Bacon, University of California, Los Angeles; and "a 'boom market' for the junior college" by Herold C. Hunt, Eliot Professor of Education at Harvard University. These views are supported by Alvin C. Eurich, Vice-President of the Fund for the Advancement of Education, who suggests, "It is entirely possible that the junior college of the future will have an enrolment three, four, or five times as large as the current enrolment."

Several letters draw an analogy between high-school graduation today and junior-college graduation of the future. President Harry E. Jenkins of Tyler (Texas) Junior College expresses the view of many other respondents as he asserts, "The junior college stands today where the American high school stood fifty years ago—on the threshold of tremendously expanded magnitude and service." Pearl A. Wanamaker, Washington State Superintendent of Public Instruction, writes, "I believe that in 1980 basic education from kindergarten through Grade XIV will be accepted as generally as high-school education is today." President Edwin H. Miner of Orange County Community College, Middletown, New York, expects that "within the next twenty-five years we will find community-college education has become as much a part of the recognized school program as has the high school today." In similar vein Erwin C. Kratt, Superintendent of Schools, Fresno, California, asserts, "During the next twenty-five years the Associate of Arts degree granted by the junior college will completely replace the high-school diploma as a device for educational measurement in job qualification."

A dissenting view is expressed by L. D. Haskew, Vice-President of the University of Texas, who believes that by the close of the next quarter of a century the pressures for more education beyond high school will be such as to by-pass the junior college and that four-year colleges will largely supplant two-year institutions. ". . . It seems inevitable," he concludes, "that most of the strong junior colleges of public character will grow into four-year, degree-granting colleges with a regional flavor." The long-term outlook suggested by Haskew seems to envisage a process of evolution under which the high-school diploma is to be supplanted by the Associate in Arts degree—which in turn will eventually be replaced by the baccalaureate degree.

Governor J. Bracken Lee of Utah shares the views of most other respondents in anticipating junior-college expansion. He foresees, however, "a decline in the number of private junior colleges and an increase in the number of public junior colleges. This trend, he writes, "in my opinion, is regrettable because there is a great role for private institutions."

A high percentage of letters comment on the desirability of the junior-college growth. Ronald B. Thompson, Registrar, Ohio State University, expresses the belief that "we shall find it best to establish new junior colleges rather than try to expand much farther our large university centers." George Meany, President of the American Federation of Labor, expresses pleasure with the anticipated junior-college expansion because "many workers' children cannot afford the full four-year course, but the junior colleges do give them an additional two years of education beyond high school." The views of many are epitomized by President J. L. Morrill of the University of Minnesota: "Here is a new and vital institution appropriately gaining in strength when existing colleges and universities reach limits of expansion and when common sense tells us we shall need the cooperative effort of all educational institutions and agencies to meet the pressures of mounting enrolments and increased demands for services from larger proportions of our citizens."

These, and similar explanations of the need for and the likelihood of junior-college expansion, lead to a consideration of anticipated developments which particularly relate to the role and purpose of the junior college during the next quarter of a century.

PURPOSES

To what objectives will the junior college address itself? Will some purposes be particularly emphasized? A. J. Brumbaugh, Director of the Study of Higher Education for Florida, anticipates the definition of functions of the public junior college to be one of the most significant developments of the next twenty-five years: "The functions of the community college will become more clearly defined," he asserts. Alvin C. Eurich feels the importance of such definition but clearly views this as a long-term undertaking: ". . . The junior colleges have a major task of clarifying the functions they are to serve. Perhaps in this area . . . great progress might be made during the next twenty-five years." It is clear that the writers of the letters here summarized believe that the purposes which most need to be achieved can and will determine the significant junior-college developments of the future. Comments on these purposes may be summarized thus:

Communtiy Service. Most frequently mentioned (in eighteen letters) among anticipated developments are those which relate to community service. As part of this service, repeated reference is made to the expansion of part-time enrolments and of services to adults.

Professor Karl W. Bigelow of Teachers College, Columbia University, explains the advances which he expects junior colleges to make in these areas: ". . . Increased national productivity and a continuing decline in the average work-week will encourage junior colleges to devote more attention to their community functions. They will become the great operating centers of a national system of adult education in which, it may be added, concern with the fundamental issues of personal and social existence will grow steadily greater." President I. Lynn White, Jr., of Mills College points out additional justification for the further education of adults: ". . . It seems clear that, as the life expectancy both of men and women increases, the community college will have an increasing function in the revitalizing of the mind and indeed the whole of life from the 40's on. We are just beginning to realize that the problems of geriatrics cannot be solved in old age: they must be solved before we get old."

The views of several other respondents are summarized by Frank W. Abrams as he writes, "If I discern any trend for the junior college of the future, I would point to the likelihood of its taking over a greater role in the adult-education activities of the community. The two-year community college offers a flexible center for training individuals who want to supplement their technical training or broaden their knowledge of the liberal arts."

President Eugene B. Chaffee of Boise (Idaho) Junior College views this anticipated trend as "the major contribution" of the junior college: "Because of mankind's greater longevity, the major contribution of the junior college, it seems to me, will be in the adult-education field."

Community-service activities clearly include more than classes and courses for adults. Charles H. Clark, Chairman of the Board of Regents of Del Mar College, Corpus Christi, Texas, points out: "The alert community college will serve local industry in more tangible ways by sponsoring clinics, workshops, institutes for management and labor, and many special classes developed and supervised by joint committees of local industrial personnel. This will be a good trend as it will attach large tax-supporting industries to the program of the community college."

Terminal Vocational Education. Increased emphasis on terminal and vocational education is anticipated as a significant junior-college development by the writers of ten letters. President Virgil M. Hancher of the University of Iowa believes that "the most important development for the junior college will be in increased attention to terminal education, technical and otherwise. . . ."

Algo D. Henderson, Professor of Higher Education at the University of Michigan, asserts that the development of vocational-terminal curriculums is still in its infancy. In supporting the same viewpoint, President Carmichael of the University of Alabama writes: "In most two-year colleges far too little attention has been given to developing programs for those who will not go beyond two years. The technical and vocational aspects of the curriculum will undergo the most drastic changes in order to meet community needs. Thus the definition and expansion of terminal programs will probably constitute the second most noteworthy development in the junior-college field during the next twenty-five years."

Mr. Randolph Van Nostrand, Director of Public Relations of the Los Angeles Merchants and Manufacturers Association, explains at some length the background for his prediction of a tremendous acceleration in the development of junior-college vocational courses:

As the first half of this century can probably be classified as the era of mechanization, the second half may well be described as the era of "automation." In the first we substituted machines for human muscle, and in the second we are substituting machines for human judgment. . . .

The challenge to our American educational apparatus which this evolution brings is well illustrated by the sharp climb in the skill levels necessary in modern business and industry. Whole new job families are being developed. There is an increasing need, and it will continue, for technicians and for more and more people in subprofessional work. . . .

. . . There is going to be tremendous pressure on public education to supply the training and the new skills which are already being demanded.

In my opinion, the most significant junior-college development of the immediate future will be a demand for, and a tremendous acceleration of, the so-called occupational courses which in two years will graduate technicians in an increasing number of fields.

George Meany likewise refers to industrial and technological developments as a basis for his anticipation of expanded emphasis on junior-college vocational programs: ". . . The junior colleges can play a very important role in connection with developments in electronics and the great potentials of atomic energy for industrial purposes. These will undoubtedly necessitate the expansion of the training program for apprentices, and here the junior colleges can serve in offering advanced technical courses. . . ."

President Julian A. McPhee of California State Polytechnic College also looks forward to expanded junior-college vocational offerings. He particularly, however, predicts that the junior college will contribute to the breaking down of a snobbery which he identifies as follows:

At one time, abstention from labor was the conventional evidence of wealth and was, therefore, the conventional mark of social standing. Today, man's attitude toward work has changed. Men work, and work hard, to earn the wealth which will enable them to satisfy their desires for comfort and beauty—beyond the mere necessities. However, we have not yet eliminated the snobbery which prevents us from giving all occupations equal dignity. But in a democratic social order we must work toward that objective.

That is the contribution which I foresee will be made by the junior colleges during the next twenty-five years.

R. H. Eckelberry, editor of the *Journal of Higher Education*, expresses a concern not unlike that of President McPhee over the relation of schooling and work. He, also like President McPhee, anticipates a junior-college development which will contribute to correcting the deficiency which he finds in contemporary education:

One of the most significant developments, in my opinion, will be the recognition and provision of work experience as an integral part of the junior-college program. Some institutions today provide this, but they are, I believe, exceptional rather than typical. I expect work experience to become an essential component of the programs of more and more junior colleges.

Such a development will have far-reaching effects on other phases of junior-college education. The problem of who should continue formal education beyond high school and for how long will take on new dimensions. As long as schooling is separated from work, many high-school graduates will and should choose full-time work rather than full-time schooling of the conventional type. By this choice they will best serve society and contribute to their own personal development. Many others, of course, will and should choose full-time schooling; in this way they best serve themselves and society.

When and as work experience becomes an integral part of the junior-college program, junior-college education will become educationally effective (and therefore desirable) for many more people than it now is. Thus this change will contribute to the growth of junior colleges. The implications for vocational and educational counseling will be far reaching. . . .

The same considerations that argue for work experience in the junior college also apply to other institutions and levels of education. But because the junior college has a short history, it has little weight of tradition to overcome. It may well be the leader in ending, on all levels of American education, the ancient and unfortunate separation between work and schooling.

Along with the various predictions of increased offerings of junior-college terminal vocational courses comes a word of warning from Dean Fred K. Eshleman of the Henry Ford Community College, Dearborn, Michigan:

As we are faced with staggering enrolments, it is going to be easy to lose our creativeness and uniqueness and to slip back into offering simply the first two years of regular college work. I am considerably worried about this danger. . . . With the large numbers of students soon to enrol in our junior colleges, it will be easy to push effective terminal programs aside for another decade. . . .

Preparation for Advanced Study. Nine letters refer to expected junior-college developments which relate to the preparation of students for advanced study. Several writers anticipate the reduction of Freshman and Sophomore offerings by four-year colleges and universities, with a consequent increasing acceptance of responsibility for lower-division work by junior colleges.

Randolph Van Nostrand points out, "As the great universities place more and more emphasis upon graduate work and research there is bound to be a very considerable decentralization of lower-division studies." Edwin H. Miner asserts, "I fully expect that the next 25 years will see a number of colleges change from conventional four-year programs to the so-called upper level of third and fourth years plus one or two years of graduate work. From an economics point of view I think such a reshuffling of higher education makes good sense. Furthermore, I think there is supporting reason from an educational point of view for such a change." Edwin C. Kratt suggests that "due to the high cost of financing post-high-school education, our junior colleges will be called upon to assume full responsibility for all course offerings at the lower-division level." Dean Peter Masiko, Jr., of Wright Junior College, Chicago, says, "I foresee the day when admission to most senior colleges and universities will be from the junior colleges."

Professor Karl W. Bigelow, Teachers College, Columbia University, expects improved understandings and relationships between junior colleges and senior colleges and universities: "As larger and larger proportions of students begin their four-year-college programs in junior colleges, some significant changes in attitudes will occur. Fewer and fewer parents and students will think of junior-college attendance plus later transfer to a four-year institution as less desirable than attendance at the latter from the start. As the four-year colleges receive more and more of their students by such transfer, they will make more positive and constructive adaptations to this situation."

General Education. Six letters refer to an expectation of increased junior-college emphasis on general education. Utah's Congressman Henry A. Dixon, former president of Weber College, writes: "The next twenty-five years will see the junior colleges becoming far more conscious of their social, civic, spiritual and religious aims. Our education will become more spiritual and social and less economic. Increasing emphasis on general education will help make it so." Howard E. Wilson, Secretary of the Educational Policies Commission of the National Education Association, also foresees "more penetrating, thoughtful concern with religion." Charles H. Clark expresses the opinion that "during the next twenty-five years there will be a merger of vocational training with cultural or liberal-arts courses.

... This is necessary due to the fact that the product of purely vo-
cational-training programs did not develop those finer points of citizenship and personality development which are so needed in our
country." Horace T. Morse, Dean of the General College at the University of Minnesota, agrees with Mr. Clark, ". . . It seems to me
inevitable that there will be less of a sharp dividing line between vocational studies and liberal or general education in the junior college
of the future."

Kenneth E. Oberholtzer, Superintendent of Schools, Denver, Colorado, expects that in the future there will be a trend to consider the
junior college much in the same way as we now consider high
school, as the basic education required to qualify for many business
and semiprofessional jobs. "If this trend does develop," he continues,
"the junior college will become increasingly a place for general education. . . ."

A hope and a recommendation, rather than a prediction, are expressed by Lynn White, Jr.:

The whole current distinction in education between the so-called
liberal arts and so-called vocationalism assumes a social distinction between a class of workers and a class of aristocrats which has been valid
through most of the many thousands of years of human history, but
which has lost its validity in our society. Thanks not merely to political democracy, but more particularly to the rise in our standard of
living, all of us are now both workers and aristocrats. The notion that
junior colleges are set up to train "hands," whereas liberal-arts colleges
are designed to educate "brains," is not merely undemocratic but anti-
democratic. If the junior colleges of the next quarter century are to
fulfil their real responsibilities, they must try to pitch their work at an
intellectual level which not many of them have as yet envisaged.

PROBLEMS AND OPPORTUNITIES

Educators who wrote to the author of this chapter refer to a number of problems and opportunities which they view as linked with
the future of the two-year college. Guidance is one of the most important of these, representing as it does both problems and opportunities.

Guidance and Counseling. L. A. Wilson, New York State Com-
missioner of Education, points out the necessity for guidance as he
asserts that "students are characterized not by their uniformity but
by their diversity." In referring to student selection and counseling,

Howard A. Campion, Associate Superintendent of Schools, Los Angeles, writes, "Here is the most critical problem facing the junior colleges. . . . The aim of having post-high-school education available for all American youth cannot be realized if the students are allowed to squander their own time on false hopes. A good program of counseling will be the foundation of the successful junior college during the next decade. . . . The guidance program of the junior college of tomorrow will not be designed to keep people out of junior college but will be set up to aid them in the selection of junior college offerings from which they can profit most. Such a program will pay for itself in reduced turn-over, in reduction of expensive repetition of courses, and elimination of failure and frustration on the part of American youth."

President Doak S. Campbell of Florida State University views the junior college as a unit of education in which young people are making far-reaching decisions regarding their future:

In my opinion, we shall look to the junior college as the institution in which final decisions are made regarding the ultimate educational plans of our young people. We do not seem able, under present conditions, to bring about a proper decision, either on the part of guidance officers or of the students themselves, during high school. Whether students are to go in for a heavy academic program that would lead to high scholarship, or into the learned professions, or into applied fields that lead directly to vocations, may well be a primary concern of the junior college. . . . I believe we have enough indication in the operation of certain outstanding junior colleges to know that this is an area to which the junior college can contribute most significantly.

Julian A. McPhee points out a dilemma which confronts the junior college—but anticipates a resolution of it with far-reaching consequence for all of American education:

To a large extent the junior colleges are on the horns of a dilemma. They know, for example, that for every professional engineer needed there are five to seven technicians required. They know, too, that industry's greatest need today and for the foreseeable future is for manpower in the *skilled* categories.

But junior-college counselors, even if they are not personally biased toward the "college preparatory" program, are confronted with the student and his parents who feel the stigma of the "nonprofessional" curriculum.

I predict that within the next twenty-five years our junior colleges will have made a major contribution in licking this bugaboo of social stigma that now attaches to all but the "university-transfer" program. They will have achieved considerable success in solving realistically the problem of sifting those who should go on to four-year colleges from those who should take terminal occupational training. As a result of these successes, the junior colleges will have assisted the cause of higher education through a most critical period when almost every college and university in the nation was being engulfed by a tidal wave of students. The success of the junior-college two-year terminal program will receive major credit for obtaining for education in general the favorable opinion of a cost-conscious public which was in 1955 on the verge of instituting ways of keeping people out of school rather than accepting the democratic principle of providing post-high-school education for all who would benefit from it.

Finance. McPhee identifies junior-college finance as a problem and suggests an approach to its solution—excellence of program, including, particularly, guidance and two-year terminal offerings. Others also anticipate problems and likely trends in the support of two-year colleges.

Roy E. Simpson, California State Superintendent of Public Instruction, predicts that "problems of plant expansion, finance, and program development will assume an importance in the next decade or two beyond anything which has been hitherto experienced. There may be many efforts by some people to economize in meeting these needs, and many of these proposals may involve reductions in the quality of the program or limitations of those to whom the program is available through the introduction of fee systems or other arbitrary ways of limiting enrolments to existing facilities. These proposals constitute a very real danger."

Howard A. Campion shares Simpson's concern regarding finance:

One of the most critical problems which will confront the junior college during the next decade will be that of adequate financial support. With inadequate financial backing, the junior college will tend to become a traditional, old-pattern collegiate institution. New types of curriculums in technical, business, agricultural, and public service require well-trained and well-paid teachers, as well as fully equipped laboratories and demonstration facilities.

". . . There will be an increased demand upon the taxing ability of local communities to meet the needs of elementary and high-school enrolments. To expect the junior college to thrive on what can be derived from an already overloaded tax basis is wishful thinking. It will be necessary to find other sources of financial support. In some states this will be greater aid on the state level. In other cases, it may be the development of new taxes which will be available for the school districts operating junior colleges. These may include income taxes, sales taxes, or other types yet to be developed.

From certain quarters will come a demand that a tuition charge for junior-college education be established at a sufficiently high level to carry a large portion of the costs. Such a move would be unfortunate. The junior college is a part of the program of education for all American youth, and it never will reach a sufficiently large group if a high tuition is imposed. Furthermore, the imposition of a tuition charge at this level will be an entering wedge which will endanger the whole structure of free public education in America.

State support is referred to by A. J. Brumbaugh, Director of the Study of Higher Education in Florida: "The community college will derive increased support from state funds. Such support will be distributed on a basis that will extend the advantages of the community college to the less favored areas in a state, thus equalizing the opportunities for post-secondary education."

A danger in increased support by states is suggested by Charles H. Clark: "During the next twenty-five years there will very likely be a trend for more assistance financially from the state level, accompanied by more and more state supervision which will automatically mean less local autonomy. This trend will be regretted and will do more harm to the local community colleges than good."

Thomas D. Bailey, Florida State Superintendent of Public Instruction, suggests that establishing two-year colleges represents a financially feasible approach to the provision of needed post-high-school education: "Our present state universities are 'bursting at the seams' because of excessive enrolments. It appears that the establishment of the community college is the only alternative to establishing one or more four-year institutions. It is my belief that the cost to the state in establishing the fifteen community colleges will be much less than that of establishing one or two four-year institutions."

A somewhat similar view is expressed by William H. Conley, Assistant to the President of Marquette University: "One of the practical educational and social reasons which may operate in stimulating junior-college extension is the financial plight of the state university. The increasing numbers of students who must be taken care of for post-high-school education . . . cannot be adequately provided for from present sources of revenue. There is no question in my mind that our elementary school and high school will get first claim on tax revenue. What will be left will go to higher education. Since the junior college can be more economically operated at the local level and can utilize secondary-school facilities, with minor modifications, there would not be the need for a great additional drain on resources."

Securing Teachers. Alvin C. Eurich refers to the problem of securing teachers for the vast numbers of new students he expects to enrol in junior colleges.

If the junior colleges tackle this problem with the same kinds of imagination and ingenuity that have been exercised in other aspects of American life, they will make their most significant contribution in this area during the next twenty-five years. In view of the fact that in every other profession outside of teaching the success of the professional worker is judged by the number of people he can serve well, perhaps the junior colleges might demonstrate how one really effective teacher can serve larger and larger numbers with sound use of various aids, both human and mechanical. The opportunities of using people of more limited capacities and training to assist the teacher and of using television, the greatest educational instrument ever devised, are really limitless. Perhaps because the junior colleges are the most flexible institutions we have in American society, they are in a position to lead the way in demonstrating how far-reaching the effects of a really great teacher can be. The next twenty-five years will tell.

Integration with High School. Leonard V. Koos, Professor Emeritus of Education at the University of Chicago, anticipates a long-term trend toward the integration of the high school and the lower years of college:

In the mind of the writer a marked and significant . . . trend during the next quarter-century will be in the direction of one of the later and, to date, less extensive recent developments in the junior college: the integration of the later high-school and early college years. This integration is desirable whatever the pattern of organization, and it is attainable in varying degrees in the different patterns. However, integration is and has been most encouraged by the 6-4-4 plan of organization.

A Pattern for Higher Education. President J. Paul Leonard of San Francisco State College suggests that other states consider the pattern of public higher education found in California:

I think that the three-system idea that we have developed in California should be considered by other states. This means that we can retain the essential character of graduate work in the universities, without filling them up with a load of students that should not be there. . . . We can also develop four-year state colleges . . . which will do the basic essential work for those who need a four-year education of general liberal arts and for a large number of the world's occupations. The junior colleges, then, will hold a very important place in continuing secondary education through two years and also provide the highly technical education for those who need no more than this for a large number of occupations.

THE COMMUNITY COLLEGE

The letters here summarized repeatedly predict and recommend the development of the junior college as a community college. Earlier reference has been made to predictions regarding the community-service function of the junior college. But views expressed in these letters go far beyond a concept of service and point to an actual and extensive integration of the college and its program with the community.

David D. Henry, President of the University of Illinois, writes, "Close to the people, the junior college will inevitably be required to serve the educational and cultural needs of the community of which it is a part. The trends in this direction have already been firmly established, and ways and means of integrating the junior college with the needs of community life will become even more effective in the future."

Ernest O. Melby, Dean of the School of Education at New York University, visualizes the junior college as a vitalizing force for the entire community:

I believe that the most important development in the junior-college field in the next twenty-five years will be a sharp increase in the emphasis placed upon the role of the junior college as an institution serving its community and receiving resources from this same community. . . .

The challenges that come to education as a result of the atomic age, both in the international scene and within our own society are such that they cannot be met within the four walls of a schoolhouse or on the campus of a college or university. It is becoming increasingly clear that we need a great education, one that uses all the resources of the community in addition to and in support of the work that is done in

schools and colleges. . . . Students of junior-college age can play a
significant part in the life of their communities if their educational
activities are appropriately planned. At the same time, the educational
resources of the community are such that the education of the youth
can be made far more dynamic if more use is made of these resources.
We will thus have a two-way street between the junior college and
the community, between the entire school system from nursery school
through the junior college and the life of the community. . . .

The above concept will, I believe, give the junior college a new
reason for being and a new vitality in the conduct of its work.

Edwin C. Kratt anticipates developments which will contribute to
the progress of the junior college toward the status of a community
college: "Greater emphasis will be placed upon recommendations
from lay committees and surveys to discover and develop the educational needs of each community, with junior colleges providing the
leadership and expanded curriculums to meet these needs."

From Baker Brownell, Emeritus Professor of Philosophy, North-
western University, also comes strong support for the community-
college concept:

I am not so sure what will be the most significant junior-college
development in the next twenty-five years, but I am sure what it ought
to be:

. . . The junior college should be primarily a service to its own community. Its curriculum and organization should be adjusted wisely to
those needs, even though it may make a college different from other
junior colleges in the country.

The junior college in its role as a community college should serve
students of all ages and all occupations within the context of the student's community and occupation.

. . . It should be a resource not only for classroom studies but for
the many services, cultural, occupational, and professional, which are
possible in such a situation but are not yet realized fully by many colleges. These service functions in turn will give the college local financial support and make its maintenance more possible. The segregation
of the town from the gown must be abolished.

Conclusion

We have looked at the public junior college as we find it today.
We have identified its role and its purposes and have noted its advances and achievements, its problems and needs. We have also
pointed to the future, observing the demand for more post-high-

school education and the contributions the public junior college can and must make in meeting this demand. We have recommended needed directions of development and have reported the expectations of selected educators and lay leaders of thought regarding the future of the junior college.

The predictions we reported are remarkably similar to the recommendations we have made in earlier chapters of the yearbook. We have proposed a sharp expansion in the public junior college; the letters summarized above predict such growth. We have identified four purposes of the public junior college (preparation for advanced study, vocational education, general education, and community service) and have urged increased and specific attention to each; educators and other leaders of thought whom we have polled anticipate greater attention to and emphasis on these goals. We have recommended the development of the public junior college as a community college; again this development is predicted by our consultants.

The future outlook for the public junior college is not, however, without its hazards, some of which might tend to minimize the high hopes and predictions previously expressed. Problems relating to finance, to the training of teachers, and to relationships with other units of education, for example, must be faced and solved if the expectations forecast in this chapter are to be realized.

There appears, nevertheless, to be much reason to believe that the predictions will be realized. The needs of youth and of adults, those of our nation and of our communities, clearly call for a notable increase in education beyond high school. The public junior college is uniquely qualified to contribute to meeting many of these needs in the home communities of students. Throughout history the American people have viewed education as a foundation of national security and of democracy itself. The citizens of our nation will, it seems to us, inevitably support the growth and strengthening of the public junior college as an element essential to our national welfare.

SELECTED REFERENCES

Readings on the Junior College

S. V. MARTORANA

This list of references has been prepared to provide interested readers an up-to-date overview of the scope and nature of available literature on the junior college. The yearbook committee concluded that this purpose would be most effectively served by a classified and annotated bibliography of recently published titles in this field. The present list, besides being a direct source of information, is also illustrative of the types of publication to which one might turn for additional references.

Since the list is selective rather than comprehensive, the bases for selection of references should be noted. First among these was the decision to use chiefly articles dealing specifically with the public junior college or some aspect of it. Therefore, many excellent works related to the more general aspects of higher education were not included. A second principle followed was that of excluding from the list most of the references which had been cited in earlier published bibliographies dealing with junior-college education. As a result, such familiar publications of the early years of the movement as Koos' Commonwealth Study[1] and Eells' *The Junior College*[2] are not included in the listings. Third, the bibliography includes only published works and does not include graduate dissertations or certain other documents such as mimeographed or processed reports of state departments of public instruction, reports of state and regional associations, and publications of particular institutions.

In the preparation of the bibliography, the authors of the several yearbook chapters were asked to suggest references. Their recommendations were treated in a manner consistent with the three prin-

1. Leonard V. Koos, *The Junior College* (2 vols.). Research Publications of the University of Minnesota, Education Series, No. 5. Minneapolis, Minnesota: University of Minnesota, 1924. Pp. xxxi + 682.

2. Walter Crosby Eells, *The Junior College*. New York: Houghton Mifflin Co., 1931. Pp. xvii + 833.

ciples just mentioned. Finally, the annotated list was submitted to the yearbook committee and the chapter authors for criticism. It was then revised in light of their suggestions.

Besides the suggestions received from the chapter authors, considerable assistance in identifying references was gained from other sources. In the *Junior College Journal*, the official organ of the American Association of Junior Colleges, the index which appears in the May issue of each volume provides an indication of the latest thinking and current issues in the movement. Similarly, the bibliographies which appear in the *School Review* are a source of information. Besides these, extensive use was made of several previously prepared bibliographies on the junior college.[3]

Though much has been written about junior colleges, it cannot be said that there has been balance in the areas, issues, or topics considered. As would be expected regarding an educational movement relatively new to the American educational scene, much attention has been devoted to the philosophical bases for the junior college and to the purposes it should serve. Likewise, much space has been given to procedures for promoting the movement and to establishing new institutions. Much less, and only in more recent years, has there been consistent and general attention to such matters as improvement of instruction, appraisal of the program of offerings, and advancement of student-personnel services. The fact that this is now taking place, however, is a noteworthy indication that the movement has become established.

There are three standard sources which are basic references concerning the junior-college movement. Besides the *Junior College*

3. Walter C. Eells, *Bibliography on Junior Colleges.* United States Department of Interior, Office of Education, Bulletin 1930, No. 2. Washington: Government Printing Office, 1930.

Walter C. Eells, *Good References on the Junior College.* United States Department of Interior, Office of Education, Bibliography No. 31. Washington: Government Printing Office, 1935. Pp. 11.

William H. Conley and Frank J. Bertalan, *Significant Literature of the Junior College, 1941–48.* Washington: Government Printing Office, 1949.

William R. Wood, "Doctoral Dissertations Accepted for Degrees in Junior Community College Education." Washington: Office of Education, Department of Health, Education, and Welfare (unpaged; duplicated).

Paul L. Johnson, "Community College Education: A Book of Readings." Unpublished report of a Type C Project for the Ed.D. New York: Teachers College, Columbia University, 1951. Pp. vii + 669.

Journal,[4] the American Association of Junior Colleges publishes annually a directory of junior colleges,[5] which lists all institutions of this type, public and private, in the United States and other countries and carries each year a summary of trends in growth in numbers and changes in status of junior colleges. A third standard reference is that published by the American Council on Education under the title *American Junior Colleges*.[6] This volume furnishes full descriptive data on the accredited junior colleges in the United States and has individual chapters covering the classification of institutions, historical developments, legal status, accreditation practices, and present trends in the movement. The following selected list, with appropriate annotations, will be a convenient guide to important writings on the particular phases of the junior-college movement which are indicated by the categories under which the titles are classified.

PHILOSOPHY AND OBJECTIVES

CONANT, JAMES BRYANT. *Education and Liberty*. Cambridge, Massachusetts: Harvard University Press, 1953. Pp. xii+168.

Compares the present status of education in England, Scotland, Australia, New Zealand, and the United States. Recommends that, in meeting the challenge of providing extended education to more youth, more institutions offering a two-year college course should be developed and these should provide a common core of general education, together with differentiated special programs. Stresses especially the need to identify, challenge, and develop fully the academically gifted youth through a revision of the curriculum in secondary and higher education.

FIELDS, RALPH, and PIKE, ARTHUR. "Community College Problems," *Teachers College Record*, LI (May, 1950), 528–36.

Defines the work of community-college administrators and instructors as determined by the consensus reached by participants in a workshop on community-college problems. Identifies the primary purpose in developing programs of offerings, instruction, and in-service staff improvement to be a more effective accommodation of the community college to the wide array of individual differences in ability and interests found among students attending these colleges.

FREDENBURGH, F. A. "Does the Community College Threaten Higher Education?" *School and Society*, LXIX, (April 23, 1949), 289–93.

---

4. *Junior College Journal*. Washington, D.C.: American Association of Junior Colleges.

5. C. C. Colvert and M. L. Baker, *Junior College Directory, 1955*. Washington: American Association of Junior Colleges, 1955. Pp. 48.

6. *American Junior Colleges*. Edited by Jesse P. Bogue. Washington: American Council on Education, 1952 (third edition). Pp. x + 604.

Attacks the notion that community colleges duplicate the services of lower-division university education and attract similar students; traces the evolutionary development of community-college educational services from their beginnings to the present time, noting in the early years the duplications of the offerings of the first two years of university programs but, in more recent times, the development of widely differentiated program quite unlike that found in the university.

GRIFFITH, COLEMAN, "The Changing Structure of Higher Education," *The Administration of Higher Institutions under Changing Conditions*, chap. ii, pp. 3–19. Proceedings of the Institute for Administrative Officers of Higher Institutions, 1947. Edited by Norman Burns. Chicago: University of Chicago Press, 1947.

Stresses particularly the need to expand the base of collegiate-level training to train the varied talents of youth in a rapidly changing technological society and the urgency of increased financial support for such an expansion. Develops the role of the community college and claims that it is essential to the complete structure of a national system of higher education.

Higher Education for American Democracy, Vol. I, *Establishing the Goals*. A Report of the President's Commission on Higher Education. Washington: Government Printing Office, 1947. Pp. 103.

Outlines the functions which a complete system of higher education needs to serve in a democratic society. After documenting the need for expansion of educational opportunity and diversification of offerings, the Commission recommends widespread increase in the number of community colleges and multiplication of their activities. The Commission further states that the prime purpose of these colleges is educational service to the entire community and that this purpose requires a variety of offerings.

MILLER, B. R., and HOOD, CHARLES E. "What Educational Program for the 13th and 14th Years: Community College or Junior College?" *National Association of Secondary School Principals Bulletin*, XXXVIII (April, 1954), 75–78.

Gives reasons why junior colleges should adopt the designation "community college" and suggests criteria for evaluating such institutions.

SPROUL, ROBERT G. "University and the Junior College," *California Journal of Secondary Education*, XXVIII (April, 1953), 229–34.

Gives an authoritative statement of the division of responsibility between the junior college and university; states that about half the students in the upper division of the University of California originate in the junior college and that these transfers do as well as those trained in the university.

HISTORY AND EMERGENCE

BOREN, CLAUDE B. "Why a Junior College Movement?" *Junior College Journal*, XXIV (February, 1954), 345–57.

Considers such social factors contributing to the development of the junior college as the changing composition of the population, technological shifts and developments, the popularization of secondary-school education, and the increasing complexity of society. Reviews some of the writings which have been published pertaining to the relationship between these social factors and the junior college.

Junior College Journal, XXV (April, 1955), 425–85.

Devotes the entire issue to discussion of the significance of the past twenty-five years of the junior-college movement. Presents articles by individual authors on features of the movement believed by each author to be the most significant development in the junior-college field in the past quarter century. Takes up the increasing adaptability of the junior college; its provision of broad programs and a broader opportunity to youth; the greater integration of college and community; adult education; and other related topics.

Koos, LEONARD V. "Rise of the People's College," *School Review*, LV (March, 1947), 138–49.

Traces the emergence of the four-year type of community college in American education from antecedent developments of the liberal-arts college and the public high school, considering the characteristics of students and faculty and the curriculums which were offered.

REYNOLDS, JAMES W. "Junior Colleges: Agencies for Community Education," *State Government*, XXVI (June, 1953), 161–64.

Summarizes the outstanding social, economic, and cultural trends that have brought about the growth of junior colleges and their gradual transformation to community colleges.

CURRENT DEVELOPMENT

BOGUE, JESSE P. *The Community College*. New York: McGraw-Hill Book Co., Inc., 1950. Pp. xxii+390.

Presents a comprehensive treatment of the history, purposes, organization, and problems of the community junior college. Provides frequent descriptions of developments in particular areas and individual institutions.

BOLMAN, FREDERICK DeW., JR. "Signs of Change in Higher Education," *Journal of Higher Education*, XXVI (May, 1955), 249–53.

Asserts that, as a result of the effects of the shrinking revenue and increasing enrolments now facing the colleges, American collegiate education may soon witness the most radical change in its three-hundred-year history. Primary feature of this change would be the widespread development of two-year colleges. Emphasizes, however, that such two-year programs must develop more effective academic and career guidance programs and present curriculums of true intellectual challenge to the students.

EDUCATIONAL POLICIES COMMISSION. *Education for all American Youth: A Further Look*. Washington: Educational Policies Commission of the National Education Association and the American Association of School Administrators, 1952. Pp. xii+402.

A revision of the document which first appeared in 1944. Reasserts the recommendation that free public education be extended upward to include general and vocational education in the thirteenth and fourteenth grades. Urges development of a co-ordinated system of guidance and initial placement through these years and financial support for all phases of the public junior-college programs.

HENDERSON, ALGO D. "What Are the Implications of the Projected In-
creases in College Enrolment for Organizational Patterns of Higher
Education?" in *Current Issues in Higher Education, 1954,* pp. 243–50.
Proceedings of the Ninth Annual Conference on Higher Education,
Chicago, Illinois, March 4–6, 1954. Washington: Association for Higher
Education, National Education Association, 1954.

> Suggests that the magnitude of the prospective increase in college en-
> rolments will, in part, be dependent upon the degree to which under-
> graduate higher education is decentralized and made low in cost to the
> student and discusses the effects which such a decentralization would
> have on the American higher educational system.

HORN, FRANCIS H. "Future of the Junior College," *Educational Forum,*
XVII (May, 1953), 427–35.

> Challenges the proposition that the junior college will provide the major
> means for continued extension of educational opportunity beyond high
> school. Summarizes the bases for arguing that the junior college is a
> transitional institution in the process of reorganization of American higher
> education. Acknowledges evidence on both sides of the issue.

JARVIE, L. L. "Plans and Programs for Post-High-School Education Outside Usual Patterns of Higher Education," *Review of Educational Research,* XXIV (October, 1954), 227–84.

> Reviews recent writings and research publications concerned with ver-
> tical extensions in secondary schools and horizontal expansions of pro-
> grams beyond the high school.

KOOS, LEONARD V. *Integrating High School and College: The Six-Four-
Four Plan at Work.* New York: Harper & Bros., 1946. Pp. vi+208.

> Compares the three predominant patterns of organization of junior-col-
> lege years in public school systems with respect to curriculum offerings,
> student-personnel services, scope of teaching assignments and background
> of instructors, supervision and costs, and physical facilities.

SEXSON, JOHN A., and HARBESON, JOHN W. *The New American College.*
New York: Harper & Bros., 1946. Pp. xviii+312.

> Deals with the basic philosophy, organization, and administration of the
> four-year junior college. Relates the four-year type of institution to other
> prevailing types in each major area discussed. Covers history and philosophy,
> organization and administration, curriculum, extracurriculum, and guid-
> ance.

STARRAK, JAMES A., and HUGHES, RAYMOND M. *The Community College
in the United States.* Ames, Iowa: Iowa State College Press, 1954. Pp.
ix+114.

> Reviews the present-day situation confronting post-high-school education
> in the United States, proposes standards for the development of commu-
> nity colleges, and presents a recommended system of community colleges
> for the state of Iowa.

STUDENTS SERVED BY THE JUNIOR COLLEGE

BURMAN, ARTHUR C. "'Emotional Adjustments of Junior College Students," *Junior College Journal*, XXIV (April, 1954), 491–96.

Examines some specific factors of emotional development as they relate to the educational experiences of the junior-college students. Stresses the need for display of emotional security by individual faculty members and administrators in the junior colleges.

CRIPPEN, RAYMOND A. "I Will Never Regret Junior College," *Junior College Journal*, XXII (January, 1952), 245–48.

A graduate of a junior college reveals the reasons behind the attitudes toward and appreciation for the education received in a junior college.

DOUGLAS, B., and RACK, LUCILLE. "Problems of Junior College Students," *Junior College Journal*, XX (March, 1950), 377–89.

Reports a study of the problems of 1,956 students representing twenty junior colleges in Texas. Analyzes findings according to type and size of institution attended. Discovers that, though junior-college students have many problems and can identify and appraise these difficulties, the problems are not differentiable according to type or size of college attended.

GOETTE, MARY E., and ROY, HOWARD L. "A Ten-Year Survey of Scholastic Aptitude of Junior College Students," *Junior College Journal*, XXI (September, 1950), 3–8.

Analyzes the changes found in records of entering students at Rochester, Minnesota, Junior College on three measures of scholastic aptitude. Compares records of incoming students to scores achieved on the same measures by a sampling of high-school Seniors in Minnesota and by the high-school Seniors in the Rochester City School system.

HOLLINGSHEAD, BYRON S. *Who Should Go to College.* New York: Published for the Commission on Financing Higher Education by Columbia University Press, 1952. Pp. xviii+190.

Estimates percentages of nation's youth who are able to profit by college education, reports percentages who do and do not go to college, and evaluates various suggestions for obtaining the college enrolment of all who have college ability. Has a special chapter by Robert J. Havighurst and Robert R. Rodgers on the special problem of motivation to attend post-high-school institutions.

JONES, BEN W. "Physical Development of Junior College Students," *Junior College Journal* XXIII (February, 1953), 306–10.

Reviews the characteristics of the students in junior colleges with respect to age, muscular bodily growth, and general physiological development. Relates this information to the curriculum offerings in health and physical education.

KEOHANE, ROBERT E. "The Challenge of the Gifted Student in the Junior College," *The Councilor*, XIV (April, 1953), 4–10. (Published by Illinois Council for the Social Studies. Charles R. Monroe, Editor, c/o Chicago Teachers College, Chicago 20, Illinois.)

Describes both acceleration and enrichment for students from fifteen to twenty years of age. Considers the problems posed and proposals for their alleviation.

LANTAGUE, JOSEPH E. "An Analysis of Health Interests of 1,000 Junior College Students in California," *Junior College Journal*, XXI (April, 1951), 429–33.

Finds that the health interests of 1,000 junior-college students, when considered according to major health areas, showed a correlation coefficient of .94 when compared to a similar study, using the same index, made of the health interests of high-school students. Makes recommendation for instruction in health and physical-education classes.

WEDEMEYER, CHARLES A. "Use of the Morale-type Survey on the Junior College Level," *Junior College Journal*, XXI (April, 1951), 434–43.

Attempts to appraise the use in junior colleges of a survey technique developed in industry. Concludes that the morale-type survey has value when used to augment information available from other sources and to provide cues for institutional action.

PROGRAM: GENERAL EDUCATION

Evaluation in General Education. Edited by Paul L. Dressel. Dubuque, Iowa: William C. Brown Co., 1954. Pp. viii+333.

Offers series of reports on the practices of evaluating programs of general education in thirteen colleges and universities over the nation, including two junior colleges, one public and one private. Has a concluding chapter on the present state of evaluation in general education, pointing out the administrative patterns of evaluation agencies, variations in emphasis on evaluation, and the relation of evaluation to instruction.

Explorations in General Education: The Experiences of Stephens College. Edited by Roy Ivan Johnson. New York: Harper & Bros., 1947. Pp. ix+262.

Reports the thinking which has been done and the program which has been developed in one institution in an attempt to meet the general-education needs of students. Sets forth major problems found with respect to staff attitude and abilities, curriculum areas, and relations of the formal and informal phases of college life of the student. Describes methods employed to attack these problems and suggests solutions.

General Education. Fifty-first Yearbook of the National Society for the Study of Education, Part I. Chicago: Distributed by University of Chicago Press, 1952. Pp. xiii+377.

Treats comprehensively the theory and practice of general education in American higher education. Discusses the meaning of general education, its philosophical and psychological bases, the social processes supporting it, and its implementation in each of several subject-matter fields. Takes up also the problems of effective instruction, organization and administration, and evaluation of general-education programs.

General Education in Action. Prepared by B. Lamar Johnson for the California Study of General Education in the Junior College. Washington: American Council on Education, 1952. Pp. xxvi+409.

Describes general-education practices in California public junior colleges. Bases results on a 14-month study covering 57 institutions. Includes chapters on the needs for and goals of general education and on each of the major subject areas in such a program.

JARVIE, L. L. "A Pattern of General Education in Technical Institutes," *Journal of General Education*, I (April, 1947), 224–31.

Describes the development, content, and organization of the general-education program of New York State's institutes of applied arts and sciences.

JOHNSON, B. LAMAR. "General Education in the Junior College," *North Central Association Quarterly*, XXIV (April, 1950), 357–63.

Presents the case for improvement and extension of general-education programs in junior colleges.

KUGLER, ISRAEL. "The Technical Institute and General Education," *Junior College Journal*, XXI (March, 1951), 387–92.

Presents the special problems of the general-education program of the junior college and the technical institute.

PUTNAM, HOWARD L. "A Survey of New-Type General Education Courses in American Junior Colleges," *Junior College Journal*, XXI (March, 1951), 401–9.

Presents statistical summary of 1,673 of the more frequent new-type general-education courses found to be offered in 425 junior colleges. Makes a regional analysis of frequency with which each course is offered.

REYNOLDS, JAMES W. "General Education in Public Junior Colleges," *Junior College Journal*, XVI (March, 1946), 308–12.

Reports the results of an intensive analysis of general-education content in the curriculums of junior colleges in all sections of the country. Uses data from catalogues and documentary and interview data gathered on junior-college campuses. Evaluates findings against a list of objectives for general education.

———. "Inadequacies of General Education Program," *Junior College Journal*, XVI (April, 1946), 363–86.

Evaluates the general-education content in various terminal programs in the junior college in comparison to that found in the general cultural program and in the arts and sciences preparatory curriculum. Reports that all measures used show a meager recognition of general education.

PROGRAM: PREPARATION FOR ADVANCED STUDY

DOUGLASS, HARL R. "How Can a Junior College Best Serve the Needs of a Student Going on to Senior College?" *North Central Association Quarterly*, XXVIII (April, 1954), 404–10.

Summarizes a panel discussion on the procedures which can be followed to articulate effectively the course offerings and student personnel services of junior colleges and higher institutions.

MARTORANA, S. V., and WILLIAMS, L. L. "Academic Success of Junior College Transfers at the State College of Washington," *Junior College Journal*, XXIV (March, 1954), 402-15.

Reports a statistical study of the academic work of 251 junior-college transfers as compared to a matched number of students entering directly from high school. Summarizes results according to areas of specialization chosen by the students.

McGUIRE, RUTH E. "Syracuse University Looks at Its Junior College Transfers," *Junior College Journal*, XX (October, 1949), 95-98.

Follow-up study at the university level of graduates of both university-parallel and terminal programs in junior colleges. Finds no significant relationship between type of program taken in junior college and probability of success in later college study. Rather general success in junior-college studies was a more reliable indicator of success in upper-division work.

RODES, HAROLD P. "Successful Transfer in Engineering," *Junior College Journal*, XX (November, 1949), 121-27.

Documents the success in later study in the engineering curriculums of students at the University of California who took their first two years of training in the California junior colleges. Discusses the examination procedures used and the prediction techniques which have been refined through the years.

SAMMARTINO, PETER, and BURKE, ARMAND F. "Success of Junior College Transfers in Eastern States," *Junior College Journal*, XVII (April, 1947), 307-10.

Summarizes the results of a questionnaire study of practices in eastern colleges concerning junior-college transfers. According to the registrars participating in the study, there is a general disposition on the part of higher institutions to accept the junior-college graduate and to allow him due academic credit for work completed.

PROGRAM: PREPARATION FOR QUICKER EMPLOYMENT

EMERSON, LYNN A. "Post-Secondary and Technical Education in the United States," *Educational Outlook*, XXV (January, 1951), 87-95.

States that the age and grade level of vocational education is definitely rising. Takes up the socioeconomic changes causing this rise, the different types of vocational curriculums found in post-high-school institutions, the structural patterns found, and the nature of likely future development.

HARRIS, NORMAN C. "Technical Education in the Community College," *Junior College Journal*, XXV (December, 1954), 200-208.

Shows the need for technical training and the procedures for developing up-to-date technical curriculums. Includes discussion and illustrations of problems encountered as well as procedures for appraising community needs and planning plant and facilities.

LOMBARDI, JOHN. "Vocational Education in the Junior College," *School and Society*, LXXIII (April 14, 1951), 225–28.

Explains the reasons for the trend among junior colleges to extend their terminal vocational programs beyond the provision only of semiprofessional and technical curriculums and to include trade-training offerings.

RODES, HAROLD P. "Cooperative Technical Education—Pro and Con," *Junior College Journal*, XXIV (February, 1954), 362–66.

Discusses the advantages and disadvantages of co-operative technical-education programs in junior colleges. Considers the students' point of view as well as that of the college and the co-operating companies.

WARD, PHEBE. *Terminal Education in the Junior College*. New York: Harper & Bros., 1947. Pp. xii+282.

The last of a series of monographs prepared by the Commission on Junior College Terminal Education of the American Association of Junior Colleges. Reports the principles and practices of terminal education as disclosed by analysis of junior-college programs over the nation. Has general findings on the philosophy and development of terminal programs and personnel services for terminal students, followed by chapters on specific tasks such as making community surveys, planning co-operative work programs, evaluating curriculums, and providing placement, follow-up, and continuation training.

WILSON, J. DOUGLAS. "Junior College and Apprenticeship Curriculum Construction through Advisory Committees," *Junior College Journal*, XXI (December, 1950), 207–16.

Describes the use of lay advisory committees in the development of junior-college vocational programs.

PROGRAM: COMMUNITY SERVICES

BRITTON, ERNEST R. "Making the Community Self Survey Study," *National Association of Secondary School Principals Bulletin*, XXXVII (April, 1953), 385–92.

States steps and principles to be followed in making a community survey and illustrates the advantages which result to curriculum development.

HARRINGTON, JOHNS H. "Blueprint for Developing Community College Curriculums," *Junior College Journal*, XXII (December, 1951), 193–200.

Outlines and discusses the procedures evolved in one community college to develop a program for adults in response to a specific and strong demand from community agencies. Traces the procedures from first awareness of demand to follow-up results.

KEMPFER, HOMER H. "The Community College and Adult Education," *Adult Education Bulletin*, XIV (August, 1950), 166–72.

Defines the term "community college" and examines the educational approaches upon which the community college might draw to ascertain needs for and to develop educational programs for adults.

KEMPFER, HOMER, and WOOD, WILLIAM R. *Financing Adult Education in Selected Schools and Community Colleges.* Federal Security Agency, Office of Education, Bulletin 1952, No. 8. Washington: Government Printing Office, 1952. Pp. 27.

Summarizes comparative costs and sources of income for adult education in high schools and community colleges based on the results of a "case study" investigation of 45 communities in 19 states.

MARTORANA, SEBASTIAN V. "Status of Adult Education in Junior Colleges," *Junior College Journal*, XVIII (February, 1948), 323–31.

Summarizes the results of a study of the number and types of junior colleges offering programs for adults. Covers enrolments in these institutions and types of programs offered.

WOOD, WILLIAM R. "The Community College," *NEA Journal*, XLIV (April, 1955), 16–17.

Defines a community college as an institution which is a vital part of its community and ideally having a program of studies and activities custom-made to the needs of its students. Describes the social phenomena of decentralization of urban population and over-all population increase in the country and relates these to the flexible type of educational services offered by community colleges.

PROGRAM: STUDENT PERSONNEL SERVICES

BRUMBAUGH, A. J. "Student Personnel Work in Transition," *Junior College Journal*, XXV (September, 1954), 11–18.

Raises questions as to the bases on which junior colleges can justify expenditure of resources on student-personnel work. Identifies the ends of student-personnel work and describes different procedures being tried to achieve these ends.

COLVERT, C. C. "Administering the Student Activity Program," *Junior College Journal*, XVIII (March, 1948), 394–99.

Suggests administrative measures for achieving a desirable balance in student experiences. Asserts that the activities program, although secondary in importance to the subject offerings, should nevertheless be considered a regular part of the curriculum.

HARDEE, MELVENE DRAHEIM, and POLLOCK, DOROTHY M. "A Process of Investigation for Occupational Interests," *Junior College Journal*, XIX (December, 1948), 177–84.

Describes the procedures and principles followed in occupational counseling at the junior-college level and illustrates their applications.

HUMPHREYS, J. ANTHONY. "Facts Concerning Student Personnel Programs," *Junior College Journal*, XIX (September, 1948), 8–13.

Synthesizes the findings of a questionnaire study asking junior-college administrators to report on the student-personnel practices and programs in their colleges. Observes that actual practices in this area of student service is far behind stated claims of the importance of the student-personnel function by junior colleges.

Junior College Journal, XXIII (January, 1953), 245-79.

Presents a series of articles treating various aspects of guidance at the junior-college level and affording examples of good practices.

PUNKE, H. H. "Junior-College Admission and Non-Curricular Provisions for Students," *School Review,* LX (January, 1952), 39-45.

Makes an analysis of admission policies and provisions of a noncurricular nature in 196 junior colleges as disclosed by their annually published catalogues.

INSTRUCTION IN THE JUNIOR COLLEGE

DAVIS, J. B. "Administrative and Supervisory Practices for Improving Instruction III," *Junior College Journal,* XVIII (March, 1948), 365-73.

Covers instructor ratings, intervisitation practices, demonstration teaching, and encouragement for advanced study.

DONOVAN, TIMOTHY P. "Problems of the Instructor in Junior College," *Junior College Journal,* XXII (May, 1952), 494-97.

Reflects the burdens and tensions faced by the classroom teacher. Claims that junior colleges must afford instructors benefits and advantages similar to those in university situations.

INGALLS, ROSCO, C. "Problems of Staffing the Community College," *National Association of Secondary School Principals Bulletin,* XXXVII (April, 1953), 393-401.

Relates the traits believed to be basic qualifications of effective community-college teachers to the program of offerings and administrative policies.

JOHNSON, B. LAMAR; LINDSTROM, ELOISE; and OTHERS. *The Librarian and the Teacher in General Education: A Report of Library Instruction Activities at Stephens College.* Chicago, Illinois: American Library Association, 1948. Pp. xi+69.

Shows how, at Stephens College, the work of making the library an integral part of the teaching program was accomplished by the physical layout of the libraries, by the organization of the services of the several units, by the co-operative work of librarians and teachers in course development and teaching.

Junior College Journal, XXIV (November, 1953), 123-98.

A special issue on teaching; has articles on language-teaching for gifted students, instructional bulletins, students deficient in written expression, assembly programs, evaluation of student achievement, and the problems of student-cheating in the classroom.

KOOS, LEONARD V. "Junior-College Teachers' Co-operations," *Junior College Journal,* XIX (March, 1949), 399-411.

Reports the result of a study of forty-eight local public junior colleges to discover the types of activities of a noninstructional nature expected of instructors, their relation to the instructors' subject-matter specializations, the time spent on them, and the implications for teacher preparation.

————. "Preparation for Community-College Teaching," *Journal of Higher Education*, XXI (June, 1950), 309–17.

Recommends a program for preparation of community-college teachers stemming from an analysis of actual conditions and practices in the junior colleges and in the universities and from a consideration of the degrees held and graduate study attained by junior-college teachers, their backgrounds of experience, preparation in education, and "other duties" in the college community.

LEGAL STATUS OF THE JUNIOR COLLEGE

COLVERT, C. C., and HEYL, ARNOLD A. *Qualifications of Junior College Teachers, Administrators, and Board Members in the United States.* Research Bulletin of the American Association of Junior Colleges, Vol. II, No. 2. Washington: American Association of Junior Colleges, 1951. Pp. 55.

Digests the legal and regulatory requirements in the forty-eight states for certification of junior-college teaching and administrative personnel as well as the qualifications, number, and tenure of junior-college board members.

MARTORANA, S. V. "Recent State Legislation Affecting Junior Colleges," *Junior College Journal*, XXIV (April, 1954), 459–71.

Summarizes recent statutory enactments affecting junior-college education in the forty-eight states.

YOUNG, RAYMOND J. "General Legislative Needs for the Public Junior Colleges in the North Central Area," *North Central Association Quarterly*, XXVI (January, 1952), 287–94.

Scrutinizes provisions found in the general legislative enactments pertaining to junior colleges according to a statistical weighting of ratings given by administrators and specialists in junior-college education.

————. "Junior College Prospects and a Guide for Its Legal Propagation," *Junior College Journal*, XXI (April, 1951), 444–52.

Based on a review of the legal provisions for junior colleges in the several states. Recommends that items of general legislation provide more for flexibility than for rigidity and tight control.

FINANCING THE JUNIOR COLLEGE

BADGER, HENRY G. "Expenditures of Junior Colleges," *Higher Education*, X (September, 1953), 11–12.

Presents a financial report of total expenditures made by 501 junior colleges in the continental United States in 1949–50 for different budgetary categories, including capital outlay. Draws comparisons for some categories between figures cited for 1949–50 and those discovered in two earlier studies, 1939–40 and 1929–30.

COLVERT, C. C. *Legally Prescribed Methods for Allocation of State Aid for Public Junior Colleges.* Research Bulletin of the American Association of Junior Colleges, Vol. III, No. 1. Washington: American Association of Junior Colleges, 1952. Pp. 35.

Supplies a state-by-state summary of the procedures found in fourteen states in which financial aid is provided for public junior colleges.

————. "Sources of Income for the Junior College Budget," *Junior College Journal*, XX (September, 1949), 34–36.

Recommends and describes procedures for budgeting the revenue received for operating junior colleges. Takes up local and state taxes, private support and gifts, endowment, student fees, and auxiliary sources.

FALLON, BERLIE J. "Modernizing Junior College Budget Practices," *School Executive*, LXXII (March, 1953), 86–87.

States that the junior colleges must define their objectives in a positive manner which is based on the needs of the communities served. Relates objectives to classifications of functions in budgets.

HACKETT, ROGER C. "Tuition Rates in Public Junior Colleges," *Junior College Journal*, XXV (December, 1954), 229–30.

Tabulates and reports statistical measures pertaining to the tuition charges, exclusive of special fees, required by 267 public junior colleges.

JONES, BENJAMIN WILLIS. *Costs of Buildings and Equipment of Junior Colleges in the United States*. Research Bulletin of the American Association of Junior Colleges, Vol. II, No. 1. Washington: American Association of Junior Colleges, 1950. Pp. 26.

Analyzes the building costs of 73 new junior-college buildings and of the equipment placed in 83 buildings recently completed. Translates costs to a 1948 index and reports results according to geographic regions of the nation.

MARTIN, A. B. *Per Student Cost of Administration, Instruction, and Operation and Maintenance of Public Junior Colleges*. Research Bulletin of the American Association of Junior Colleges, Vol. I, No. 1. Washington: American Association of Junior Colleges, 1949. Pp. 24.

Attempts to arrive at measures of "unit" costs in each of the stated areas. Bases conclusions on a questionnaire survey of 135 public junior colleges.

ORGANIZING AND ESTABLISHING JUNIOR COLLEGES

DAVIS, ALVA R. "Place of the Community College in a State Educational System," *Educational Record*, XXX (January, 1949), 79–92.

Relates the organization and administration of community colleges to the university and state colleges in a state system of higher education with particular reference to California.

FRETWELL, ELBERT K., JR. *Founding Public Junior Colleges: Local Initiative in Six Communities*. New York: Bureau of Publications, Teachers College, Columbia University, 1954. Pp. 148.

Describes how public junior colleges were established in six communities. Bases accounts on interviews with leaders in the development in each locality and on documentary records of the establishment in each locality. Seeks from the analysis of common factors found in each of the six cases to arrive at basic principles for use in establishing public junior colleges.

JENKINS, H. E. "A Guide for the Organization and Evaluation of Community Junior Colleges," *American School and University*, 1950–51 Edition, pp. 113–18.

Constructs a checklist scheme for appraising junior colleges, based on an analysis of the standards for accrediting associations covering five regional areas of the country.

KOOS, LEONARD V. "Essentials in State-wide Community College Planning," *School Review*, LVII (September, 1949), 341–52.

Presents ten generalizations to guide state policies for establishing community colleges. Based on extensive investigation in the junior-college field, the recommendation is advanced for free junior colleges with broad programs and organized as part of public school systems.

MARTIN, PHILIP, and WOOD, WILLIAM R. "Organizing Education for the 13th and 14th Years." *Bulletin of the National Association of Secondary School Principals*, XXXV (March, 1951), 257–63.

Suggests that the techniques for organizing junior-college education will vary from state to state. Develops the steps believed to be generally desirable in a procedure to establish junior colleges.

MARTORANA, SEBASTIAN V. "Where and How New Community Colleges Are Likely to Develop," *School Review*, LIX (January, 1951), 25–31.

Bases conclusions on analysis of distribution of population into cities of various size groupings, on size of student enrolments in junior colleges, and on organizational plans of junior colleges. Foresees a wide growth of these colleges in small cities.

MINNESOTA COMMISSION ON HIGHER EDUCATION (Dean M. Schweikhard, Chairman). *Higher Education in Minnesota*. Minneapolis: University of Minnesota Press, 1950. Pp. xv+419.

Parallels for the state of Minnesota the work done for the nation as a whole by the 1947 Report of the President's Commission on Higher Education. Has extensive treatments of the student potential for post-high-school education and junior-college service in the state. Makes recommendations for future extensions of service.

Higher Education for American Democracy, Vol. III, *Organizing Higher Education*. A Report of the President's Commission on Higher Education. Washington: Government Printing Office, 1947. Pp. 74.

Gives a basic plan for widespread extension of community-college education. Discusses the organization of the community college and its relationship to other units in a state-wide educational program. Covers the principles for administering such a system of community colleges.

YOUNG, RAYMOND J. "School District Reorganization and the Public Junior College," *Junior College Journal*, XII (October, 1951), 72–75.

Argues that the two current movements in American education involving basic district reorganization and development of community colleges should augment one another. Discusses the evidence from legal and quasi-legal regulations of junior colleges in the several states to support his contention.

INDEX

Index

Teacher shortage in junior colleges, 217

Technical changes in relation to the provisions for post-high-school education, 23–27, 37–38

Technical Institutes of New York, standard program of general education in, 132

Technical trends, influence of, on junior-college vocational education, 96

Terminal curriculums in junior-college vocational programs, 99–101

Terminal Education Study of the American Association of Junior Colleges, 184–85

Terminal programs, need for student counseling on nature of, 54–55

Testing procedures employed in administration of student personnel services, 198

Thompson, Ronald B., 60, 306

Timing of intended use of vocational training, 99, 113–14

Todd, Lindsey O., 45

Transfer curriculums, 94

Transfer function in junior-college administration, importance of, 78–80

Transfer students: advantages of junior-college courses for, 70–71; collegiate records of, as evidence of quality of junior-college teaching, 215; numerical importance of, in junior colleges, 79–80; success of, in senior colleges, 79–85

Traxler, A. E., 59

Trends of junior-college enrolments, 60–61

Tuition charges in public junior colleges, 255

Types of junior-college programs, 1–3

United States Supreme Court, decision of, on segregation in public schools and colleges, 21

Unity of general education, 120–21

Universities, role of, in meeting increasing demand for higher education, 64–65

University parallel curriculums, 94

Van Nostrand, Randolph, 308, 310

Variation in characteristics of college students, 56–58

Vocational advantages of junior-college education, 52

Vocational education, responsibility of junior college for, 71–72

Vocational education in the public junior college: approach to learning in, 95; various patterns of, 94

Vocational problems of junior-college students, 45

Ward, Phebe, 171

Wedemeyer, Charles A., 47

White, I. Lynn, Jr., 307, 312

Williams, L. L., 83

Willis, Benjamin C., 305

Wilson, Howard E., 311

Wilson, L. A., 312

Women in employment, types of training in junior colleges for, 33–34

Wood, William R., 217

Young, J. B., 279

INFORMATION CONCERNING THE NATIONAL SOCIETY FOR THE STUDY OF EDUCATION

1. PURPOSE. The purpose of the National Society is to promote the investigation and discussion of educational questions. To this end it holds an annual meeting and publishes a series of yearbooks.

2. ELIGIBILITY TO MEMBERSHIP. Any person who is interested in receiving its publications may become a member by sending to the Secretary-Treasurer information concerning name, title, and address, and a check for $5.00 (see Item 5).

Membership is not transferable; it is limited to individuals, and may not be held by libraries, schools, or other institutions, either directly or indirectly.

3. PERIOD OF MEMBERSHIP. Applicants for membership may not date their entrance back of the current calendar year, and all memberships terminate automatically on December 31, unless the dues for the ensuing year are paid as indicated in Item 6.

4. DUTIES AND PRIVILEGES OF MEMBERS. Members pay dues of $4.00 annually, receive a cloth-bound copy of each publication, are entitled to vote, to participate in discussion, and (under certain conditions) to hold office. The names of members are printed in the yearbooks.

Persons who are sixty years of age or above may become life members on payment of fee based on average life-expectancy of their age group. For information, apply to Secretary-Treasurer.

5. ENTRANCE FEE. New members are required the first year to pay, in addition to the dues, an entrance fee of one dollar.

6. PAYMENT OF DUES. Statements of dues are rendered in October for the following calendar year. Any member so notified whose dues remain unpaid on January 1, thereby loses his membership and can be reinstated only by paying a reinstatement fee of fifty cents.

School warrants and vouchers from institutions must be accompanied by definite information concerning the name and address of the person for whom membership fee is being paid. Statements of dues are rendered on our own form only. The Secretary's office cannot undertake to fill out special invoice forms of any sort or to affix notary's affidavit to statements or receipts.

Cancelled checks serve as receipts. Members desiring an additional receipt must enclose a stamped and addressed envelope therefor.

7. DISTRIBUTION OF YEARBOOKS TO MEMBERS. The yearbooks, ready prior to each February meeting, will be mailed from the office of the distributors, only to members whose dues for that year have been paid. Members who desire yearbooks prior to the current year must purchase them directly from the distributors (see Item 8).

8. COMMERCIAL SALES. The distribution of all yearbooks prior to the current year, and also of those of the current year not regularly mailed to members in exchange for their dues, is in the hands of the distributor, not of the Secretary. For such commercial sales, communicate directly with the University of Chicago Press, Chicago 37, Illinois, which will gladly send a price list covering all the publications of this Society. This list is also printed in the yearbook.

9. YEARBOOKS. The yearbooks are issued about one month before the February meeting. They comprise from 600 to 800 pages annually. Unusual effort has been made to make them, on the one hand, of immediate practical value, and, on the other hand, representative of sound scholarship and scientific investigation.

10. MEETINGS. The annual meeting, at which the yearbooks are discussed, is held in February at the same time and place as the meeting of the American Association of School Administrators.

Applications for membership will be handled promptly at any time on receipt of name and address, together with check for $5.00 (or $4.50 for reinstatement). Applications entitle the new members to the yearbook slated for discussion during the calendar year the application is made.

5835 Kimbark Ave. NELSON B. HENRY, *Secretary-Treasurer*
Chicago 37, Illinois

i

PUBLICATIONS OF THE NATIONAL SOCIETY FOR THE STUDY OF EDUCATION

NOTICE: Many of the early yearbooks of this series are now out of print. In the following list, those titles to which an asterisk is prefixed are not available for purchase.

POSTPAID
PRICE

Distributed by
THE UNIVERSITY OF CHICAGO PRESS, CHICAGO 37, ILLINOIS
1956